Political Transition
in Cambodia
1991–99

Political Transition in Cambodia 1991–99

Power, Elitism and Democracy

David W. Roberts

CURZON

First Published in 2001
by Curzon Press
Richmond, Surrey
http://www.curzonpress.co.uk

© 2001 David W. Roberts

Typeset in Garamond by LaserScript Ltd, Mitcham, Surrey
Printed and bound in Great Britain by
TJ International, Padstow, Cornwall

All rights reserved. No part of this book may be reprinted or reproduced or utilised in any form or by any electronic, mechanical, or other means, now known or hereafter invented, including photocopying and recording, or in any information storage or retrieval system, without permission in writing from the publishers.

British Library Cataloguing in Publication Data
A catalogue record of this book is available from the British Library

Library of Congress Cataloguing in Publication Data
A catalogue record for this book has been requested

ISBN 0-7007-1283-6 (Hbk)
ISBN 0-7007-1424-3 (Pbk)

*To the memory of
Stephen P. Riley, my mentor and friend,
and to the memory of David Munro,
who first opened doors for me;*

*in loving memory of
Rita and Mary Hammond;*

*and for Leo de Frettes and
Edward Hawksworth*

Contents

Preface ix
Acknowledgements xvii
Acronyms xviii
Tables xx
Maps
   SOUTH EAST ASIA xxii
   CAMBODIA xxiii

    Introduction 1
I   Peace Seeking 6
II Assumptions of Peace 31
III A Critical Overview of the Operation 50
IV Early Challenges to Transition 83
V Elite Challenges to Transition – the Khmer Rouge 93
VI Elite Challenges to Transition – the CPP 104
VII From 'Coalition' to Confrontation, 1993 to 1997 121
VIII Peripheral Challenges to Transition, 1993 to 1997 150
IX Recreating Elite Stability, July 1997 to July 1998 168
X Conclusion 202

Notes 214
Bibliography 248
Index 256

Preface

Over the course of the last decade, the number of independent states facing a form of political transition and embracing different types of democracy has increased dramatically.[1] Such states may have enjoyed a relatively unhindered progression from, for example, socialism or variants of communism, to political liberalism, as some former Soviet satellites have. Other states have experienced a more traumatic passage to pluralism, invoking United Nations peacekeeping forces to oversee or implement the transition, such as in Angola, Mozambique, or Cambodia. But regardless of the nature of the transition, few would contest the claim that democracy or democratic principles in a broad, if not necessarily western constitutional liberal, sense are becoming globalized. Echoing this sentiment, US President Clinton commented in 1993 that 'democracy is on the march everywhere in the world'.[2] This process, argues Schwarz, 'has been the avowed aim of every US President since FD Roosevelt'.[3] It is inimically linked to the Liberal American tradition, and through that, the rest of the Liberal world.

There are a number of forces involved in this process. The call for freely elected, open and accountable government comes from grass roots movements, such as those in the Philippines in the 1980s, or in Romania and Czechoslovakia in the late 1980s, or in Nigeria in 1993. Demands for more open, democratic and accountable government come from the World Bank and the International Monetary Fund in the form of lending conditionality.[4] Some international institutions and individuals also propose democracy as a panacea for post-Cold War conflict resolution, although this has only been a fairly recent phenomenon. Indeed, the speed at which democratisation has moved geo-politically since the late 1980s is matched perhaps by its slothful progress since the end of World War Two. One of the principal impediments to the spread of liberal democracy since 1945 has been resistance from states eschewing this form of political organisation in favour of the single party communist or authoritarian capitalist state. The USSR, the People's Republic of China, the east European bloc, and numerous states in the developing world offered an alternative to western Liberalism.

The further development and consolidation of the communist, socialist or capitalist single party state model of political organisation after 1945 lay at the heart of the limits on the immediate spread of the Liberal ideology which had triumphed over the Fascist assault. In the period following the second world war, until the late 1980s, the relationship between the various states adopting Communism or pursuing liberal democracy was strained at best; the two represented conflicting views of the world with little room for ideological conciliation. This was to change dramatically, however, if not with the 'collapse' of 'communism' as a political *modus operandi*, then with the pre-eminence of the 'capitalism' attached to most of the developed democracies, as well as to some of the dictatorships. There are, of course, many reasons why the 'Cold War' ended the way it did, and at the time it did; however, this book is more concerned with one of the many consequences of that ending.

The removal of a key barrier to the spread of what Young refers to as 'The Liberal Project' at the end of the Cold War had as a consequence the further spread of liberal democracy as the dominant ideology for political organisation globally.[5] Burbach, Nunez and Kagarlitsky described the phenomenon well when they wrote that 'the capitalist democracies have vanquished their twentieth century antagonist, communism, and with this victory the liberal democratic ideal has become ascendant'.[6] The decline of this 'antagonist' represented for some, such as Lawson, an opportunity for the West to universalise political organisation 'to assume moral authority in areas such as human rights so as to pursue hegemony by other means'.[7] A related consequence of the decline of an alternative to liberal democracy has lent further momentum to the credibility of democracy as a replacement for the regimes around the world which sought or had thrust upon them political transition. The outbreak of wars in such areas has necessitated UN intervention to settle the many emerging post-Cold War disputes. The Cold War relationship between the superpowers had capped, for a number of decades in some cases, civil conflicts in the developing world that permitted confrontation to exist by proxy for the dominant world powers – the USSR, China and the US. Civil conflicts, fought between the members of the United Nations Security Council Permanent Five (Perm-5) and long condensed into the rigid framework of bi-polarity, burst onto the world stage at the end of the Cold War, demanding responses. The end of the political confrontation between the superpowers permitted attempts to settle the many wars in the developing world fought partly at the behest of Washington, Moscow or Beijing.[8]

Accordingly, a coincidence of forces evolved which led some to believe that this 'final' stage of democratisation had arrived. It represented both the pre-eminent form of political organisation, proven and necessitated by the decline of its main rival; and also represented a vehicle for the resolution of the many civil wars 'breaking out' around the globe. Thus, democracy offered, at the fall of the Berlin Wall and after, both a replacement for the departing single party communist systems, and a solution to the phenomenon of the global 'outbreak' of civil wars.

The two forces – democratisation through political transition and civil war settlement – merged into an evolving phenomenon that has been a significant characteristic of the international politics and relations of the post-Cold War period. Assumptions regarding the validity of democracy as the 'best' form of political organisation, on the one hand; and the necessity to settle wars in which there may be several sub-national contenders for political leadership, on the other, pointed towards a fusing of concepts. Political settlements to civil conflict would take the form of elections to permit mass participation in the liberal tradition, reflecting the primacy and dominance of liberal values and precepts in the 'new world order'. It also meant that many states would experience the trauma of political transition.

Another force for change at the end of the Cold War was linked with the movement towards using pluralistic elections for the resolution of the multiplying civil conflicts. Many of those conflicts involved states and contenders for political authority with little or no interest in, or experience of, holding multi-party elections. Furthermore, because of the nature of the conflicts, few parties to the wars would trust one or the other to conduct impartial elections. Thus the utility of a neutral interventionist force was elevated as a potential solution. In this context, the United Nations as an ostensibly neutral arbiter could, perhaps, facilitate the mechanisms of power transfer in such a manner that all sides might trust and respect. Countries fractured by civil war could turn, it was hoped, to a United Nations newly-empowered to wield its original mandate of preserving peace by the terms of the 'new world order'.[9] The restrictive conditions of superpower confrontation had to a degree tied that organisation's hands and blunted its teeth throughout the Cold War. However, they seemed no longer to apply in a world order which was viewed in many quarters as representing, if not the 'end of history', then at least near complete global ideological unison – with a few notable exceptions such as China, Viêt Nam and Cuba, and the more democracy-resistant regimes in Africa, the Middle East and South Asia.[10]

It did not take long for national and organisational policy makers to realise the implications of and possibilities for a significantly increased role for UN intervention forces. Conflicts which had been 'off-limits' to intervention during the Cold War because of superpower confrontation were debated in a fresh context which was no longer primarily dictated by such considerations. The UN could now broach resolution of the many conflicts contained within the framework of superpower hostility. Examples would come to include Angola, Cambodia, El Salvador and Mozambique, as well as Namibia and, to a lesser degree, Western Sahara.

The nature of the conflicts, and especially their multi-layered complexities where multiple contenders often vied for power in conditions of extremes of poverty and destruction, necessitated fresh approaches to intervention. Indeed, one of the characteristics of the new operations is that they are determined by increasingly complex and comprehensive political mandates. Thus, whilst in the Cold War some mandates had been as simple as the patrolling of a dividing line, such as in Cyprus, the complex nature of the post-Cold War conflicts required far more sophistication. Sometimes they would necessitate the transfer of refugees from second states. Other times they would need not just the separation of fighting groups but also their disarmament. In other cases they might require the provision of elections under UN supervision; and in yet others they might need a reconstitution of government and civic principles.

Reflecting this, the role of intervention forces expanded dramatically for some early operations. The mandates were generally a political document that would establish certain conditions from which specific outcomes would educe. These conditions have tended to reflect the issues outlined above. These included the rise of multi-party liberalism and elections as a mechanism for conflict resolution, and the absence of any significant competing ideology for political organisation.

Preface

Thus, where several parties competed through arms for political legitimacy, the conflict would be resolved by mass elections determining political authority and thus ending the war through a peaceful contest for power. Pluralism and the ballot sought to replace armed confrontation whilst simultaneously embracing western liberalism, facilitated by United Nations peacekeeping operations framed by complex mandates.[11]

The design of such mandates reflects the dominant assumptions of the 'victors' of the 'Cold War'. The application of the 'Liberal Project' to post-Cold War conflict resolution underpins the view that peace can be arrived at in conditions of war by transferring the competition for power away from the elite and towards the masses through the vehicle of popular participation in multi-party elections.[12] This may appear a timely panacea reinforcing the end of the ideological 'enemy'. However, its utility in some circumstances, either as a form of appropriate political organisation, or as an effective cure through liberal elections for deep rooted political conflict, raises many questions as yet either left unanswered or denied amidst the sanctity and inviolability of the western liberal democratic ethos.

Cambodia is just one of those cases, and there are good reasons for emphasising this particular instance of intervention, and, equally importantly, its aftermath. First, that operation reflected a joint, unified role for members of the Perm-5 previously engaged in confrontation and disunity through which they could end their conflict in Southeast Asia. China, the US and the USSR all agreed to the provision of a force for change, the intended consequences of which had also been agreed. Second, it permitted wider rapprochement between China and Viêt Nam as well as between the US and Hanoi, which in turn would accelerate the integration of all Southeast Asian states into the Association of Southeast Asian Nations (ASEAN). This in turn was believed to offer the opportunity for greater political stability and improved economic development, as well as implying greater accessibility to regional resources for foreign states and companies. Third, a settlement in Cambodia using such an approach clearly offered an opportunity for the further spreading of the Liberal credo in the fashion enunciated by many who argued along the lines of an 'end of history'. Fourth, it offered an opportunity to test the degree to which, in the 'new world order', constitutional, pluralist liberalism and the assumptions behind the globalisation of political ideology would be transferable to developing states with limited experience of such forms of organisation.

Preface

Accordingly, in 1991, the Perm-5 concluded the settlement of the long-running Khmer conflict in Paris. This bitter war and its conclusion reflected the values of both the Cold War in which it was born and the 'new world order' in which it would be resolved, standing as it did on the cusp of both eras. In 1991, Cambodia, like its capital Phnom Penh, stood astride the confluence of mighty forces. Just as the flow of the Bassac and Mekong rivers converge on Phnom Penh, so too did the ebb of communism and flow of democracy; the emerging utility of elections for conflict resolution; and the utilisation of the new peacekeeping ethos, straddle Cambodia in that year.

The operation that ensued in Cambodia over an eighteen-month period, concluding with elections in May 1993 was, at the time, the most sophisticated of the post-Cold War UN interventions. A massive peacekeeping force implemented a mandate to hold multi-party elections to allow Cambodians to chose their own leader and in so doing extend legitimacy to a national political body, organised along democratic lines. The elections were indeed unimaginably successful, but the reliability of the transitional process, and the degree to which democracy has persisted in Cambodia, were more doubtful. 'Democratisation' in Cambodia was still very much an experiment in 1999. The operationalization of that transition was characterised as much by trauma as security, and the nature of Khmer politics in the post-UN period did not reflect the overt ideals of the Paris mandate which ordered the UN's conflict settlement efforts. In July 1997, for example, fighting erupted in Phnom Penh, and in other parts of Cambodia, between the incumbent Cambodian People's Party's (CPP) military and their opposition; effectively, between representatives of the two co-prime ministers.[13] This fight represented the consolidation of the domestic balance of power in Cambodia, and resulted in the exile of some key leadership elements of the Royalist FUNCINPEC party which won the 1993 elections. Thus, whilst the international community claimed to have 'settled' the war in Cambodia in 1991, Cambodians appeared to settle it themselves in 1997.

There is, this book will argue, a clear connection between the Liberal assumptions underpinning the mandate established to remove Cambodia from the international agenda, and the resistance to the transitional process from 1991-1999. It will argue that the political settlement ordained primarily at the behest of the superpowers explains in no small part both the travails of transition under the UN, and the continued challenge to democratisation in Cambodia.

Preface

Furthermore, it will argue that the externally derived settlement has, in fact, created a different and new context in which the original conflict was fought. The institutionalisation and re-contextualisation of conflict, away from the battlefield and into the coalition body which governed Cambodia in 1993, created the conditions in which the underlying tenor of the Khmer conflict continued to dominate Khmer political evolution to the detriment of secure transition to western constitutional democracy. This statement neither endorses nor rejects the much debated concept of 'Asian values'; rather, it seeks an explanation for the transitional challenges experienced in Cambodia.

If it was the purpose of the United Nations to settle the political conflict in Cambodia which underpinned the war, by establishing democratic norms and procedures resulting in a sustainable political peace, it failed to do so at the time. If it is true to say, as Zakaria does, that western-anointed liberalism is best symbolised 'not by the mass plebiscite but by the impartial judge', then Cambodia did not have such a democracy by 1997.[14] The pre-eminence of democracy as the 'highest' form of political organisation further presupposes that the central tenets of liberal democracy, which include multi-party elections and powersharing where there are many contenders for leadership, are appropriate to settle conflict. However, the central political issues that created conditions of instability were not addressed in the settlement and mandate. Further, notions of conflict resolution implicit and explicit in the 1991 Paris Peace Agreements (PPA) did not ease directly Cambodia's transition from war to peace, and from authoritarianism to democracy.

The PPA is the most visible evidence of the over-arching assumptions concerning liberal democracy and its agency as a peacemaker. The peace agreement constituted the institutionalisation of democratisation, providing the key ingredients and the mechanism for super-imposing them on the subject country: Cambodia. However, it will be argued that there were few signs by Spring 1998, six years after the arrival of the UN force, of the type of durable political peace in that country which reflects the institutions the international community, liberalisation, and UNTAC brought to Cambodia. It is the purpose of this book to question the degree to which the peace settlement was appropriate to Cambodia's conditions and experiences, and use this approach to offer an explanation of Cambodia's deeply troubled political transition to 'democracy'.

Jarat Chopra wrote, in 1994, that 'failure is not part of the institutional memory of the United Nations', and that 'lessons are left to be learned only from successes'. He went on to observe that 'obscuring mistakes has meant they have been repeated. Reluctance to keeping UN history honest has slowed the development of more effective operations'. He moved to express the concern that 'lucky strikes recorded as organisational accomplishments have led the UN to assume more challenging tasks', arguing that the UN 'has been heading toward a disaster, as UNTAC nearly illustrated...'. He added that 'a self-congratulatory mood ... following the balloting process threatens to obscure the valuable lessons to be learned from ... mistakes'.[15] This book seeks to demonstrate and explain the weaknesses of the approach to resolving Cambodia's conflict through democratisation and the ensuing trauma of the transition necessary to undertake this. It also seeks to expunge some of the myths that claim intervention in Cambodia 'brought to a successful conclusion' war and suffering; and that 'the curtain has closed on a great human tragedy'.[16] Such denial of Cambodia's circumstances underscores the accuracy of Chopra's 'institutional memory' and requires closer scrutiny if Cambodia's political transition into the 'new world order' is to be better understood. As importantly, it perhaps offers a criticism of the broader acceptance of democratisation and the innate problems of transition that accompany this phenomenon.

Acknowledgements

This book is a product in part of the support I have been lucky enough to enjoy from a number of people and institutions, especially in the concluding stages. I would like to thank everyone who lent me invaluable support, be it for material, advice, criticism, or who rendered my research possible in other ways. This work could not have been completed without the friendship and trust of Sarah Burgess, Patricia Donnelly, Marcus and Regine de Frettes, David Munro, John Pilger, Graham and Many Pin-Shaw, Stephen Riley, Candice Sainsbury, Sim Sambo, Yothin Tho and Michael Vickery. It is regrettably not possible individually to thank the numerous interviewees, Cambodian, non-governmental, United Nations and many others, who provided so much material, and without whose experiences this book would be much less valuable. Nor could some of the research exercises have been conducted without the kind support of the British Academy. I am grateful to them all; I alone bear responsibility for any flaws in this work.

Acronyms

ASEAN	Association of Southeast Asian Nations
BLDP	Buddhist Liberal Democratic Party
BLP	Buddhist Liberal Party
CC	Constitutional Council
CGDK	Coalition Government of Democratic Kampuchea
CPAF	Cambodian People's Armed Forces
CPP	Cambodian People's Party
DES	District Electoral Supervisor
FUNCINPEC	Front Uni Nationale pour un Cambodge Independent, Neutre, Pacifique et Cooperatif
ICK	International Conference on Kampuchea
ICM	International Control Mechanism
IMF	International Monetary Fund
IRI	International Republican Institute
JIM	Jakarta Informal Meetings
KID	Khmer Institute for Democracy
KNUFNS	Kampuchea National United Front for National Salvation
KPNLF	Khmer People's National Liberation Front
NADK	National Army of Democratic Kampuchea
NDI	National Democratic Institute
NEC	National Election Committee
NGO	Non-Governmental Organisation
NPE	Neutral Political Environment
NUF	National United Front
PAVN	People's Army of Viêt Nam

Acronyms

Perm-5	Permanent Five members (of the UN Security Council)
PICC	Paris International Conference on Cambodia
PPA	Paris Peace Agreement
PRK	People's Republic of Kampuchea
PRPK	People's Revolutionary Party of Kampuchea
PRC	People's Revolutionary Council
RGC	Royal Government of Cambodia
SNC	Supreme National Council
SoC	State of Cambodia
SRSG	Special Representative of the secretary-general (of the UN)
SRP	Sam Rainsy Party
UNAMIC	United Nations Advance Mission in Cambodia
UNCHR	United Nations Centre for Human Rights
UNHCR	United Nations High Commission for Refugees
UNTAC	United Nations Transitional Authority in Cambodia
UNV	United Nations Volunteer
VCP	Viêt Namese Communist Party
VONADK	Voice of the National Army of Democratic Kampuchea
WB	World Bank

Tables

1. 1993 election results by party, seats in the Assembly, and vote counts. 80
2. 1998 elections, confirmed provisional results, 7 September. 182

Maps

1. SOUTH EAST ASIA   xxii
2. CAMBODIA   xxiii

Maps

Map 1: SOUTH EAST ASIA

Maps

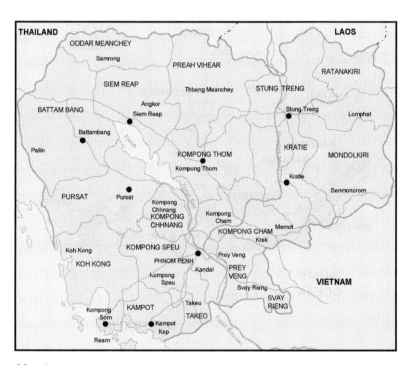

Map 2: CAMBODIA

Introduction

Although the worst disaster to befall Cambodia in recent times originated from a group of Khmers led by the late Pol Pot, Cambodia's political development since the mid-nineteenth century has been punctuated by a series of interventions which have been distinctly non-Khmer in their nature. European imperialism turned the country into a protectorate under the French Union in Indochina. It also led to the rediscovery of the ancient temples of Angkor Wat, in the Northwest of the country, recreating for Khmers the powerful identity and status they enjoyed between the ninth and thirteenth centuries, but lost after the capital moved to Oudong in the wake of Thailand's sacking of Siem Reap. After the French, Japan invaded and annexed part of the country to Thailand. By the time independence came and went in 1953, the rumblings of discontent were set in stone in Viêt Nam, directly to the East, and sympathy on the Khmer Monarch's part for Viêt Nam's plight coincided with the influence of China's political orbit to undermine Phnom Penh's neutrality.

In response, Cambodia's eastern borders attracted the attention of the secret US bombing campaign known as Operation Menu; and incited a clandestine US land invasion from the East coinciding roughly with an externally-supported coup d'etat against Prince Sihanouk, the country's leader until 1970. As the civil war inside Cambodia gave way to Khmer Rouge victory and political consolidation, so too did direct international intervention largely cease, until 1979 when, after halting the murderous policies of Pol Pot, Viêt Nam drew the wrath of China and the US for its incursion into Cambodia.

For the ensuing decade and more, much of the western international political order, in conjunction with China, ensured that the

Introduction

population and its *de facto* elite were not recognised at the UN. By denying that government its seat at the United Nations, international development aid needed to rebuild Cambodia, after Pol Pot's failed agrarian experiment, was arrested. Cambodia's development, political, economic and social, was determined in large part by these conditions imposed from beyond and tuned to fit the needs of those punishing or supporting Cambodia and Viêt Nam in the Cold War.

As these conditions of isolation persisted, limited Western influences or institutions permeated Cambodia, with exceptions such as Oxfam, UNICEF and the FAO. Political and social organisation altered little in the following decade, although significant shifts from a planned to a market economy accompanied the liberalisation of private ownership laws after 1985. This was predated by the acceptance of private trade as a pragmatic mechanism for recovery, despite the creation of *krom samakki* (solidarity groups) which have a distinctly communitarian/communist flavour.

When a Cambodian plebiscite was ordained as the Cold War drew to a close, a huge interventionist force was required to create conditions favoured by foreign agencies in which this could take place. The United Nations Transitional Authority in Cambodia (UNTAC) withdrew after an 18-month mini-trusteeship. The intention of this was to offer a semblance of political pluralism and a shift away from a single party Leninist state to one governed more by a concern with joining the path of economic development through markets and the minimal state.

Four years after the elections that engendered this change, violence swept Phnom Penh in July 1997. Many described the events as a coup, although the state was unaffected, and whilst one member of the National Assembly was exiled, he was replaced by another member of his own party. The fact that this person was the first of two co-premiers offers some clue as to the complexity and extraordinary nature of Khmer politics, and the fragility upon which Khmer political order rested. Whilst this was one of the few major domestic political events which was not *immediately* influenced by external intervention, the consequences of the power struggle received direct attention from all the aid donors.

The response was mixed. ASEAN and Japan, later joined by Europe, continued aid at a reduced rate, whilst the US took a much harder line and ceased development aid, suspending the activities of many aid organisations including those devoted to primary education, such as the Cambodian Agency for Primary Education (CAPE).

Introduction

The effect of these punctuations again had a determining effect on indigenous political development. Political instability, and the underlying causes of the July 1997 fighting, created and exacerbated conditions of insecurity, hostility and suspicion. They are not the only or immediate determinants of political instability. That derives also from the activities of Cambodian politicians and their political clans. However, if foreign intervention was a characteristic of the past, it is equally idiosyncratic of the present.

This book examines the various stages of Cambodia's most recent externally imposed political transition. The preface has outlined the post-Cold War context into which the Cambodian experience appears to fit. The introduction sketches the manner in which recent Cambodian political transition has often been a function of external interests, as well as indigenous experimentation. Chapter one will introduce the background to the most recent international intervention and the manner in which this arose and was framed. Chapter two will then examine some of the key assumptions made regarding the application of such an approach to this conflict. It will discuss the incongruity between on the one hand, the external governing concerns of the powers involved in imposing the particular peace plan; and on the other, the concerns of Cambodia's contesting leaders.

Chapter three will present a critical overview of the operation. Much of the detail has been treated in various quarters; this chapter will highlight the most demanding challenges to political transition, and will identify early indicators that some characteristics of Khmer political tradition were not catered for or understood by the Paris Peace Agreements of 1991 (PPA). Chapter four will be the first of three chapters that will examine some key problems of transition during the implementation period, between 1991 and 1993. It will examine the relationship between elements of the deployment that, although not apparently connected on first inspection, become more evident through more careful scrutiny. Chapter five will address a key deficiency of the intervention in the form of the Khmer Rouge's political withdrawal from the peace process. This, it is argued, has its origins less in the traditional view of the unreliability and untrustworthiness of the Khmer Rouge, and more in the inadequacy of the Paris Agreements which were unrealistic but which, more importantly, failed to create the conditions to which the Khmer Rouge had originally agreed. This, then, led to the first major challenge to Cambodia's planned transition to multi-party democracy through the exclusion of a key party, and identified some of the conditions which

Introduction

determined the degree of participation in Khmer politics, as well as the perception of the consequences of exclusion.

Chapter six will examine the second, and deeply significant, challenge to political transition in Cambodia. It will discuss the June 1993 secession, and will argue that it was illustrative of the deep-rooted challenges to democratic transition inherent in a political system characterised by the historical and contemporary absence of institutionalised opposition.

The next three chapters will discuss some of the major themes that have characterised political transition in Cambodia in the period since UNTAC's departure. Chapter seven examines two linked, central themes that have their origins in the Paris Agreements. These, when examined in the context of powersharing in Cambodian elite political culture, led directly and indirectly to the fighting in July 1997 which effectively demonstrated that the surgical insertion of democracy was relatively illusory. Instead, the period between 1991 and 1997 is perhaps best characterised as one where the greatest concern for the elite was power building, rather than power sharing. Chapter seven will also argue that the July fighting was a direct consequence of a struggle for the political and military resources of the Khmer Rouge as it imploded. Its armed legacy, left to it by UNTAC's inability to fulfil key terms of the Agreement, was thus thrown out of proportion.

Chapter eight will examine the fragmentation and recreation of parliamentary opposition. It will also attempt to identify some of the key power-base building that accompanied shifting political coalitions within the Assembly. It will argue that the nature of the relationships between the dominant party and its antagonists, either in terms of political parties or extra-parliamentary opposition, defines political instability and prevents the development of a stable political culture, accepting of compromise and powersharing on the path to democratic transition.

Chapter nine will examine the period between the July 1997 fighting and the July 1998 elections. It will note the recreation of political stability under the conditions defined by the absence of unacceptable opposition to elite parties of all political persuasion, and the reformation of political opposition. It will also examine the elections and attempt to explain why the CPP overawed its opposition, and identify conditions for political stability and the limitations to political transition.

Chapter ten will conclude that the nature of political transition is far from what was envisaged. It actually represents, rather than the

Introduction

termination of war and confrontation, the re-contextualisation of conflict inside the very mechanism the PPA used to end hostilities. The conclusion will then relate these findings to the utility of applying democratic, powersharing political systems in this more traditional political culture. It will thus criticise the pre-eminence of democracy as the only remaining form of political organisation, and as a global panacea for conflict resolution in the context of the Cambodia operation.

I
Peace Seeking

To understand the nature of the Paris Peace Agreement of 1991 (PPA) and its propriety, one must understand the path by which the settlement was reached. The development of a 'solution' to the Cambodia conflict followed a serpentine process. It began when Viêt Nam invaded Cambodia on 25 December, 1978, ousting Pol Pot, the chairman of Democratic Kampuchea, and formed a new government made up of defectors and the few remaining administrators and bureaucrats who survived Pol Pot's exterminations and forced labour camps.

Supporting the political and civil reconstitution of Cambodia were Hanoi's imported counterparts to the new Khmer government in Phnom Penh. The interpretation of Viêt Nam's role in this process lay at the heart of thirteen years of sustained domestic, regional and international conflict. For they revolved less around events inside Cambodia than they did around the problem, as Beijing and Washington viewed it, that Moscow-backed Viêt Nam had overthrown the Chinese client Pol Pot, who was then quickly adopted by Washington. Events befalling Cambodia took on great significance as the period of superpower détente receded and was replaced by the rapidly deteriorating international relations characteristic of the second Cold War.[1]

Background to the Paris Peace Agreement: 1978 to 1991

Viêt Nam's act of liberation and invasion in conjunction with the Kampuchean National United Front for National Salvation (KNUFNS) stirred deep concerns about alleged Soviet imperialism.

As Moscow announced its support for Hanoi in its Cambodia operation (having the year before signed a twenty-five year Treaty of Friendship), concurrently, various pro-Western figures in the developing worlds were being toppled and replaced with anti-western or pro-Soviet proxies.

Superficially, the debate was located in the terms of the United Nations Charter. Those suspicious of, or ideologically opposed to, Hanoi declared the attack and the continuing occupation a breach of the Charter and of Democratic Kampuchea's sovereignty. This in turn implied that the new administration could not represent Cambodia legitimately in terms of international norms. As a result, the UN refused to recognise the new *de facto* government in Phnom Penh, and instead recognised that of Pol Pot. Furthermore, despite a very obvious and crying need for it, Phnom Penh's exclusion from UN recognition meant it could not receive UN development aid. At this point, it probably needed it most, after the destruction wrought by Pol Pot and the Khmer Rouge, and in the light of the series of environmental disasters which beset the country in the wake of his ousting. Vickery contended that

> The international legal argument against the PRK is not only complex, but weak; and its hypocrisy is stupefying. Few if any of the countries now concerned with the Viêtnamese presence in Cambodia showed equal concern over the reimposition of French rule in Indochina after World War II, or over Thai and non-communist Viêtnamese efforts to destabilise the regime of Prince Sihanouk.[2]

However, the significance of the debate revolved more accurately around the manner in which the UN seat issue supported the interests of Soviet, Chinese and US foreign policy. Although Viêt Nam's incursion clearly put an end to Pol Pot's well-documented rule, these benefits were not the ones that were emphasised. Instead, the incursion was turned around to reinforce the Cold War view, held in the West and in China, that the USSR and Viêt Nam were colluding to expand their empires, so the UN Charter acted as a fig leaf of respectability behind which to pursue more venal anti-Soviet agendas. For the US and China, the incursion represented an opportunity to punish its Viêt Namese enemy, and its enemy's allies in Moscow. Chang Pao-min argued that in view of security considerations in Beijing and Washington, the Viêt Namese occupation of Kampuchea ... was not an "isolated event" or "local issue" ... It not only revealed Hanoi's ambition to dominate all of Indochina but also represented an important component of the Soviet attempt to further its strategy of seeking world hegemony.³

This perspective also helped retrospectively legitimise the US role in the Viêt Nam war, and spurred on a renewed confrontation between Washington and Hanoi, with Cambodia once more a 'side-show' to the larger issues.

However, such perspectives conceal alternative views of the events in Indochina. Both Washington and Beijing invented or exaggerated the meaning of Viêt Nam's actions. Still stinging from their defeat in the war in Viêt Nam, and hostile to the USSR, whilst simultaneously utilising an opportunistic vehicle for nourishing their recent alliance with Beijing, Washington turned the situation to its own geo-political advantage. In other words, Viêt Nam's actions with regard to Cambodia furnished the US with occasion to undermine the post-1975 communist regime in Hanoi. Michael Haas observed that

> Washington needed the bogey of Viêt Namese expansionism ... it was clear that no such [Indochinese] federation was intended ... [This] did not stop Washington from continuing to claim that Hanoi's action to oust the Khmer Rouge was an instance of imperialism.⁴

The general propaganda of the Cold War regarding Russo-Viêt Namese expansionism in Indochina reflected the broader ideological confrontation globally. It was easy to ascribe such a motive to Hanoi, because it fed the propaganda machine that supported the Sino-Western agenda of punishing Viêt Nam and containing the USSR. However, Turley argues that Viêt Nam's longer-term presence was not expansionist in terms of imperialism. Rather, it could be ascribed to a desire to

> deny the use of Cambodia by a country seen as hostile, namely, China ... Viêt Nam's strategy was to cement a "special relationship" with Cambodia like the one it had with Laos to strengthen the three countries' "security interdependence" ... Viêt Nam's long term [security] depended on Laotian and Khmer self-reliance.⁵

Duiker corroborates this analysis, noting that within weeks of its establishment after January 1979, the PRK had 'signed a Treaty of

Friendship and Cooperation with Vietnam. Having initialled a similar pact with Laos the previous year, Hanoi achieved its special relationship with its western neighbours'.[6] The problem for Cambodians, and for the Viêt Namese, was succinctly summarised by John Pilger, who argued that 'Cambodia's liberators came from the wrong side of the Cold War'.[7] Vickery added that it was clear that 'the problem for [the superpowers] was not so much the overthrow of Pol Pot by external force, but that the force was socialist Vietnam'.[8]

It was clearly a nonsense of a conspiracy theory, constructed from propaganda rather than evidence, and aimed at punishing Cold War enemies with the 'hidden' expense of Cambodian lives. In the first instance, it is important to note that the invasion was not merely Viêt Namese. It was spearheaded by the Kampuchean National United Front for National Salvation, often referred to as the Salvation Front, a group formed officially on 2 December 1978.[9] Despite its novelty then, it consisted of Cambodians who had already gone from Cambodia to Viêt Nam before this, including Hun Sen, Bou Thang, and Heng Samrin in 1977. It also consisted of those who had remained in Viêt Nam after their communist training had been completed, rather than returning to Cambodia.[10] Khmer refugees from Cambodia who had fled the Pol Pot destruction supplemented it. Indeed, some of its members were present at the first meeting of the Communist Party of Kampuchea (CPK) in 1951. There were clear nationalist credentials attached to this political body. Both Hood and Duiker state that the goal of the KNUFNS was the 'overthrow of the Pol Pot regime'.[11]

This raises two points. First, there was consent from the KNUFNS towards the Viêt Namese action. It is reasonable to assume that the Heng Samrin leadership of this organisation would not have been willing to act as a colonial arrowhead for Hanoi. It is also reasonable to assume that the Viêt Namese Communist Party (VCP) did not dupe the whole organisation with its 'imperial' pretensions. Second, the assault was genuinely non-imperial because it was aimed specifically at eliminating Pol Pot from politics, not at creating a form of suzerainty or colonialism on Viêt Nam's part. No documentation has been produced showing Viêt Nam's intentions were dishonourable in this sense.

This has both a domestic and an international flavour to it. Domestically, there was an elite ready to manage Cambodia after Pol Pot that sought its own hegemony and sovereignty, and which planned to introduce reforms which would not have met with particular disapproval from other states. This included prioritisation of education, repair of health infrastructure, and reintroduction of a currency, amongst others. The PRK also delivered evenly distributed land access, although all land belonged to the state and thus private ownership did not evolve until later.

Internationally, such an assault and removal would halt the murderous border raids launched frequently by Pol Pot's forces whether on his command or not on the Viêt Namese western border. These attacks have been chronicled and documented in several critical sources.[12]

However, it should also be noted that those attacks were far from unplanned, sporadic or individual 'hit and run' affairs. Nor were they limited to the late 1970s. In fact, early references to military attacks on Viêt Nam extend to May 1975. Some sources dated in 1976 have talked of plans to 'reconquer Kampuchea Krom [southern Viêt Nam] and Saigon'.[13] Signs of strong anti-Viêt Namese propaganda extend from shortly after this period.[14] Vickery's surveys in 1979 and 1980 of Cambodians who had lived near the border at the time show that 'there were [Khmer Rouge-led] meetings announcing the new policy of equality between base ['old'] and new people ... to unite in opposition to the Vietnamese'.[15] Hanoi was accused of using these 'attacks', which amounted to open and co-ordinated warfare, as a pretext to launch an imperial war of domination and subjugation. If this was case, the most obvious question to raise, is 'why did Viêt Nam wait until the end of 1978 to do this?'

Thus, not only was there a great deal of misleading propaganda that identified Viêt Namese intensions as despicably imperial in their nature, but Hanoi was also blamed for attacking Cambodia. This was despite the clear evidence to show that their attack was necessitated by the Khmer Rouge's behaviour towards Viêt Nam, and that it was a reluctant intrusion that they could well have done without. Furthermore, the fact that Cambodians spearheaded the attack was ignored, as was the fact that some of those involved had long-reaching connections historically with the early originators of the Communist Party of Kampuchea.

This debate about the legitimacy of Viêt Nam's actions is important, because it frames the international views and agendas of the wider participants in both the Cambodian conflict, and in its resolution. Quite clearly, any peace settlement would naturally reflect the values of the international actors involved as much as the prosecution of the war would. In this sense, the terms of victory for either the US and China, on the one hand, or the USSR on the other, would reflect their interest on the ground. Thus, Washington and Beijing aspired to the defeat of Hanoi and Phnom Penh during the course of the war; and Moscow and Hanoi sought to defend the positions of their clients from the Sino-Western strategy.

As early as 1981, the parameters of any settlement were clear, and differed little in objective and format (but greatly in scope and intrusion) from the agreement signed ten years later. The Soviet Union demanded the removal of the Khmer Rouge from the UN seat and recognition of its' clients in Phnom Penh. The US and China sought the inclusion of the Khmer Rouge and removal of the *de facto* Phnom Penh government.

By 1991, the US and China, the former having 'won' the Cold War, could ensure their Khmer Rouge clients a position in the 'comprehensive' settlement; but the Soviet Union, beaten, could not demand the preservation of Hanoi's position on Cambodia, or of the government in Phnom Penh. The terms of the PPA reflected these conditions, and influenced the manner in which implementation of those terms could be conducted, as well as influencing the durability of the settlement. In the decade between the definition of the problem and its conclusion, the war continued, with neither side gaining sufficient advantage to deal the other a final military blow that would close the conflict permanently.

The War

The conflict was conducted at three levels. First, the Viêt Namese-installed People's Revolutionary Party of Kampuchea (PRPK), having established the People's Revolutionary Council (PRC) and the People's Republic of Kampuchea (PRK), faced a tri-partite coalition nominally headed by Prince Norodom Sihanouk. Sihanouk had, until being ousted in March 1970, led Cambodia as a royal descendant and Monarch. The strongest element of this coalition was the Khmer Rouge. Based in and around a series of refugee camps along the Thai-Cambodian border, Sihanouk's supporters and the Khmer Rouge were abetted by the Khmer People's National Liberation Front (KPNLF).[16] Although this coalition reflected socialist, liberal and Royalist interests, they were united by a common desire to rid Cambodia of the Viêt Namese 'invader-occupiers'. The Coalition Government of Democratic Kampuchea (CGDK) became by 1982 the institution 'around which international support largely coalesced'. As a result, it was the CGDK, rather than the incumbent *de facto* leadership in Phnom Penh, which represented Cambodia at the UN from 1982.[17]

At the second level, regional alliances revolved around this conflict and the divisions they engendered at the superpower level. The pro-western capitalist ASEAN states lined up behind the US and China, because they all shared the common purpose of preventing or containing alleged Soviet or Viêt Namese expansionism. Although both the Khmer Rouge and the Chinese reflected, if perhaps inaccurately, a Communist mantle, ASEAN's alignment acted as a buffer against the perception of a Soviet threat. In fact, although the Khmer Rouge Central Committee dissolved the Communist Party of Kampuchea (CPK) in order to create an illusion of a capitalist organisation, that body remained ideologically committed to key elements of socialist thinking.[18] The Communist states of Viêt Nam and Laos lined up behind Moscow and the Warsaw Pact countries.

At the third level, the Cambodian parties were quickly adopted by superpower patrons keen to use the Khmer conflict as a vehicle for their own which would continue the Cold War pattern of avoiding direct superpower confrontation through the use of proxy wars primarily in the developing world. However, the relationship was more complex than at first appears. Not only was the US using the KNUNFS/Viêt Nam's invasion to politically assault the USSR; it was also using the coincidence of Chinese antagonism towards Viêt Nam to buttress and build upon Nixon and Kissinger's pro-Beijing diplomacy of the early 1970s that reinforced the Sino-Soviet split. Thus, Beijing saw the utility of supporting Pol Pot because doing so represented indirect accomplishment of Beijing's plans to 'bleed Viêt Nam white' for leaning towards the USSR in the American War in Viêt Nam and for Hanoi's wartime 'disloyalty' to the People's Republic of China (PRC).[19] Furthermore, it represented an opportunity for Beijing to punish Moscow, both for the deepening divide ideologically between the two superpowers; and for the latter's support of Hanoi and Hanoi's so-called 'puppets' in Phnom Penh. The Khmer Rouge and Pol Pot thus became a double-headed, two-handed stick with which Beijing and Washington could beat Hanoi and Moscow, for the US's humiliation in Viêt Nam and Beijing's regarding the choice Hanoi made between China and the USSR.[20]

The KNUNFS/Viêt Namese invasion polarised the international community into two distinct camps, led on the one hand by Washington and Beijing; and on the other by Moscow.[21] In the context of the Cold War, argues Pilger, 'there [was] essential agreement

Peace Seeking

between the United States and the People's Republic of China with regard to strategic perspectives and particularly as they relate[d] to ... the invasion of Cambodia by Soviet-backed Viêtnamese'.[22] Accordingly, China and the US denied the PRK political legitimacy in 1982 'to prevent Cambodia's UN seat from falling into Soviet hands via the Viêt Namese client regime in Phnom Penh'.[23] This act further underscored the political axis of support that would later strongly influence the formulation of the Paris Peace Agreements a decade later. It is well established that in order to accomplish Sino-US objectives, 'the US and China brought the [Khmer Rouge] ... back to life'.[24] Sihanouk confirmed this thus: 'To save Cambodia, all you had to do was let Pol Pot die ... and you brought him back to life. It is true.... From the ashes the Phoenix rises! Was reborn and sent to the battlefield to kill! To kill! To kill!'.[25]

It is important to understand that the international origins of the conflict help explain the manner in which it was settled. Had the Khmer conflict been devoid of an international context, then the nature of a settlement would probably have reflected such conditions. Efforts aimed at resolving the international problem did not automatically consider or address the internal conflicts, political and military, being waged in Cambodia and along the Thai border. In a sense, it was not the Khmer war that caused the Perm-5 distress; it was the consequences of that war for the engaged foreign powers.

Three reasonably distinct phases characterise the period from 1979–1991. The first stage reflected intransigence on the part of one axis or the other to accept change that either benefited or disadvantaged each side. Thus, Soviet initiatives met with disapproval from the Sino-US quarter, and vice versa. The second stage reflected domestic changes within the USSR, and to a lesser degree, in Viêt Nam after 1986, which effectively represented a change of position permitting the Sino-US axis to maintain and advance its own geo-political position. As Soviet resistance waned, the framework acceptable to the US and China pushed forwards to a degree, only to be met with resistance from Phnom Penh and Hanoi, leading to a halt in the movement of the peace process. The third stage reflected Sino-US disdain at this brake on their interests and objectives, and resulted in the removal of the 'peace' initiative from the local level, where it stalled regularly, to the domain of the Perm-5, where it could be more readily influenced. This stage was also marked by the continued withdrawal, to a large degree, of Soviet pressures for a settlement that reflected their own geo-political interests in the issue and the region.

Stage One: 1979–c1986

Although clearly at the beginning of the conflict most national and international actors took a fairly intransigent line, Heininger observes that during this stage of the war, and in the efforts at diplomacy surrounding it, '[m]uch of the stalemate of the 1980s owed to [the] outside powers'.[26] Certainly, China and the US had no interest in seeing their Khmer Rouge clients marginalised by Viêt Nam and the USSR. This clear divide, the UN record shows, impeded effective diplomatic intervention in the Cambodian imbroglio.[27] The external actors would not agree to anything that shifted a *status quo* that suited their positions of rivalry within the UN Security Council.

Resistance to various peace proposals found expression in Moscow, Beijing and Washington. The International Conference on Kampuchea (ICK) in 1981, for example, recommended a variety of proposals not dissimilar to the PPA a decade later. The Conference was convened 'with the aim of finding a comprehensive political settlement of the Kampuchean problem....' which, at the insistence of the US and China, necessitated inclusion of the CGDK.[28] Predictably, the USSR and Viêt Nam boycotted the ICK because of its insistence on a 'comprehensive' settlement and a Viêt Namese withdrawal.[29] Clearly, this would have been unacceptable, as the strength of Moscow's axis would have diminished in conjunction with that of the opposition's being enhanced. The power equation would have been out of balance.

Although the Soviet-led Eastern axis was demonised for vetoing the ICK, the US and China also caused peace proposals to founder. A solution to the Kampuchea problem without the Khmer Rouge ran counter to Sino-Western interests, because the mechanism of punishing Hanoi would be undermined, and because preserving the *status quo* was a vehicle for maintaining the confrontation with Moscow. Furthermore, although China's policy paralleled that of the US, Beijing had individual and independent reasons for continuing the war. Beijing clearly stated such objectives, admitting that they did not 'love the Khmer Rouge for themselves, they love[d] them as a cheap weapon for bashing the Viêt Namese'.[30] Deng Xiaoping thought that it was 'wise for China to force the Viêtnamese to stay in Cambodia, because that way they will suffer more and more'.[31] Further, Deng 'did not understand why some people want[ed] to remove Pol Pot'. Beijing was using the Khmer Rouge to protract the confrontation with Viêt Nam. Accordingly, Beijing and Washington rejected the 1981 ICK because it would have represented an impediment to their foreign policy objectives regionally and internationally, although in slightly different ways. The situation in the first stage clearly benefited US and Chinese interests, as the Khmer Rouge enjoyed a form of international legitimacy; and the 'client' regime of Hanoi's was punished as a direct consequence of this. Viêt Nam and the USSR incurred heavy penalties economically in supporting Cambodia's precipitous recovery, at times when Hanoi itself was still economically impaired and unevenly and unreliably developing politically. Furthermore, Sino-American allies were better placed financially to support their side of the process, which primarily involved aid to the refugee camps on the Thai border, and the supply of weapons and finance to the Khmer Rouge. In an article which concluded that international aid should not be sent to the Cambodians in Cambodia, Heder notes that such 'politically blind border aid almost certainly rescued the [Khmer Rouge] remnants from a potentially fatal crisis. If it had not been for international aid from across the border, the Viêtnamese would have succeeded in literally starving [the Khmer Rouge] to death by the end of 1979'.[32] This situation permitted major Sino-US objectives to be achieved. It was thus 'the US and China that brought the [PDK] ... back to life'.[33]

This superpower-determined framework had consequences for the regional level peace initiatives proposed during the 1980s. Because the situation was useful for the Sino-US, anti-Moscow axis, it had to be preserved. Beuls, for example, observed that 'whenever a regional consensus developed [it] was regularly boycotted at the international level'.[34] Kiernan offers the example of Australian Foreign Minister Bill Hayden's attempts to encourage regional diplomacy regarding Cambodia in 1983. US Secretary of State Schultz deliberately discouraged his attempts. Schultz gave Hayden 'an extremely tough time [and] a hell of a hammering'.[35] Despite strong support for Hayden's initiative, which found currency with some of the ASEAN states, 'Schultz managed to force Hayden to abandon [the plan]'.[36]

Regional and local interests were subsumed to confrontation within the Perm-5 that had already set, and continued to inform, the tenor of peace negotiations and the likely character of any settlement. The situation had changed little, in this respect, by 1985. In response to various Thai initiatives to settle the problem, driven in part by a vision of Indochina as a market place rather than as a battlefield, Schultz again intervened. He warned ASEAN states with this view 'to be extremely careful in formulating peace proposals for Kampuchea because Vietnam might one day accept them'.[37] Schultz's threat played on ASEAN fears of an expansionist Viêt Nam; concerns which Washington deliberately aggravated, according to Haas and others, with black propaganda deliberately conceived to mislead external views regarding Viêt Nam's intentions.[38] Such intervention was far from unique; nor was it restricted to the early phase of hopeful regional negotiations. Indeed, it had established an unhealthy precedent, argues Vickery, which was vigorously pursued from Washington throughout the 1980s. In sum, 'all practical attempts to promote peace without the Khmer Rouge [were] obstructed by the US'.[39] Washington continued to take advantage of the seeds of doubt within ASEAN. Reinforced by misinformation, it ensured by covert means with Beijing's co-operation that the political organisation which left dead over a million people in forty four months would be succoured, nourished and nursed back to health with the intention of persecuting Viêt Nam and the USSR. Despite the moral bankruptcy of these programmes, they should be essentially unsurprising in the Cold War context.

Stage Two: 1986 to 1989

This impasse may well have continued to paralyse international relations regarding Viêt Nam's position in Cambodia but for changes affecting one side of the political equation at the international and regional levels. Gorbachev's Vladivostock Initiative and Hanoi's Sixth Party Congress reforms, both outlined in 1986, led to quite radical changes in the international and regional balance of power, which Pao-Min describes as 'the crucial catalyst for a new eagerness to expedite a resolution of the Kampuchea conflict....'.[40] Noting the role of the USSR, Tessifore and Woolfson argue that 'no real progress was made toward a political solution of the Cambodia conflict until Mikhail Gorbachev took the reins of government in the Soviet Union'.[41]

At a speech made in Vladivostock in July 1986, Gorbachev announced a review of Soviet foreign policy as it related to Eastern Asia. The reform-minded Soviet leader, confronted with economic problems at home, saw an opportunity to achieve a number of objectives. First, changing the degree of Soviet involvement in Indochina would release revenue that might be better used domestically. Second, by such a pragmatically driven approach, a key stumbling block in the political economy of Sino-Soviet and Soviet-US relations would be removed. This in turn might then encourage acceptance from the key capitalist states and integration into the world economy. The opportunity cost was that influence in Indochina would diminish; but clearly, for the pragmatic Gorbachev, this was outweighed by the benefits of an enhanced domestic economy.

Moscow, then, began to retreat from its fixed position regarding a Cambodian settlement. Pao-min claims Gorbachev had

> his eyes firmly set upon domestic reforms and major diplomatic breakthroughs in Moscow's relations with ... the United States and China ... Gorbachev could no longer sustain ... sponsorship of Viêtnam's occupation in Kampuchea.... It is clearly the combination and confluence of the above-mentioned developments that ... caused the ... remarkably stable coalition between Moscow, Hanoi and Phnom Penh to ... crumble.[42]

As a result of Gorbachev's changed foreign and domestic priorities, Moscow was ready to attempt to influence Hanoi and Phnom Penh to adopt similarly pragmatic positions for the sake of its longer term policy objectives which would suit Beijing and Washington and smooth Soviet rapprochement with the US and China.[43]

At roughly the same time, Viêt Nam held its Sixth Party Congress, at which more reform-minded leaders began to replace the orthodoxists in the Viêt Namese Politburo. Pragmatists recognised the economic consequences of Gorbachev's new posture for the already largely impoverished Viêt Namese state. Hanoi continued its strategy of withdrawal that further undermined Phnom Penh. A physical withdrawal had been underway since 1983 due to the costs, material, financial and human, of remaining in Cambodia fighting the civil war.[44] Hanoi's policy, then, aligned with Moscow's, and did not cause confrontation between the allies. Pao-min notes this was because of

> the urgent need to bring Viêt Nam out of the abyss of economic stagnation and social misery [and of] a basic re-examination and reorientation of Hanoi's external postures and policies, all of which required a new approach towards the question of Kampuchea.[45]

Heavily compromised economically, both the USSR and Viêt Nam chose to pursue desired economic policies by acquiescence to the wishes of the US and China through the expedient of reducing commitment to Phnom Penh and being seen to lean on its *de facto* leadership to accept Sino-US peace conditions. Thus, although Gorbachev's policy shift had been relatively significant, the fact that Viêt Nam was already withdrawing and recognising its domestic

Peace Seeking

economic constraints meant influence from Moscow to Hanoi was less important than some maintain.

This had a predictable effect on Phnom Penh's capacity to pursue the conflict militarily or diplomatically. Whereas the Khmer Rouge retained their voice in the Perm-5 through China and the US, Moscow's withdrawal left Phnom Penh with limited international influence. Equally, the withdrawal of financial and military support marginalised Phnom Penh's capacity to wage war. As a result, Pao-min notes, 'under the combined pressure of both Viêtnam and the Soviet Union, the [Phnom Penh] regime had no choice but to modify its own posture and policy'.[46]

This process undermined Phnom Penh's capacity to refuse to enjoin negotiations with the Khmer Rouge. The more the USSR and Viêt sought to normalise their relations with the US and Beijing, the closer Phnom Penh was forced to come to a consensus on the Cambodia problem with the CGDK. Similarly, this progress set in motion the process by which the peace settlement would be determined in large part by the 'winners' in this 'conflict': namely, the US and China.

This in turn permitted the Sino-American opposition and its Khmer allies in exile to take a definite negotiating lead for perhaps the first time since the war began.[47] The outcome was increasingly orientated towards the original objective of securing the Khmer Rouge a place in any settlement, and simultaneously towards marginalising their Viêt Namese-installed opposition in Phnom Penh. The closer they came to an agreement, the quicker the peace process could move forward; correspondingly, the more the Russo-Viêt Namese axis acquiesced to the deal, the greater the negotiating gain accrued to Washington and Beijing as they pushed for the inclusion of the Khmer Rouge in any settlement.

US and Chinese approaches contrasted clearly with the pragmatism of the changing regional outlook. Possibly sensing the inevitability of the Viêt Namese withdrawal from Cambodia, and hence ASEAN borders, Thai PM Chatichai Choonhavon expressed interest in turning Indochina 'from a battlefield to a trading ground'.[48] He opened bi-lateral relations with Hun Sen, the Cambodian Prime Minister, on an independent initiative, which was contrary to western policy because it afforded the PRK a form of recognition. By December 1987, a Hun Sen–Sihanouk alliance brokered by Bangkok looked likely, and prior to this, according to Leifer, 'Vietnam ma[d]e approaches to Sihanouk through the Romanians ... in order to engage him, either directly or indirectly through the Phnom Penh government in a dialogue'.[49]

However, such regional diplomacy was as unsustainable as it had been in the early 1980s. US State Department representatives called a halt to the proceedings. Interestingly, Ieng Sary, the Khmer Rouge Foreign Minister during the Pol Pot regime, claimed that the US had supported this proposal, but no other evidence was offered to support such an assertion.[50] The Thai administration was blackmailed economically and warned in no uncertain terms that if it continued to pursue this line and, in so doing, rejected the Khmer Rouge in favour of economic ties with Phnom Penh, then 'it would have to pay a price'. Kiernan records that US representatives warned the Thai administration that it 'should consider whether the total value of any new Indochinese trade would even cover the US trade access privileges it still [enjoyed] under the Generalised Special Preferences...'.[51] The US told Sihanouk, 'no Khmer Rouge, no deal'.[52] Because Thai policy and what it promised potentially confronted the emerging consensus in the Perm-5 that suited Washington, it was arrested. As Kiernan observed, 'the only lasting solution to the Cambodia conflict was to be found in Southeast Asia. But that avenue was blocked by the great powers'.[53]

Phnom Penh's allies were also forced to compromise. Even when the USSR or Viêt Nam disagreed with the conditions gradually being forced upon Phnom Penh, it was not in their interests to react to this in a manner consistent with pre-1986 policy. Moscow's normalisation with Beijing and Washington rested upon the Kremlin accepting to a significant degree Phnom Penh's situation. Accordingly, Moscow acquiesced in the marginalisation of the PRPK.[54] Similarly, some of Hanoi's reform-minded leaders resisted little and actively sought to persuade Phnom Penh of the benefits of such acquiescence. Hanoi depended on Phnom Penh's concessions if it were to normalise with the US and gain access to the international funding it needed for development; and it required China's support if it were to be able to withdraw from its own military quagmire in Cambodia.

This combined pressure led Prime Minister Hun Sen to recognise the inevitable prospects for Cambodia, which required rethinking PRK policy to accommodate these positions.[55] Despite his reluctance to accept later aspects of the PPA as it evolved, Hun Sen recognised that resistance was useless, and that it was therefore essential to make the best of a worsening situation that was not under his control.[56]

The situation at this stage was characterised on the one hand by the decline of the international pro-PRK axis and the empowerment of its opposition; and on the other, by continued resistance from Phnom

Penh despite their weakened position. Recognising a deadlock, regional initiatives came again to the fore. The difference this time was that the regional powers recognised the limitations of the diplomacy they might invoke in the context of Sino-US interests. A series of meetings in Indonesia, the first of which was known as the 'cocktail party', delivered the possibility of a quadripartite bargaining process involving all four Cambodian parties, in the wake of Hun Sen's agreement to meet some members of the Khmer Rouge.[57] The first Jakarta Informal Meeting (JIM) was astute and sensitive diplomacy. It created a complex politico-cultural framework that permitted the four Cambodian factions to meet in the unofficial presence of Prince Sihanouk, without any of the Cambodian parties losing face from the implicit assumptions of political recognition of an enemy otherwise derived from such a meeting. Furthermore, the meeting did not automatically mean Phnom Penh being officially 'recognised', for the sake of Sino-US interests.

Despite this diplomatic event, there was no agreement among the Khmer leaders regarding some of the most fundamental elements of the proposed solution. The 'comprehensive' aspect was problematic, but it was not the only issue on the table. A significant role for the UN was envisaged in a peacekeeping capacity of sorts, which irked Phnom Penh. Correspondingly, the timetable for the withdrawal of Hanoi's troops from Cambodia frustrated the Khmer Rouge. There was also disagreement on the nature of political organisation in the interim, transitional period.

This was unsurprising. At issue were the very notions that had kept the Khmer parties at each other's throats for almost a decade: Viêt Namese 'imperialism' and Khmer political legitimacy.[58] Although encouraging reconciliation, Hun Sen himself was still opposed to the inclusion of the Khmer Rouge and the nature and size of the intervention force, but was also ultimately 'still aware of the necessity' for their presence in the agreement because of the intractability of the Chinese and US positions.[59]

A Cambodian Solution

That these issues could not be resolved led to reconsideration of the number of possible options available to the domestic combatants. Vickery contends that since Angkorean times, there has been 'no serious conception of self-reliance ... in a crisis everyone looked to a powerful saviour from above or outside rather than seeking a local solution'.[60] This is probably true, especially with reference to the manner in which the Cambodian elite has used variously Thailand and Viêt Nam, as well as France, to solve its international problems. However, evidence that this approach may not have been a norm in the 1980s is provided by local attempts managed by Khmers to resolve the war. Sihanouk, the Cambodian Monarch-in-exile, had been moving away from the CGDK. He saw in Hun Sen the possibility of a fresh merger that might afford him some of the power he had been used to, and which would avoid a complicated and potentially divisive powersharing arrangement between the PRK and the CGDK. Such an arrangement would also be favourable to Hanoi, as it excluded the Khmer Rouge. Sihanouk realised Hun Sen's resistance would delay a political settlement and his return to his country. He was also aware of the relative position of strength the Prime Minister enjoyed. With this in mind, Sihanouk tabled a proposal that would see himself joining Hun Sen in Phnom Penh and leaving the Khmer Rouge politically isolated. *The Economist* recorded that the Prince offered to 'throw [the Khmer Rouge] over if Mr. Hun Sen accept[ed] the right terms' for Sihanouk's return.[61]

This had a predictable and inevitable outcome, based on the previous experience of foreign reactions to locally brokered non-comprehensive arrangements. The Hun Sen–Sihanouk alliance was 'torpedoed by the [US] State Department' because Sihanouk's move towards Phnom Penh would have legitimised the latter and reduced the credibility of the CGDK.[62] Sesser notes that 'the United States played a key role in the collapse of the [Hun Sen–Sihanouk] alliance by not offering Sihanouk support if he cut ties with the Khmer Rouge and its sponsor, China...'.[63] The PRK, it was claimed, 'could have worked out a deal with Sihanouk in November 1989 that kept the Khmer Rouge out. [They] offered him his throne and he accepted it. But the Perm-5 would have none of it' without the Khmer Rouge.[64]

In a very real sense, the Hun Sen–Sihanouk alliance offered an opportunity to achieve what UNTAC later could not. Hun Sen would not have been challenged; Sihanouk would have had presidential power immediately; the KPNLF, according to Ieng Sary, would have moved with Sihanouk and adopted court politics to a degree; and the Khmer Rouge would have been isolated. However, the success of such a venture could have been facilitated only with the permission of the US and China, who would have been unlikely to recognise the new regime. If the venture had been allowed to proceed, the political will to permit this would also have ensured international recognition and then development aid. However, that crucial political will on the part of the US and China was absent.

Stage 3: Reform

This 'crisis', of Sihanouk's unilateral diplomacy with Hun Sen, had arisen for the US and China in no small part because the locus for the meetings had been regional to a degree that limited direct influence from the two superpowers. Lack of close supervision leading to a departure from the Sino-US line persuaded the Perm-5 'to organise an international conference where ... enough pressure could be applied to the four factions [sic] to force a breakthrough on the issue of national reconciliation'.[65] In this way, bi-partite solutions, such as those postulated at various points by some ASEAN states and Australia (above), could be avoided. The Paris International Conference on Cambodia (PICC) of July-September 1989 provided such a framework. The Perm-5 had largely agreed that they could co-operate. Beijing had hinted that it would review its position as arms supplier to the NADK, and US President George Bush had publicly declared that he 'didn't like those Khmer Rouge guys', but was clearly prepared to tolerate their inclusion for the sake of Sino-US relations.[66]

Despite being a very international stage, the PICC was to be dominated as much by the Cambodian combatants as it was by international actors. During the early phase, several points of resistance from Cambodian actors had to be overcome. These included powersharing in the transitional body; the nature of the intervention force; exclusion of reference to the term 'genocide' in ensuing documentation; the presence of Viêt Namese in Cambodia; and the nature of any cease-fire. Thus, despite 'progress' having been made, it was only one-dimensional. The key causes of contention which had hobbled peace in the past not only remained, but had been joined by others which derived from the momentum towards a UN intervention force still as yet unidentified. That momentum towards 'peace' led to a number of problems in terms of understanding the depth and importance of the issues which held up the development of a political settlement. Two of the core issues were the transitional arrangements and the nature of powersharing it might entail. This was reflected in one of the more popularly cited problems of the PICC, which was the seating arrangement at the conference. It was widely reported that the Khmer participants could not agree on who would sit next to whom. The term 'squabbling' was used.[67]

Peace Seeking

The use of such terms reflected the degree of ignorance of Khmer political culture and the significance of its recent history in the context of the competition for political power. The Cambodian parties 'squabbling' over seating positions reflected far deeper powersharing and legitimacy issues. To have accepted the proposed seating arrangement would have meant accepting

> the legitimacy of an equal distribution of power when we did not accept the legitimacy of the Khmer Rouge. To sit with them was to sit with the illegitimate; to sit with them was to recognise them. It was not like the [Jakarta 1988] meetings. There, we could meet but not have the formal recognition, or the diplomatic status. This was not the same. If we accepted this, we acceded to the argument. I would not do this.[68]

Hun Sen expressed in emotional terms what acceding would have meant for him:

> They proposed that I sit in the delegation of Democratic Kampuchea [the Khmer Rouge-CGDK] as the second man, to the right of Sihanouk [as if they and the CGDK were on the same side]. I said I would not sit with the tripartite delegation. They told me that if I sat with them they would invite me to sit again at the UN. I rejected that idea, saying that I could not sit in the chair of Democratic Kampuchea which is stained with the Cambodian people's blood. I said I would not do that. Sihanouk then proposed that they should drop the name Democratic Kampuchea and keep only the name Kampuchea.... I rejected the offer.... I did not want to sit in the bloodstained chair just because the name was dropped....[69]

It is unsurprising and not at all unreasonable that Hun Sen rejected these and the other conditions. Other key elements of the plan were as untenable as the seating arrangement Sihanouk attempted to foist on Hun Sen. No settlement on disarmament of the four Cambodian parties could be reached on the part of Hun Sen's party because the Viêt Namese had agreed to withdraw by the end of September 1989 (one month after the PICC), leaving his defences weakened. Yet the new arrangement involved inclusion of the Khmer Rouge. The International Control Mechanism (ICM), which would oversee the transition, was not as yet clearly defined. The pro-Khmer Rouge forces argued for a considerable UN presence of an international character, whilst Hun Sen supported the International Control Commission which had

Peace Seeking

supervised the 1954 French withdrawal from Viêt Nam (composed of PRK ally India, and neutral Canada).

In a sense, the diplomatic process was raising as many problems as it was resolving. This of course is not unusual in peace negotiations. As new parameters are defined, they inevitably lead to new challenges. However, in this case, so fundamentally important were these issues to all the Khmer parties that they in fact laid the seeds for many longer-term problems that would only be cloaked as long as the peacekeeping force was in place. It is no surprise that almost as soon as the UN left Cambodia, the same problems that characterised the peace process resurfaced violently, and were still not fully resolved by 1998.

The outcome was that intra-party conflict was bitterly aggravated. Sihanouk once again took centre stage when, having learned from his previous venture with Hun Sen that he could not maximise his own interests with the PRK, he rejoined the Khmer Rouge and the CGDK. He demanded

> the dismantling of the Phnom Penh regime [and] joined China ... to denounce the draft resolution which read that the Cambodian peoples must be protected from a return to the policies and practices of genocide of which they have been victims and demanded the deletion of the word genocide.[70]

These were key issues to Hun Sen, who was still fighting to retain the references to genocide which the Khmer Rouge denied, and which the China and US sought to sweep under the carpet.

The political conflict between the Khmer Rouge and Phnom Penh was reignited as Sihanouk swung back into the Khmer Rouge's orbit and the anti-Phnom Penh alliance realigned. In response to Sihanouk's fresh pact with the Khmer Rouge and Beijing, Hun Sen's government demanded the dismantling of the guerrillas, declaring that 'the King of the Khmers Rouges has his hands stained with blood'.[71] Once again, the conflict was trivialised and its deepest causes and rationale misunderstood in many parts. Hun Sen viewed any alternative course of action, in the light of Sihanouk's return to the CGDK, as 'political suicide.... Can you imagine our concerns?' he continued:

> Our enemies were multiplying. Now we faced Sihanouk, China and the Khmer Rouge. But we also faced the UN because they supported the comprehensive plan. The UN and its members were denying that genocide took place. It was hard to accept ...

very hard. It was as if history was being re-written; as if a million Khmers did not die.[72]

Despite the Perm-5 achieving their own consensus for a political settlement, the initial hurdles remained. One overriding characteristic of the failure of the PICC was that the four indigenous elements could not agree to the process put forward by external interest seeking to determine a particular outcome. At this stage, although there was external consensus, *The Economist* claimed that 'the Paris peace conference ended in failure on September 3rd because Vietnam and Mr. Hun Sen were utterly unbending, and Russia either could or would not force Vietnam's hand'.[73] Of course, they were not the only ones to be recalcitrant; neither the US nor China were making relevant concessions. More accurately, the PICC failed because the Khmer parties would not agree on how to distribute power. The lack of interim arrangements was compounded by the absence of a satisfactory model of power-management acceptable across the divides. In the end, as the Australian Foreign Minister Gareth Evans put it, 'We spent the first day of this Conference establishing that the settlement process was ... dead. We spent the last two days writing the obituary'.[74]

Whilst the PICC had failed to break the impasse, it had clearly identified where the Conference had run aground, and thus the prerequisites sought by all parties were fairly clear. The US and China still remained fixed in terms of what they would and would not accept, and this in turn affected the rate at which peace would evolve, and the character of any peace that devolved from such one-sided diplomacy. In a very real sense, the expectations of the dominant actors at this stage continued to reflect their positions of the early 1980s. Those same motives drove the development of the settlement, but now enjoyed both less opposition, and more opportunities to have their favouritism built into any ensuing agreement. The real peace involved in these negotiations was the necessary rapprochement between the superpowers and, to a lesser extent, Viêt Nam. In many ways, Cambodia was as much a 'side-show' to the peace process as it had been to the war in Viêt Nam.

While the issue of powersharing had been identified at the PICC as central, the composition and structure of the embracing institution which would contain such an ambitious concept was still not clear. In August 1990, however, a proposal known as the 'Framework Document', which had grown from an Australian proposal known as the 'Red Book' (because of its cover), was adopted voluntarily by all except Phnom Penh, which was forced into signing the deal and had few other viable options.[75] This plan did not treat the problem of political confrontation at its roots, however. Rather, it overwrote the Khmer conflict. Leifer, Evans and Grant observed that the Red Book proposal, endorsed within the Perm-5, appeared to circumvent the powersharing problem.[76] It created a quadripartite body deemed 'the unique legitimate body and source of authority in Cambodia' during the transitional period and to be known as the Supreme National Council (SNC).[77]

This notion was perhaps one of the more illusory of the peace process. The final composition of the SNC involved six members from Phnom Penh, and two from each of the three factions. Sihanouk represented the thirteenth member to whom the membership of the SNC would submit when consensus could not be arrived at. In the absence of a decision by Sihanouk, the future head of the as yet unconceived transitional body would have the final say. However, the SNC did not have much power in real terms, because that transitional head had a right to veto any decision appearing not to underscore the values and *modus operandi* of the Paris Accords-to-be.

On the other hand, the provision of the SNC had a number of advantages in ways other than practical administration. In fact, all the actors except the Phnom Penh party accrued significant benefit from it. The Khmer Rouge was inside a framework, with their allies, that they would probably never have had access to in other circumstances. The dismantling of the State of Cambodia was implicit in the framework. Sihanouk had a nominal Presidency and oversight over all four groups; and the Viêt Namese army was already out of Cambodia. The US and China had achieved their primary objectives of removing Viêt Nam from Cambodia, whilst simultaneously ensuring the inclusion of the Khmer Rouge.

On the other side of the equation, Phnom Penh had lost a large portion of its defences. It had been forced to accept the presence of the Khmer Rouge at the negotiating table and in the SNC; and was about to face 'the virtual dissolution of [its governing body] through United Nations' control...'.[78] It also faced an intervention force from the same United Nations which had denied Phnom Penh recognition and development aid, and overwritten genocide with the euphemistic 'policies and practices of the past' committed by the Khmer Rouge; and of which it was suspicious.[79] It is no coincidence that these issues were vehemently opposed originally by Phnom Penh (and earlier by

Hanoi), but the pressure on them to acquiesce had been unrelenting and unmanageable. Clearly, these conditions were not those sought by the Hun Sen government, known since 1989 as the State of Cambodia (SoC). Thus, while a powersharing framework had been created which overcame the problem of the interim transitional allocation of political authority by having it all vested in the SNC, the grievances implicit in the relationship between the four main groups remained and were simply re-housed. Simultaneously, the innate resistance to power sharing in Khmer political culture remained extant, subsumed only to an artificial body trusted by none of its members as a fair vehicle for political leadership. It was also resented by at least one of the main actors aggrieved by its inevitable and intended political marginalisation consequent upon the creation of the SNC.

In other words, the SNC represented little more than an artificial, externally imposed set of boundaries of political behaviour inside which was located the unresolved causes of over a decade of national conflict. The politically-underpinned military conflict in Cambodia was thus temporarily institutionalised at the behest of the superpowers in a powersharing coalition which relocated armed confrontation in a political framework without addressing the Khmer causes of the war and the domestic political grievances which had sustained it over the decade of the 1980s. The SNC became the vehicle by which the Khmer combatants would persecute each other after the military cease-fire.

The Pattaya Meeting (Thailand), June 1991

Negotiations to overcome the remaining problems led to a meeting in Pattaya in June 1991. Members of the Perm-5, especially China, were to continue their role in pressing the Cambodian groups to come to an agreement which would result in a peace plan being endorsed which would remove finally the Cambodian problem from the Perm-5 agenda. Hun Sen still had reservations regarding the seat of the SNC and military support for the Khmer Rouge and its contemporaries. However, he was mollified to a large extent with the developing deal secured by a softening Sihanouk under Beijing's aegis, although this still did not improve his weakened position to any great degree.[80] Further complaints from Phnom Penh brought abrupt responses from Washington, which in retaliation slowed down the 'normalisation' process with Vîet Nam. Clearly, it was the case that 'even though Phnom Penh had been forced to give away almost everything but their formal existence, the US [still] objected that it was not the 'comprehensive' solution which had been sought'.[81] In a clear demonstration that Viêt Nam was rolling over, Hanoi indicated surrender and support of the process by

> sacking the anti-Chinese pro-American Foreign Minister Nguyen Co Thach ... and applying pressure to the Phnom Penh regime to go along with the plan and let the UN administer the country and also organise and conduct elections.[82]

This forced the reticent Phnom Penh regime to make concessions under pressure from a Viêt Nam seeking US normalisation. Hun Sen's resistance dwindled as he allowed the process to develop further by hinting that he may accept the removal of references to genocide, the electoral model of Proportional Representation (PR), and the problematic disarmament plan (see below). Phnom Penh's sole support had conceded defeat, and with it had gone Hun Sen's only remaining bargaining 'chip'.

Hun Sen finally agreed to drop all reference to the term 'genocide' and its inclusion in the forthcoming agreement. The genocide issue had been important because its absence contributed to the legitimisation of the Khmer Rouge whose track record in national politics is irrefutable. Its significance demonstrates the extent to which Sino-US interests had made Hun Sen compromise. The issue was never about 'genocide' per se. Rather, the removal of the term overcame some of the distastefulness in the international community about the clearly loathsome, repugnant and offensive inclusion of the Khmer Rouge in any agreement. There was a sense of absolute defeat and exhaustion about Hun Sen when he said:

> we no longer had control. What could we have gained? The Viêt Namese wanted a settlement. The Chinese wanted a settlement. The US wanted a settlement. They all wanted a settlement on their terms.[83]

The Paris Peace Agreement was signed on 23 October 1991. The much-heralded settlement suggested an end to the war and the possible beginning of a new epoch in Khmer history. However, in Hun Sen's sentiments, and the processes that aroused them, lay the seeds of dissent. His pragmatic rhetoric disguised the reality of his relative impotence before the convergence of Chinese and American interests, underscored by the triangular relationship with Viêt Nam and exacerbated by Moscow's changing ways. The agenda followed by China and the US, determined the manner in which the final agreement was arrived at. It established the framework and the bare, most basic conditions acceptable to the interested external parties, but did not provide grounds for a durable settlement of a far more complex confrontation.

At the very heart of this lay the powersharing problem, alien to the Khmer elite political culture of the legitimacy of absolutism. With the price of defeat so high, and with the most powerful party also the most marginalised and with the most to lose, the essence of confrontation was intensified by the provision of enforced powersharing. Leifer contended that 'the impasse over the chairmanship and composition of the Supreme National Council reflected the fact that power sharing is not part of the Cambodian political tradition'.[84] The solution did not address the basis of Khmer discontent, leaving the issues unaddressed and simmering in a framework that regulated tension in a similar fashion to the effect the superpowers had on regulating Khmer-organised settlement of the problem. And in much the same way as, after the Cold War, multiple sub-national conflicts reignited around the world as the regulating effect of the deadlocked superpowers receded, so too did the departure of the UN after September 1993 remove the restrictions on the Khmer management of the Cambodian political contest.

The PPA, democratisation, and peace

The 'conclusion' of the Cambodia conflict reflected the dominant views and assumptions of the pre-eminent form of political organisation at the end of the twentieth century. The most utilised way for western intervention to settle conflict is to apply the format of liberal, multi-party elections. In conjunction, human behaviour is guided to respect the values implicit in unfettered free choice for the individual in choosing leaders. This helps resolve the problem of multiple, sub-national contenders to political thrones. The PPA introduced all these values into Cambodia with the intention of settling a complex war in a society with some very differing values where the cost of losing the struggle was higher for the elites than the cost of continuing the conflict.

It has not worked in the manner it was intended to. Elections did not bring democracy as it is known in the West and as it was intended in the peace settlement. The role of the PPA, and the manner in which it was arrived at, reveals much about both the implementation of the mandate and the degree to which the settlement proscribed has

Peace Seeking

endured. In reality, the peace process was aimed at foreign powers, not at Cambodians. Ratner argues the peace process was 'an amalgam of global powers and regional actors motivated by intentions both self-serving and beneficent'.[85] Heininger records the purpose of the PPA as 'largely to allow the central players in the region ... to disengage from Cambodia in face-saving manner'.[86] Ott noted in 1997 that

> many of the key participants in Paris had little real concern for Cambodia itself.... Paris provided a useful opportunity to jettison some embarrassing baggage. For many in the US, the agreements were a means to artfully disengage from a nasty little problem'.[87]

Ashley concurs, adding that 'the interest of the international community was not primarily in the development and democratisation of Cambodia but rather in stopping a prolonged military conflict involving major external interests'.[88] Jeldres states the PPA was 'pressed on [the Cambodian factions] by their respective foreign backers, who had decided that it was time to stop the carnage in Cambodia'.[89] *The Independent* concluded that this was why, if the peace plan failed in implementation, 'a few leading powers would be embarrassed, but few vital interests would be harmed'.[90]

The Perm-5's cynical attitude to Cambodia ironically paralleled the often-cited Khmer Rouge posture to their people during the Pol Pot regime: 'preserve them, no profit. Kill them, no loss'.[91] The PPA, although satisfying the Perm-5, 'did not equate with a desire by the Cambodian factions for peace'.[92] The following chapter discusses in more detail some of the key assumptions upon which the PPA rested, and then reviews their propriety both to the international organisers of peace; and to Cambodian elite and civil society and the institutions, values, traditions and norms which govern them.

II

Assumptions of Peace

The previous chapter has discussed some of the conditions under which the PPA evolved, and the consequences of superpower competition in determining an outcome that would benefit those dominant at the end of the Cold War. The limitations upon a viable peace process of such imposed political will are evident in the assumptions upon which the peace plan rested. This chapter discusses the degree to which these assumptions were meaningful, in the context of utility derived for those powers which dominated its evolution; and in the context of their applicability to the Cambodian situation.

The Paris Peace Agreements were not concluded to the absolute satisfaction of all Khmer parties – few peace arrangements enjoy universal and comprehensive support. Whilst a degree of consensus had been arrived at within the Perm-5, however, a key characteristic of relations between the four Cambodian political groups was mistrust and suspicion.[1] The superficiality of the gathering momentum for 'peace' had been evident in the concluding stages of negotiations. The antipathy with which each group had viewed the other had in no way been addressed, prompting one *Newsweek* reporter to observe that after one 'successful' meeting, 'the four Cambodian leaders beamed as if none of them had ever dreamed of slitting the others' throats'.[2] The intensity of the competition had ensured that hostility was to continue to characterise relations between the Khmer political elite both throughout the operation; and in the years to follow before the creation of the unelected Senate in 1998. In a very real sense, whilst members of the Perm-5 enjoyed satisfaction, the Khmer political elite did not. This is not an uncommon paradox. Taylor generalises that 'in their ideal form, elections [as proposed for Cambodia] are means of resolving political conflicts without resorting to physical force. But they may be merely masks for coercion that is occurring or has taken place in a different context or a different time'.[3] In other words, forcing a settlement without addressing the causes of the conflict may have a disappointing outcome.

The PPA did not terminate the conflict in Cambodia, when conflict is defined in both an armed military and relatively less armed political fashion. It merely changed the vehicle for communicating hostility and confrontation, from war to elections. The *Phnom Penh Post* remarked, perhaps with the benefit of hindsight, that the political parties at the signing of the PPA

> did not reach out to one another to signal their rapprochement. There was no joint celebration. Perhaps the signing marked another stage of their war in Cambodia and that they needed to carry on fighting until their final victory as had been done in the past.[4]

The significance of the conflict had not changed. It remained a vital struggle for political survival in an extremely hostile environment where the consequences of absolute defeat and marginalisation could be dire, and far more exaggerated than in western systems upon which the chosen model of polling was based. Power in Cambodia, both traditionally since pre-Angkorean days and contemporarily since the 1970s, has been of an absolutist nature, with little tolerance of opposition.

Underpinning this is a system of patronage and clientelism that seeks to ensure the preservation of elites by lower ranks, and to ensure as far as possible positions of economic and sometimes social privilege by elites. Loyalty passes upwards, ensuring leaders remain leaders, and loyal clans undermined challenges to their patrons' authority at grassroots level. Gifts, such as positions that ensured socio-economic security and privilege, passed downwards, so ensuring that loyalty would be offered in return, sealing the circle and perpetuating the lineage of power and position. Brown refers to the well-known *khsae*, or string. This is a series of hierarchical relationships that saturate Khmer society and determine relationships and politics. The Cambodian model is 'particularly pervasive'.[5] The PPA made no attempt to alter this model to fit democratisation. Frieson observed specifically in the context of the intended elections that 'patron-clientelism was … a formidable obstacle to voter autonomy'.[6]

Assumptions of Peace

Kofi Hadjor generalises that 'under conditions of scarce resources, political patrons will fight any attempt to democratise society'.[7] His observation fits the Cambodian system with regard to the assumptions of the Paris Agreements. Such tensions as would be created by 'Liberalising' Khmer politics had not existed prior to the UN mission. The settlement would simultaneously offer legitimacy and possibly authority to the newly empowered opposition leaders; and would also expose all parties, to one degree or another, to the consequences of political defeat where there existed no institutionalisation or peaceful experience of such a concept.[8] Underscoring this paradox, the consequences of defeat or political marginalisation characterised by a lack of access to the state and privilege were potentially dangerous in a wider sense, especially for any incumbent, whether Royalist, Buddhist or former Communist. As many Cambodian politicians attempt to maintain their support base through political clans cemented internally through patronage and clientelism, those networks too would be marginalised.

The system of dependency and patronage prevalent before the French has in effect changed by degree more than by character. Then, Vickery argues, 'everyone below the King had a fixed dependent status'.[9] Later, that social status-derived hierarchy responded to increasing changes in economic access and privilege. Thus, whilst Frieson is right to note 'the relationship between state and society was considerably loosened' as a consequence of UNTAC's presence, the phenomenon of grass-roots systems of organisation distinct from those prescribed by the elite was not new.[10] As more of the population generated a greater degree of personal wealth through a combination of an expanded bureaucracy and private economic freedoms, the nature of the hierarchy around them altered to reflect the new primacy. Thus, although the French presence had an effect, 'there was not a corresponding change in attitudes and values'.[11]

Reflecting the experiences of the UN in the 1990s, and illustrating the inherited systems of patronage for wealth accumulation and consumption, government representatives viewed their jobs as they have traditionally viewed them, as one method of wealth accumulation. Ward argues that in Cambodia, administrative organisation is 'a legacy of a vast, thinly disguised and widely spread system of patronage' which represents 'the main means through which ordinary Cambodians tap into the state apparatus to guarantee a personal social security net'.[12] In such a system, not only would marginalised or defeated politicians lose power and wealth, but their clans of supporters would also lose access to the privileges passed their way by their incumbent political masters. One observer argued that the majority of Khmers from all levels and walks of life

> have backers, supporters, patrons. Their livelihood depends on patronage. They have been given access to benefits unavailable otherwise, and if they lose their patronage, there is no safety net and so far, few other choices.... Not having a patron means vulnerability.[13]

Furthermore, the intended separation of the bureaucracy from the incumbent party of the State of Cambodia, led by Hun Sen, aggravated this problem by having the effect of separating mutually interdependent patrons and clients. Whilst this could be argued to be deft planning and deliberate policy to overcome a cultural and economic platform of resistance to democratisation, the PPA is conspicuously bereft of any such notion, as was the process by which the agreement was arrived at.

The organisers of the PPA missed several crucial issues in their attempts to democratise Cambodia. One of the most important was that they attempted to implant equality and individual choice in a society governed, and financed, through hierarchical inequality and group loyalties. Free choice would be desirable if the consequences of making that choice did not have negative economic ramifications. That is, it could not be meaningful to vote altruistically for a personality if that leader could not return the favour in the traditional manner. This tension lay at the heart of the disintegration of FUNCINPEC between 1993 and 1997.

This situation was further aggravated by the manner in which the PPA shifted the balance of power in Cambodia away from the incumbents and towards the opposition, by the simple expedient of inclusion of opposition. It is quite clear that the Khmer Rouge viewed the PPA as an improvement in their efforts to return to some form of political authority in Cambodia (see chapter five). For the first time, the Khmer Rouge elite had access to the broad population of Cambodia through a nationally contested and pluralist electoral system. Equally, their performance on the battlefield did not appear to indicate that they could have won militarily in armed conflict.[14] The PPA both removed them from the military situation in which they were not winning, and simultaneously lent them a platform from which to compete politically that they would never have achieved otherwise, so accruing advantages they could not have hoped for in war.

The converse appears true of the incumbents. The Cambodian People's Armed Forces (CPAF) were preserving to a large degree the *status quo* and advancing very little – often being pushed back but not to any degree that altered the overall outcome of the conflict. The PPA changed this and dissolved that advantage. However, unlike in a cease-fire, the process was not arrested at this stage. Rather, the process involved the Khmer Rouge in the CPP's political arena, which would not have happened in the absence of Sino-US intervention. Whilst in a very clear sense a peace settlement should probably attempt to neutralise such advantages, the consequences of doing so remain to be considered. The CPP's marginalisation made them acutely aware that their chances of preserving their power were also being reduced; and the consequences of defeat were more severe than they wished to contemplate. Hun Sen said in 1994

> Thank you for raising this question. We knew that we would have to give up the power in some ways with so many parties competing. We knew that we would lose a lot of things. We would lose our country, because no-one of the other parties had the [capacity] to take over from us. If this happened, we would all be losers.[15]

It was thus inevitable that all efforts would be made to redress the imbalance, as the CPP saw it.[16]

Competition explicitly begets opposition. However, whereas in the western liberal tradition, the notion of loyal Opposition is legitimised in its role as a further check and balance to the system of government, in elite Khmer political culture, a loyal Opposition is a contradiction in terms. Jarat Chopra noted that although a particular constitution may imply separation of powers and limitations upon the executive, 'in practice, power always has been exercised exclusively by the executive and the Cambodian population has not been protected by checks and balances on authority'.[17] Exaggerating the issue yet further is a direct consequence of this view of loyal Opposition within indigenous elite circles. Since it has never taken a formal part in Khmer political society, it has been neither institutionalised in the elite context nor socialised in the wider, mass, sense (see below for a fuller discussion).

The PPA, then, created conditions where arch enemies were forced into a powersharing arrangement that had as its conclusion an election which might remove at least one group from political power, in a system which did not cater for the notion of opposition, or for the transfer of power, or for the possible consequences of such an event. Quite clearly, this seems to be a not unusual approach; but equally clearly, it was not sustainable in the longer term, as the history of coalition confrontation after 1993 and the July 1997 fighting suggest. These conclusions are unsurprising. The content of the PPA was not designed originally to deal with such political issues in Cambodia. Its origins lay in the need to settle a wider war among the superpowers and Viêt Nam, as well as to allow Thailand to put an end to its refugee problem. Therefore, the settlement reflected concerns at the international level which over-wrote the reality of settling a potentially zero-sum political contest in a highly armed country where the contest for power amongst the elites was virtually absolute. Indeed, the 'comprehensive' nature of the settlement was a Sino-US requisite based on a view of conflict resolution which reflects the Kissinger dictum: 'the standard method of solving civil war ... is to make [contestants] govern jointly'.[18] According to Schwarz, this concept includes 'coalition governments, the guaranteed division of key offices [and the inclusion of defeated political] groups ... in national and political affairs'.[19] These assumptions reflect what Schwarz refers to as an 'ahistorical and naïve paradigm' which is 'guided by faith in the nostrums of the liberal tradition'. This faith, he continues, leads US policy makers to believe that 'a community is built by balancing competing interests'.[20] These assumptions do not, however, reflect values, mores and traditions in Khmer society and politics, where rather than maintaining an even balance of power amongst several groups, the tradition of absolutism has historically underwritten a 'winner takes all' belief. Schwarz moves to conclude that such approaches 'depend on a host of faulty assumptions' about, for example, Khmer political tradition, especially with regard to the conventional wisdom that 'the strongest group in a divided society will be willing to make major concessions-concessions that will jeopardize its preponderant position'.[21] This was both explicit and implicit with regard to the main political parties in Cambodia.

The PPA enshrined this approach to conflict resolution, ignoring the evidence to the contrary. It also failed to prepare alternative plans, explicitly assuming that there would be broad co-operation generally. It assumed that the Perm-5 would continue to be a source of positive influence, as it had previously coerced the combatants into ending the military conflict and signing the PPA. It also assumed that all parties would disarm as the Agreement stipulated; that they would transfer power in a peaceful manner which would reflect the outcome of the polls; and that they would not revert to armed conflict or separatism or secession. These are mighty assumptions.

Yet there was in 1991 little evidence to support them. A key question must ask how reasonable the assumptions were. Broadly speaking, two positions can be adopted. First, it was appropriate that elections be utilised to settle the conflict because the Cambodian electorate deserved, on the cusp of the twenty-first century, to have the right to choose their leaders. This process would then end the war; development would then ensue, furthering yet more the broader goals of Khmer society. As all parties sought such an outcome, including the Khmer Rouge, according to their statements to this effect, and as all parties agreed that this was the way forward, the Paris Peace Agreement was valid, and represented a reasonable way to approach the Khmer war.

From this perspective, the assumptions regarding disarmament, power sharing and power transfer in the event of a shift from the *status quo* via the elections have a degree of validity. All parties signed the PPA and agreed to be bound by its rules. Theoretically, each side had a fair and equal chance of achieving its objectives because UNTAC would, through disarmament, protection of human rights, and separation of the incumbents from the state apparatus, create the 'neutral political environment' necessary for fair and meaningful elections. Therefore, all sides stood to benefit equally if they adhered to the PPA.

However, it was not the Khmers that lay at the centre of the issue. Each aspect of the peace settlement was only acceptable if it fulfilled certain conditions that included reinforcing rapprochement with China; and the punishment of Hanoi and, to a lessening degree as time wore on, Moscow.[22] As this failed to take into consideration those elements of elite Cambodian culture discussed above, it was unwise, disingenuous or deceitful to perpetrate the belief that the PPA was anything other than a tool for superpower disengagement with no real concern for Cambodian people. Had genuine concern existed over any of these issues, which were publicly raised either by political Khmers resisting such approaches or by western scholars, then alternatives might have been developed to underpin the peace process. None were. Davies claims this was not 'a settlement born out of reconciliation or the healing of national wounds, and herein lies its paucity'.[23] Rather, it was the settlement of a different war, the terms of which were incongruous with the needs of the Khmer conflict. This point cannot be overstated. The following section reviews the implications in the Khmer context of the failure to create a propitious settlement with Khmer interests as defining elements of that process. It may also be considered a departure point for later debates regarding the durability of the settlement.

Assumptions of Co-operation

Outside of the Perm-5 concerns, the UN carried over the task of implementing the peace formulae. In many of the pre-deployment analyses of the impending operation, it was as much hoped as assumed that a sufficient degree of co-operation would prove possible and sustainable between the four main parties and with UNTAC. Such conclusions may have been based on the perception that the PPA would be equally beneficial to all the Khmer groups.[24] They were not. The CPP, for example, having enjoyed absolute power, stood to be marginalised; whereas the Khmer Rouge, previously denied a political role, now enjoyed one.

The consequences of non-co-operation clearly varied depending on the level of withdrawal, the numbers refusing to co-operate, and the issue over which withdrawal might occur. Again, the assumption of co-operation might have been little other than the triumph of hope over superpower politics. However, no contingency plans were prepared for any kind of deviation from the original proposal, because it had been hard enough developing the PPA to the degree that it was accepted, however tendentiously, by the Cambodian parties. In the event of a failure to co-operate, some maintained that antagonists might be delivered back to the consensual fold by pressure from their former patrons.[25]

However, such expectations were somewhat deficient. For example, a UN representative involved in the formulation and implementation of the refugee repatriation programme explained that:

> The whole Paris Accord was weakened because there was no contingency or strategic planning. China influenced and weakened the content of the Accords because at that stage it was still if not supporting, then defending, its former clients. There was no contingency plan because the plan was cast in stone by the Chinese and the US.... Those involved in pressuring the Cambodian parties were very short-sighted to expect that parties who hated each other would accept anything that marginalised them against the others.... You don't go into a twenty-year situation without a contingency plan.[26]

The UN representative voiced a number of fears that were rejected in the absence of any alternative to which all parties, domestic and international, might acquiesce. They were also rejected, he claimed, because to have addressed them would have been harder than to press ahead with the only plan that had been accepted by all the parties. Thus, to reconsider issues over which some were already decidedly unhappy, or which were central to the demands of one actor or another, or over which a reasonable degree of concern could justifiably be expressed, would likely open a Pandora's box which would undermine the progress and signing of the Agreements.

In essence, to assume co-operation from some groups was overly optimistic. The CPP incumbents were expected to release their control of the state organs, in the context of having signed an agreement under pressure from a loss of international patronage and a wrecked economy which simultaneously politically legitimised their reviled Khmer Rouge opposition. It was naive in the extreme to expect co-operation to the degree that the Accords anticipated in Paris. Indeed, long before UNTAC's tardy deployment was underway, the various organs of the state of Cambodia had been transformed such that real power lay elsewhere, denying UNTAC the capacity to neutralise the political environment. It was naive also to assume that a party as entrenched in political power as the CPP would relinquish that control when its political future depended largely upon securing support for itself through the labyrinthine networks that were characteristic of the communist model of bureaucracy and politics in Indochina.

It was not unreasonable, however, to expect co-operation from the Khmer Rouge. Because the PPA empowered and suited the Khmer Rouge, in part because its patrons had created the conditions from which the guerrilla group would benefit politically, it was to be expected that the Khmer Rouge would co-operate as long as the plan was implemented. At the signing of the PPA, many questioned the likelihood of their co-operation, but this was based normally on a limited understanding of the role the PPA was playing for the party of Pol Pot. However, it is crucial to qualify the nature and type of co-operation involved, anticipated or achieved. The evidence clearly demonstrates that up until the signing of the Paris Agreements, the Khmer Rouge were planning to hoard weapons and arms caches in remote jungle locations invisible to the UN's inspectors. It is equally clear from interviews with all ranks of the organisation that they intended to participate in the elections. This would occur as long as the

UNTAC operation appeared on time and fulfilled those elements of its mandate that created conditions amenable to their objectives (see chapter five). This means that because the PPA offered the guerrillas something they had failed to achieve through warfare, and because it undermined a key element of their CPP opposition's innate advantage, they had nothing to lose by participating while UNTAC executed the mandate.

The two other main parties which had made up the 1980s resistance group, the BLDP and FUNCINPEC – not unlike the Khmer Rouge – had a vested interest in participating, and according to Schear, 'stood to gain the most from the settlement itself'.[27] The PPA permitted for them political participation where the electorate would decide who would lead Cambodia, rather than the choice being made on the battlefield. FUNCINPEC, headed by Sihanouk's son Prince Norodom Ranariddh, clearly believed working within the PPA would be politically more productive than fighting the Phnom Penh government. Hun Sen declared that

> For Ranariddh and Son Sann and Pol Pot, the Paris Accords were useful. How else can they join the politics and compete politically with Hun Sen? How else can they take political power?[28]

As long as the UN executors of the mandate adhered to the terms of the Agreement, the fight was easier, and FUNCINPEC carried the Royal seal and association with the still-respected Prince Sihanouk. Equally, the BLDP, with little fighting capacity on its own and therefore tied to FUNCINPEC and the Khmer throughout the 1980s, had much to gain by co-operating. Son Sann, their political leader, was a political doyen, somewhat venerated in part because of his role in the Sihanouk government and Court of the 1960s.[29] This view of him is reflected in his current title of *Ta* (Grandfather) and his senior role in the National Assembly.

Thus, from this somewhat Realist perspective, co-operation from the Khmer Rouge was not an unreasonable assumption. The most likely to co-operate were those most advantaged; and vice versa. As long as the conditions which advantaged the three leading parties opposing Phnom Penh remained *in situ* throughout implementation, their continued participation on their path to the election could be anticipated with some degree of validity. On the other hand, from this perspective, the co-operation of the CPP might not be as readily achieved, because its relative position of power was being progressively weakened and would be further undermined if UNTAC implemented its mandate the way the PPA dictated. This approach to thinking about co-operation is borne out by the CPP's resistance to UNTAC's civil administration objective.

Assumptions of continued Perm-5 influence

As a general assumption derived from the experience of enforcing participation in the PPA, the notion of Perm-5 corrective influence seemed to offer a similar system of coercion during implementation to that which had endured through the formulation of the peace.[30] Brown observed that China, for example, 'would retain a degree of leverage over its Cambodian clients that would lead to a constructive participation by the Khmer Rouge...'.[31] Hong concurs with this view. Others observed that Viêt Nam and Moscow might enjoy the same influence over the CPP based on vague ideological loyalties.[32] Furthermore, as the US had been so tenacious in its attempts to manipulate the Khmer Rouge against Viêt Nam and Phnom Penh, it was also expected in some quarters that Washington might be able to bully the Khmer Rouge should they become reluctant to participate.

This was not to be the case. In both serious withdrawals of consent, UNTAC's sponsors did not change the situation to the degree that co-operation was restored. The Khmer Rouge refusal, in June 1992, to disarm and demobilise was never reversed; however, they did not revert to active non-co-operation by, for example, declaring war on Phnom Penh or UNTAC.[33] In the second instance, the secession after the elections in June 1993 was reversed not by international pressure, but by Hun Sen. He was not the architect of that event, emanating as it did from disaffected former party loyalists (see chapter six). However, he was directly responsible for the negotiations with his brother that terminated the secession.[34] Radio Australia reported that Hun Neng, the Provincial Governor of Kompong Cham, 'notified the UN of the decision [to reject the secession] in a letter after he was visited by his brother, Hun Sen. He said he wanted to drop all demands to hold new elections and would accept the election results'.[35]

Until that point, UNTAC and other international intervention had not ended the secession; Hun Sen's activities did.[36] Many reviews of the UNTAC operation, during and since 1992, argue that international pressure has acted upon the Khmer parties to control their actions. However, interviews with elite cadre such as Ieng Sary, and top government party officials, such as Hun Sen, confirm the relative impotence of foreign intervention.[37]

Assumptions of disarmament and demobilisation

The success of the Paris Agreement depended to no small degree on the capacity of UNTAC to disarm all the parties. The notion of disarmament itself had been difficult to pursue during the peace negotiations, providing a persistent stumbling block. The only proposal acceptable to the government of Cambodia was that 70% of all sides would disarm and be put into holding camps in a process known as cantonment. It was especially important to the CPP who had lost their Viêt Namese military support to the peace negotiations, whilst having to accept the inclusion of the Khmer Rouge and its army in the final settlement. Cantonment would be followed by demobilisation and reintegration into the rural or urban economy, with some provision for retraining to facilitate this process.

The importance of effective and meaningful disarmament has become perhaps more apparent since UNTAC departed. The excess of armed soldiers, combined with the unemployment of the demobilised, and coupled to the ready provision of weapons, has ensured that Cambodia remains characterised as a heavily armed state. It also means that it was as hard in 1998 to create a neutral political environment as it was in 1992, but for different reasons. Whilst one key problem was the unity of state and government structures in 1992, in 1998, another was the capacity for armed men to intimidate in favour of the CPP-dominated Royal government, or for their own apolitical interests. The presence of easily available weaponry has also undermined processes of political arbitration, business conciliation and domestic conflict settlement.

Considering the heavily armed state, unemployed soldiery, stark economic choice, and a brutalised society accustomed to the arbitrary use of violence, it was less than reasonable to expect disarmament to work. However, in a less obvious sense, it was almost naïve to expect that this process would be adhered to in the sense the PPA anticipated. From the point at which the PPA was signed, and before, evidence existed that the Khmer Rouge, for example, would make no effort to reduce their caches unless by submitting poor quality weapons whilst preserving the sound stocks. This could not have been a surprise; neither side would have taken chances with an armed opposition either winning or losing the polls. Furthermore, it was widely held that there would be a significant difference in the capacity of UNTAC to disarm the government and the guerrilla troops. Kiernan argued that disarmament 'would be much more difficult to do to the Khmer Rouge, who [were] located in remote, jungled areas, than to the SoC army, which defends fixed positions such as bases, cities, and populated areas'.[38] Most observers seemed to recognise that the NADK were deliberately misleading the UN, and were 'roundly suspected of hiding large amounts of arms for later use'.[39]

In the face of this obvious recalcitrance, the creators of the PPA had few alternatives. Accordingly, they 'made no serious attempt to spell out how all the Khmer Rouge forces [were] to be located, supervised, disarmed, and cantonized'. The day after the PPA was enshrined in law,

> one source revealed the existence of a secret Khmer Rouge army of "several thousand" troops, which ha[d] long been camped in isolated jungles.... A second source said there were several "completely" inaccessible

Khmer Rouge base camps in the mountains, which the UN would find 'very difficult to inspect.[40] Most of this evidence had long been available before the UN endorsed the PPA. At no point was it ever really assumed that the parties would disarm; however, the understanding that they *should* was implicit in the Agreement, and the Agreement depended on this wish list to a certain degree.

Assumption of Electoral Obligations

The terms of the PPA provided for an election, with certain technical and political parameters, and with certain conditions for judging credibility. The PPA made no provision for the rejection of results after polling, other than it being strongly urged that all parties abide by the results derived from the framework to which they had agreed in law. Furthermore, and perhaps more importantly, there was no provision for the post-electoral transitional period, in which the secession occurred. The PPA therefore, by not providing alternatives, assumed all parties would abide by the results. It also presupposed the transfer of power would proceed peacefully.

In a misguided sense, from the Perm-5 perspective, these might have been reasonable assumptions. Those who orchestrated the PPA had achieved a fair degree of 'success' through coercion and bribery. Viêt Nam had leaned on Phnom Penh with the offer of access to 'normalisation'; and Beijing had implied they would cut off supplies early to their guerrilla clients. Given, then, that this created a perception of a continuing power relationship between international patrons and Khmer clients, there was little to suggest that this should not have continued to be the case.

Assumptions of Power sharing

The PPA stipulated PR by party slate. The all but inevitable outcome of a PR election in a politically-cleaved environment, where, as in the Cambodian case, a 66% majority is demanded, and where twenty parties compete, is a coalition which ultimately involves sharing power. In the Cambodian case, according to one United Nations Volunteer (UNV) with experience in the field, 'a coalition was the inevitable outcome.'[41]

This presupposed that the parties would accept a power sharing equation after elections. This assumption is perhaps the most flawed of all those underpinning the creation of the PPA and the mandate it lent UNTAC, with direct ramifications for UNTAC's ability to fulfil its tasks. It also illustrates the limitations of the assumption that key parties might accept election results, if their power base was distorted by the presence and challenge of other parties in a new coalition. Furthermore, it assumed that this contradictory process would set Cambodia on the road to peace and stability, whereas in fact it has ensured the continuity of the political conflict it appeared set to resolve.

It has been noted that in Cambodian elite political culture, the notion of sharing power is antithetical to absolutist traditions. In this sense, power would not be shared; it would be continually contested. Those sharing power would not be viewed as co-operative, but as a form of Opposition, but within Parliament. In most Western systems, a coalition government is supposed to present a unified front to a parliamentary opposition. In the Cambodian case, the members of any coalition would be viewed by other members of that same coalition as contesting power, not co-operating in the interest of the country. Cambodia's political culture has not developed in the same manner as the western system. Simone and Feraru generalise that 'the traditional Asian concept of authority is the notion of the superior-inferior status in all relationships'.[42] Therefore, they argue, a 'loyal opposition' is an oxymoron and majority rule a threat to continued elite dominance...'.[43] In this sense, Zakaria is right to argue that Cambodia is little different from many regimes in East Asia which 'make their elections ratifications of power rather than genuine contests'.[44] Since the Angkorean period, political leadership has been based on regal hierarchy and descent, rather than competition and transparency. Until 1970, this system was only slightly abused by the rise of an informed educated opposition. Even since the rise of the Far Left in Cambodia, there has been no history of universal, multi-party, democratic elections in Cambodia since independence in 1953.[45] Jennar reminds that 'Cambodians have never been able to enjoy the basic political freedoms of democratic countries. On the contrary, arbitrariness has been a permanent feature of Cambodia since its independence'.[46] Whilst few feel Cambodia's recent political leaders can appropriate such divinity as in the past, there are distinctive similarities if not in personalities and positions then in political processes with the Kings from which tradition derives.

Perhaps the dividing line comes in 1970. If Sihanouk represents the last of the Royalty with political legitimacy and moral authority deriving from Angkorean tradition, his successors since then have not enjoyed such right or intrinsic respect. First, the right-wing Republican Lon Nol overthrew the traditional source of legitimate authority in 1970, thus ending centuries of monarchical organisation. Then, in 1975, he in turn was violently ousted by the pseudo-Maoist Pol Pot. Finally, in 1979 the Viêt Namese helped install a new political party which governed the country ostensibly, but inconsistently in practice, as a single party Leninist state.[47] This period is dominated by tensions between authoritarian leadership and opposition. Sihanouk's treatment of the Far Left is well documented.[48] The Republican Lon Nol's totalitarian leadership rejected opposition, and the rule of the Khmer Rouge was least tolerant of all.[49] The single party Leninist state of Pen Sovan, Heng Samrin and Hun Sen also tolerated little dissent.[50] Thus, through all the regimes since independence, and the different state nomenclature reflecting ideology, there has been little attempt to imbue the Cambodian body politic with notions of a democratic nature that include or involve the concept of sharing power or opposition.[51] Indeed, for some, the notion of holding elections to decide who would take power was regarded with both mirth and dismay in Cambodia before the polls.[52]

Whilst challenges to traditional authority from Lon Nol and Pol Pot came from quite markedly different sources in one sense, in another they continued a familiar pattern. Each leadership was unchallengable in the peaceful sense: change could only come about through violence and revolution. Heder notes that there is a 'general refusal of elite culture to recognise the legitimacy of difference and opposition'.[53] The nation's political culture had not really changed from the regal system, insofar as it remained a fixed system of leadership the elites of which did not accept competition. Curtis maintains that the 'home-grown solution to the problem of sharing political power should have been anticipated by the architects of the Paris Agreements, as well as by UNTAC'.[54] He goes on to observe that the PPA should not have expected UNTAC, or any other intervening body, to create a peace by forcing powersharing. Rather, he argues, they should have 'devoted much more effort to helping the Cambodians develop a new and distinctly "Khmer" form of consensual politics through efforts directed towards the art of compromise, including improved negotiation techniques for "national reconciliation".[55] While there is a strong vein of truth in this argument from a theoretical perspective, in practice it is less likely to have worked within the declared time frame. The culture of conflict management in Cambodia is not one that can easily be changed, as long as the conditions underpinning it, of wealth scarcity and patronage, remain the dominant norm. Other values will have to change as well, not least of all the efficiency and validity of the model of economic organisation.

The Supreme National Council – a portent of powersharing problems

Clear warning signs were visible at all points of the Cambodian peace process that sharing power could potentially cause more problems than it resolved. The torturous experience of the formation of the Supreme National Council (SNC) reinforced the possible problems inherent in applying such a model of government to Cambodia. The SNC represented a scaled-down version of a coalition government that would follow PR elections but without the legitimacy of the mass plebiscite. This ignored the experience of the Coalition Government of Democratic Kampuchea.

This model, however, worked temporarily throughout its existence for a number of reasons. First, each side had an equal vote and political 'say'. Second, many of the topics they debated were already framed in the PPA, and this could not be changed. Third, their decisions could be adjudicated over by the thirteenth member of the twelve person Council, Sihanouk. Fourth, in the event of a deadlock at that level, the head of UNTAC, Yasushi Akashi could over-rule any decision in order that it would reflect the conditions of the PPA. However, according to two of its opposed members/advisors, even in this context the rivalry was bitter and contained only by the inability to change the constitutional process of the Council and its location in the PPA framework.[56] Such a body was unlikely to succeed peacefully when the key restraints to its confrontational nature were removed upon the departure of the United Nations.

The evidence was quite clear. The problems UNTAC would face in implementing the (then futuresque) PPA were reflected when Hun Sen declared at the 1989 Paris Conference that 'you can talk about sharing power in Paris, but not in Cambodia'.[57] Five years after the political conditions of the PPA had been imposed, the notion of opposition was still being renounced. Hun Sen warned Cambodians parading against his leadership in Paris in 1996 that 'You can hold a demonstration in France but do not do it in Cambodia'.[58] In the period between these two statements, Leifer made the observation that 'genuine compromise and power sharing among adversaries have not been a part of the political tradition and experience of Indochina. Power has been treated as a possession to be enjoyed on an exclusive basis, not as a commodity that might be shared with adversaries'.[59]

In other words, the Cambodia interim arrangement, and the inevitable coalition that would follow an election of the proposed nature, brought together political combatants for whom the election was a continuation of the war, rather then the basis for sharing power agreeably. The final settlement went stages beyond this. It forced two leaders who, because of their own views on rights to power, would have no option but to contest the validity of the other, and take the necessary precautions to ensure that their position remained or became dominant and unassailable. Forcing this power sharing arrangement on Cambodia merely took the fundamental conflict into a different domain; the actual fight went on. The PPA did not resolve this or prepare a mechanism through which it could be resolved.

Such assumptions underpinned the PPA. Their tenuous nature provides a clue as to why they were made. It is possible to speculate that there were several reasons for these expectations rooted in the fragility of the peace plan and the problems that were encountered during its design. First, there were very few, if any, alternatives to a powersharing arrangement while external actors such as the US and China defined the parameters of peace. In a sense, then, powersharing was inevitable; it was the most likely product of a nation-wide democratic election contested by so many parties whose form of contest was determined by a western liberal model imposed from and endorsed by members of the Perm-5.

Second, this inevitability may have over-ruled considerations of the propriety of such political organisation in Cambodia's political culture. Although the creators of the PPA may well have known that the framework into which plurality would be inserted might reject such a notion, no other formula was presented which satisfied all parties, including by necessity the international actors with a stake in the outcome.

Third, again there was little that the UN would be able to do in the event of massive non-co-operation, such as a universal return to arms. The conditions to which the Cambodian parties had agreed had been tortuously achieved through compromise and coercion; it was possibly the only approach that offered a reasonable probability of success as defined by China and the US. Furthermore, the party considered the most volatile and dangerous, which was also least likely on their past record to co-operate, had been well-provided for in the PPA. Several aspects clearly offered them an advantage that it may have been assumed would be sufficient to retain their co-operation.[60]

The PPA's formulation was fundamentally determined by a number of external objectives which, when contrasted with the needs of Cambodians, resulted in an incongruity or paradox. The dichotomy of this situation and the tensions it created were sufficiently clear that one noted author was prompted to presciently observe that 'read carefully, [the peace process] seems to have been designed to ensure further destabilisation rather than lasting peace'.[61] Whilst the PPA clearly resolved the international confrontation over Cambodia, it did not address meaningfully the real problems which underscored Cambodia's civil war. The PPA reflected the need for peace among the Perm-5 first and foremost; the operation was thus determined by the necessary considerations attached to this perspective. In essence, because of the larger issues at stake in resolving the fight, Cambodians unwittingly, and with the tragic irony that the Cambodia historian David Chandler illustrates in some of his work, became a 'side-show' to the peace settlement.[62] Raoul Jennar pointed out from a long term analysis of the peace process and the UN operation that, 'on the one side there are the Cambodians and, on the other side, a UN operation. One ha[s] to let oneself be intoxicated by official rhetoric to be persuaded that the latter concerned the former'.[63] In this way

Cambodia and Cambodians were again relegated to the spectacle of being a side-show in their own peace.

The compromises that permitted the PPA to be signed reflected incongruities between what was being imposed, and what was appropriate or practically achievable. Schear claims that 'few people had any illusions about the Paris Accords. They were fragile instruments, a product of intense pressure applied upon the parties by external powers operating in a climate of co-operation that did not exist inside Cambodia'.[64] What the superpowers required to settle their own conflict did not translate directly into what might either be implementable or workable on the ground. This incongruity lay at the heart of UNTAC's inability to implement its mandate. It also demonstrates the inappropriate framework established by the PPA, which in turn undermined political transition in the implementation phase as well as in the period between the two elections in 1993 and 1998. The following chapters explain how and why this incongruity manifested itself, and how stable democratic political transition was temporal in the short, UNTAC-term, and untenable in the longer term.

III
A Critical Overview of the Operation

This chapter presents an overview of the Cambodian peacekeeping operation in practice. It does not dwell on great detail or minutiae, which are already covered in a number of texts, but instead discusses the issues raised in the context of the PPA.

The UN planned to enter, in order to fulfil its mandate, a country with a painful recent history, much of it relevant to Cambodia's present and to UNTAC's presence. The country had been secretly bombed by the US between 1969 and 1973, and had then experienced a five-year internal war, followed by an appalling genocide perpetrated by the Khmer Rouge. The devastation wrought between 1975 and 1978 left Cambodia socio-economically brutalised with a severely depleted educated elite and civil bureaucracy, a ruined physical infrastructure, and the conspicuous absence of many of the elements that constituted pre-Pol Pot Khmer civil society.

Compounding the problem of rebuilding Cambodia was the diminished supply of engineers, lawyers, doctors and skilled technicians who might begin the process of re-assembling the remnants of Khmer society into something recognisable as a modern state. The conditions Cambodia faced in 1979 cannot be over-emphasised; they had an obvious effect on UNTAC's capacity to implement its mandate, as well as the crippling significance to Cambodia and Cambodians themselves.

Viêt Nam's role in staving off further socio-economic decline in the immediate aftermath was important. Despite much anti-PRK/Viêt Namese propaganda, Viêt Namese officials were ready to co-operate with aid deliveries that were made available, according to early missions from Oxfam organised by Jim Howard.[1] British representatives in

A Critical Overview of the Operation

Thailand had told Howard that there would be major problems if any attempt were made to fly directly to Cambodia. No such problems existed.

Furthermore, Viêt Nam contributed supplies from its own citizens. Many Khmers surveyed recount incidents of Viêt Namese soldiers being so shocked by their surroundings and the levels of food availability that they themselves contributed from their own meagre rations.[2] Furthermore, Cambodians refuted disinformation regarding the distribution of supplies once inside Cambodia. Priorities initially revolved around 'rice and children's clothes; and the rice ... was all foreign aid ... [that] also got out on the roads to Battambang, Kompong Speu, Kien Svay, and Koh Thom'.[3]

However, the Viêt Namese presence also had the effect of compounding the socio-economic crisis already in full swing, because of the dim view taken internationally of Viêt Nam's actions (see chapter two). As a consequence, Cambodia was denied development aid at a time when the social, economic and environmental consequences of Pol Pot's agrarian 'reforms' were undermining institutional capacity to counter the disastrous effect of famines, droughts and floods that followed Pol Pot's ousting.[4] Other than limited support from the eastern Bloc and a few independent States, international aid was generally private in nature and channelled through a small number of NGOs. In fact, the type of support required to both restore and repair Cambodia's social, economic and environmental structure necessitated massive multi-lateral developmental and emergency involvement.[5]

Thus, UNTAC, and its early predecessor the United Nations Advance Mission in Cambodia (UNAMIC), found itself tasked with undertaking a peacekeeping operation in a country characterised by a near complete absence of viable sealed roads along which its logistics might run, and a population depleted of the numbers of skilled specialists one would normally associate with a nation-state in 1991, and which would also support the UN operation at the grass-roots level. It also faced a single party state control system which extended deeply into many aspects of civil society; which had enjoyed tenure for over a decade in a political vacuum and which, as a consequence, was reluctant to cede any form of political authority to the UN body, or to any form of political opposition.

Furthermore, as a result of the years of civil war, bombing and genocide, some societal values had been transformed in the period since the late 1960s into ones which, on the one hand, had high

A Critical Overview of the Operation

expectations of what UNTAC would be able to achieve but, on the other, had little absorptive capacity to deal with such a massive intervention. A number of social, economic, societal and political characteristics reflected these conditions, and influenced UNTAC's capacity to discharge its responsibilities in the manner of the PPA.

Human Rights and a Culture of Violence

One series of perspectives on the pre-transition environment paints a picture of effects derived predominantly from the extremities of the Khmer Rouge rule. Raoul Jennar, for example, has argued that Cambodia, as a consequence of its recent past, has had some innate fundamental values challenged. Responses to normal life situations have been perverted by its brutal and traumatic recent historical experiences. It has become, argued Jennar, 'a society governed entirely by the law of the strongest'. Jennar went on to note that

> the price placed on a human life [was] less than that placed on a motorbike. There [was] a total lack of concern for the common interest.... Killing [wa]s ... an everyday act, the automatic, almost direct, consequence of the negation of differences.[6]

The experience of the 'Pol Pot time' seems, the *Far Eastern Economic Review* mooted, to have left many Cambodians with such a deep loss of meaning that they seem incapable of practising the age-old Buddhist values of respect for life and the dignity of individuals, tolerance and solidarity.[7] Whilst this is a sweeping and somewhat flawed generalisation, it should be noted that Cambodia's international isolation ensured it was not meaningfully exposed to, or pressured to co-operate with, the conventional human rights norms and values that constitute Western-dominated international law. Phnom Penh had been largely left to get on by itself, and in that time, the ways in which power and justice were disbursed went loosely checked. Those in power, unsurprisingly, did not seem to feel the need to acquiesce to the often-hypocritical demands of Western institutions. Such bodies as the United Nations, with the connivance of the US (amongst others), had financed, armed and fed the orchestrators of Cambodia's genocide, but simultaneously demanded that the Phnom Penh leadership conform to western human rights norms. Amnesty International and the Lawyers' Committee, for example, made various reports and allegations against Phnom Penh, but no reports were published regarding the Khmer Rouge genocide. It is unsurprising that one-sided western moralising had little impact on Cambodia in the 1980s.

The combination of extremes of poverty, and a diminished respect for human rights, had exacerbated and aggravated a culture of violence and impunity. This appears to have become largely self-reinforcing, underscored by the socialisation of brutality accruing from Cambodia's experience of bombing, war and genocide and located within a closed, sometimes self-serving political elite.[8] Oxfam commented that Cambodians

> seem to have lost something and when they see something they want, they just snatch it.... Violence is a means of survival and it won't change in this generation. With something so seriously damaged you can't just mend it just like that....[9]

Such conditions were not, however, exclusive to or created by the Pol Pot experience alone. From his experience of living in various parts of Cambodia in the 1960s, Vickery chronicles examples of extremes of violence that are less interesting for the fact of their existence than they are for the often brutal and crude justifications which accompanied them. Indeed, there are many obvious parallels between the general practices and treatment meted out to those assumed to be 'pro-French' government workers by the Khmer Issarak anti-colonial (protectorate) resistance, and by the Pol Pot-ists. Thus, such 'patterns of extreme violence ... have very long roots in Cambodia ... [it] was still part of the experience of many rural Cambodians in the 1940s, 1950s and 1960s.... Probably few Cambodians entertained doubts that ... enemies should be killed'.[10] They are far from a direct product of the Pol Pot period alone, as many explained them. Vickery contends that

> for the rural 80–90 percent of the Cambodian people, arbitrary justice, sudden violent death, [and] political oppression ... were common facts of life long before the war and revolution of the 1970s.[11]

Vickery documents several examples with which he has been familiar, the details of which mirror in several cases the brutality more usually associated with the Pol Pot regime.

It is also to be noted that such behaviour can be connected to Cambodian cultural heritage and tradition. The concept of 'face' is not unique to Cambodia. However, in Khmer relationships there is no mechanism or system for managing disputes. Furthermore, the intolerance of others' opinions characteristic of political, as well as social, culture aggravates the likelihood of confrontation and the inevitable loss of face for the 'loser'. The absence of institutions to resolve conflicts that derived from intolerance of 'other' views leads to their settlement in more violent ways. These traditions and cultural aspects of Cambodian relationship management clearly predate the Pol Pot time, and are thus useful in explaining continuity in social and political relationships. Ovesen *et al* noted that

> There is no cultural tradition for reconciling contrary opinions (or even for the acceptance of the [legitimacy] of contrary opinions. Nor are there any socially accepted behavioural rules for resolving conflicts. To the extent that conflicts stem from contrary opinions, it follows that one opinion is perforce more correct than the other; and the one who holds the incorrect opinion will have lost face ... [Cambodians'] "cultural heritage" offers no way out of a humiliating ... or ... difficult situation.[12]

Such long-standing values and attitudes combined with some of the Pol Pot experiences and an exceptionally harsh decade following the removal of the Khmer Rouge. They were then coupled to envy and surprise at the sudden and obvious flouting of enormous wealth after UNTAC arrived with its equipment, salaries and disproportionate *per diems*, to underscore and encourage an unsurprising and self-serving bonanza.

It is perhaps a combination of such circumstances that prompted one observer to observe that there was 'no sense of community, no sense of greater good, no sense of nation building. It [was] every man for himself and his family'.[13] Nine years after that was written, an incident with an aid worker in Ratanakiri, in the north-east of the country, demonstrated that some of these issues persisted. The volunteer lost her house and motorcycle keys in the mud of wet monsoon Ratanakiri. A passing Khmer found them, but tried to charge her US$ 10 to return them.[14] Furthermore, when a Viêt Nam airways airliner crashed at Pochentong airport, killing almost everyone on board, Khmers stole private property from the dead. They also stole the black box flight recorder, and charged investigators a fee to return it. The sense of self above all is apparent in both examples close to a decade after the UN's arrival.

In a sense, whilst not everyone endorsed it, violence and crime became almost legitimised through socialisation and a corrupt police force. These circumstances were further aggravated by a lack of lawyers and a government hampered in its goals by an international embargo, elements of which were sometimes key sources of the marginalisation of human rights. These issues, in the context of a western interpretation of human rights, were further compounded by the organisational nature of socialist government, in which the separation of executive and judiciary is not necessarily a given.

Exacerbating this further was the extent of political corruption, aggravated by the ruined economy that further legitimised and underscored corruption and nepotism. In much the same way that arbitrary violence pre-dates Pol Pot, some of these characteristics have been extant in Cambodian society since the Angkorean period. Then, filial duty ensured for some individuals and groups access to socially prestigious positions. However, rather than a sense of filial and social obligation, in Cambodia's extremes of poverty, a survival necessity reinforced the problem of corruption. The traditional arms of the state, including the judiciary, the civil service, and the legislature, as they existed in Cambodia, were indeed corrupt in many ways. However, it is perhaps overly facile to criticise these conditions without putting this corruption in context. The country did not recover anywhere near fully from the Pol Pot period, or from the environmental disasters that characterised the early 1980s. This then compounded the problems further and exacerbated the necessity for corruption for self-preservation, as well as, of course, for private greed.

Such circumstances were underpinned by dwindling external fiscal and physical aid, especially as the Soviet Union and Viêt Nam had progressively extricated themselves, and their sponsorship, from the international dimension to the problem.[15] Partly as a consequence of this, and of internal corruption, the government army, separating the country from the Khmer Rouge in 1990–1991, endured uneven supplies and unreliable compensation, and accordingly would 'freelance' to support itself. The civil service, as well as being understaffed in terms of expertise and bloated in terms of efficiency, was also paid at rates which would not feed a civil servant's family. Underlining the gap between the fundamentals of political survival and the need to stave off poverty, the state police were also embroiled in the endemic corruption which characterised Cambodian society, economics and politics before, during and after the UN arrived.[16]

Many local level political representatives and servants of the government and those that supported it and carried out its orders were petrified at losing power, and therefore losing status and access to resources that separated them from some of the conditions noted above.[17] To preserve their positions, which also meant preserving the social security of extended families as well as the political clan they represented, was crucial. Violence and the culture it reinforced in Cambodia could also be explained in part, Jennar maintains, because 'local leaders who fear losing power and do not have ... the resources to guarantee themselves a financial future, do not hesitate in resorting to violence to "neutralise" political adversaries'.[18]

This trait explains in part the regular intimidation outside Phnom Penh of those who challenge the state by affiliating with an opposition political party. Those who become exposed to potential removal from power often confront that challenge at grass-roots level. Those whose position, and therefore power, is threatened, use that power to further their own ends irrespective of whether their actions serve the interests of the state. By removing the local challenge, they also remove that aspect of the challenge to the higher authority on which their privilege often rests. Chopra observes that 'extortion, murder, death squads, secret detention centres, intolerance of opposition, racial violence, and intimidation have all been facets of [the] administration'.[19] Frieson observes that this was the same during Sihanouk's reign. She notes with regard to the 1955 election that Sihanouk's party led 'a violent campaign during which several opposition party workers were killed, their supporters harassed and ballot boxes disappeared'.[20] However, in both periods, this is predominantly independent of central planning and occurs as localised responses to immediate, tactical threats, rather than necessarily institutionalised efforts at the more strategic level. Accordingly, the view that such behaviour is necessary and therefore legitimate is more widely externalised, and therefore begins to constitute a 'right', to protect the family from the debilitating consequences of poverty. In a sense, the process becomes legitimised, institutionalised, and regarded, if not necessarily accepted, almost as a norm within the state and the society, and manifests itself in political violence in the course of the preservation of political power upon which social and economic wealth depends. Thus, social violence joins political brutality to permeate opposing networks of political loyalty.

As UNTAC deployed in 1992, extremes of poverty contrasted with the sudden explosion of urban wealth for a minority class of emerging entrepreneurs preparing to service and supply new cash-rich markets. On the eve of the UN's deployment, many Cambodians with access to state resources took advantage of their positions to feather their own nests, worried no doubt in part by the possible political losses to come.

A Critical Overview of the Operation

The UN's arrival, and the consumption that naturally accompanied it, fuelled this process. In a country where sometimes often basic goods and services were not readily available, many took the opportunity to exploit a hide-bound bureaucracy and a corrupt constabulary in the process of providing for the sudden upsurge in market demand. In so doing, *The Economist* observed, they accelerated 'a lurch from communism to *capitalisme sauvage* [where] privatisation Phnom Penh-style [became] a euphemism for corruption'.[21] Thus, the issue of corruption, in the context of political survival before possible tumultuous change in access to political power and the attendant privileges, derived great nourishment from the UN's arrival and its spending power and service and product demand.

The Party, the state and Political Control

The nature of politics in Cambodia drew on the legitimisation of violence and reinforced state control over people and resources to ensure access to power and privileges along political clan lines. One characteristic of the state was the use of power relatively arbitrarily and with only limited checks and balances, in a western democratic sense. Although there was sometimes a direction stemming originally from a form of Leninism, the vagaries of political doctrine were a subject of more random external forces than domestic pro-active decision-making.[22] Leifer argues that the use of political power in States such as Cambodia corresponds to a harsh version of 'developmental authoritarianism', whereby 'the state intervenes to dampen political opposition in the declared interest of social order and economic development'.[23] Attempts to achieve political and development objectives were thus sometimes managed by some members of the SoC through intimidation and fear in the face of consistently adverse conditions ranging from famine to war during the 1980s.

However, these policies might appear only relatively unreasonable, according to some. Vickery, for example, argues that

> what would have seemed to the former Cambodian bourgeoisie and officials unacceptably and oppressively revolutionary and authoritarian before 1975 could be offered as a return to social freedom and personal liberty

under the post-1979 leadership.[24] In other words, what the PRPK dictated was far better than anything experienced in the five years preceding its arrival in January 1979. Vickery notes that 'not only [did]

A Critical Overview of the Operation

the PRK/Viêtnamese performance look good in absolute terms, but relatively, in comparison with the available alternatives, it look[ed] even better'.[25]

Some media elements contrived to assail this view, with questionable evidence to support it. Shawcross, for instance, argued to this effect in an article entitled 'The End of Cambodia?'. In the face of the evidence that was even then emerging from both Cambodia and Thailand, Vickery argues, such 'uncritical repetition of assertions' represented 'a position [that] could not be maintained by anyone but an abject propagandist'.[26] Thus, evaluation of conditions in 1980s Cambodia must consider what Vickery refers to as the Standard Total View (STV) of the type expressed by Shawcross. Well-known contributors such as Barron and Paul, and Ponchaud also expressed it. These writings have sometimes been limited by type of source, misleading, factually inaccurate or analytically lacking.[27]

Whilst this point is raised, it is worthwhile noting the degree to which discrepancies exist between the arguments presented in national or international media, and in some sources of scholarship, on the one hand, and evidence offered from inside Cambodia, on the other. The general view was that the Viêt Namese were regularly unspeakably cruel to their colonial subjects. Several incidents were used to demonstrate, or 'prove' this point, as has been noted above.

However, the statements of many surveyed in the early 1980s do not reflect such assertions. For instance, a wide range of peasants, rather than former bourgeoisie, surveyed by Vickery after 1979, showed the Viêt Namese in a more positive light. The manner in which that research was undertaken was more broad and credible than some of the methodology applied to some of the other material, in the sense that it was geographically more broad and focused on a wider range of citizenry. It revealed for instance, that counter to beliefs which persisted in 1999, the lower level of Cambodia's administration was exclusively Khmer. Whilst there was of course a Viêt Namese presence in various hamlets and villages, the interviewees surveyed

> did not consider the extent of Vietnamese administrative intervention to be in any way oppressive. The officials they dealt with were all Khmer, and the Vietnamese troops they encountered did not bother them.[28]

More recent surveying of opinion regarding this issue was conducted in 1991, before the UN arrived and whilst the Viêt Namese presence was still relatively fresh in people's minds. In Takeo, Svay Rieng, Prey

A Critical Overview of the Operation

Veng and Kandal, Cambodian commentary suggested no mistreatment at the hands of the Viêt Namese. They reported reasonable living conditions and showed no animosity towards the Viêt Namese who had settled in the area. Those people were not viewed as imperialists, but often as friends and co-workers. They sometimes brought invaluable skills that Cambodians did not possess in large enough numbers. The Viêt Namese therefore contributed to the community and were respected broadly.[29] The immediacy of their location near to the Viêt Namese border, and a longer experience of tolerance, could explain this. However, similar interviews conducted further from the border in the same research exercise at roughly the same time, in Kompong Chhnang and Kompong Speu, indicated similar experiences. One cannot generalise from such limited sources and with limited time available. However, the purpose here is to demonstrate that there are two sides to the story, and that the demonisation of Viêt Nam is based as much on hostile political agendas as it is upon an alleged 'traditional hatred' of Viêt Namese in Cambodia.

This is not to say that there is no documented research or evidence that testifies to individual acts of cruelty or brutality. However, the allegations which were extant in the early 1980s, and which persist or are still insinuated in 1999, were and are imputed or inferred from a statistically inadequate survey of incidents from which crude and inaccurate generalisations have been made and have become 'truth'. That they were picked up in the Western Press was a function of that body's willingness to present the evidence as argued in the wider contest of the Cold War against the Soviet Union. There has clearly been a demonstrable degree of misinformation coupled to weaknesses in some interpretations of the period. Such processes have interesting precedents, particularly with reference to Viêt Nam. Whilst the phenomenon of 'smears' reproduced as truth in the media and in some scholarship has a broad and lengthy history, a recent example refers to 'atrocities' during and after the 'reintegration' of Viêt Nam after the Geneva Accords. Hanoi was accused of creating a 'bloodbath' in areas of Viêt Nam that resisted integration both geographically and in terms of labour organisation. The information upon which this accusation was based was later proven to have been erroneous, and designed to create an illusion of bad management in Viêt Nam to justify support for the 'capitalist' South.[30] The tradition of demonising Viêt Nam in Cambodia is an extension of processes begun much earlier.

Thus despite the many reports which demonised Hanoi's activities in Cambodia and ascribed to them the characteristics of the Pol Pot regime, human rights existed on a relative scale, with Pol Pot's atrocities at one end and the SoC's relative benevolence at the other. In between lay the Viêt Namese period in which, by most reasoned and reliable accounts, simply bore no comparison with the Pol Pot regime. In fact, an alternative to the Standard Total View is that the Viêt Namese presence contributed in many significant ways to Cambodia's shaky recovery.

Whilst this is to suggest a period of greater stability and recovery than is normally insinuated, there is no doubt that the SoC faced real and imagined enemies. At a time of imminent political change administered by a foreign body perceived as hostile to the SoC, two characteristics emerged. First, reports of SoC/Viêt Namese brutality increased. Second, the state sought to limit the damages accruing from this and from the planned intervention. Most states when so threatened would undertake increased internal security when threats to their existence or interests were identified. The SoC at the time also had to counter the effects of negative propaganda emanating from foreign journalists and scholars. The SoC thus legitimised civil control towards emerging opposition groups in a number of ways. First, they could compare the rights they 'permitted' with the policies of their predecessors. Then they could point to biases in the UN which politically institutionalised the enemy they militarily had kept at bay for more than a decade. Finally, they could argue that the processes at work were naturally destabilising and had to be managed. As is the case with most political parties world-wide, their self-preservation drive should not be underestimated.[31] UNTAC thus faced an entrenched elite used to non-competitive tenure on power, coupled to an infrastructure often inadequate for Cambodian needs, let alone the needs of 22,000 foreigners. It also faced a variety of misperceptions about Cambodia which would do little to help its institutions interpret and understand the challenges it faced, in many instances without even realising that this was the case

There is another view of the context into which UNTAC was to deploy. UNTAC would bring with it enormous opportunities for the burgeoning informal sector and market entrepreneurs (economic liberalisation had commenced in 1985, despite the statements of anti-SoC propagandists), which would cater to the UN's needs and enrich Cambodians embracing the 'free market'.[32] In fact, contrary to some popular perceptions, the Cambodian government had permitted such laissez-faire economic organisation at least as early as 1981.[33]

All would benefit from this because it would enable UNTAC to do its job better and more quickly given unrestricted access to various

A Critical Overview of the Operation

materials which might be procured in a sometimes-unofficial fashion. UNTAC's arrival would also prompt the re-birth of Phnom Penh, by recreating a high-spending expatriate social scene that had been restricted in summer 1991 to one functioning night-club (the Café Royale attached to the *Samakki* (Solidarity) Hotel, now part of the 'restored' Hotel Royale). From the expansion of this sector of the market would come vastly increased dollar revenue, the more so as the daily *per diem* of many troops only just fell-short of the yearly Cambodian *per capita* income. Some of the gaiety and multi-culturalism of a happy, thriving Phnom Penh would be reinvigorated by the UN. This would be justified by the arduous nature of the work the UN had to undertake. But as much as this, UNTAC's arrival signified for some a return to a halcyon vision of Cambodia as recalled or imagined by Sihanouk, in his 'golden age of peace' in the early 1960s.[34] Sihanouk contentedly trilled in late 1991 that 'there is *joie de vivre here again*'. He pointed out that 'night-clubs have reopened with taxi dancers. I am sure they will allow the opening of massage salons. It is a good way of life. It is our way of life'.[35]

This 'liberalisation' is perhaps borne out to a degree by developments in Cambodia. Frieson maintains that 'before UNTAC's arrival ... access was made difficult through complicated visa procedures and travel restrictions.... Foreigners ... were rarely allowed outside the city limits'.[36] However, this was not the case almost a year before UNTAC arrived. Visas could be obtained quickly and painlessly by faxing the Ministry of Foreign Affairs, which despatched by airmail letters welcoming applicants to Cambodia. The flight to Phnom Penh from Viêt Nam, in 1991, was neither complicated nor obstructed. Phnom Penh was busy, industrious, and its hotels were not all state owned. Fuel supplies were poor for the government, and electricity lasted between three and six hours per twenty-four. However, all but the heaviest of industry compensated by private purchases, and supply was not a problem.

Nor did security appear as tight or Orwellian as some imply. There was no requirement, as there had been in Saigon, to register with the local police. No official observations were made on my presence, except in a salutary sense, and I was not followed, except by children and cyclo drivers. Phnom Penh's main markets, with which many readers will be familiar a decade later, were full of consumer goods, including advanced VCRs and televisions. Khmers I asked spoke and travelled freely at that time. Most showed no hesitation in approaching non-Khmers, and most would engage freely in political conversations, with some exceptions. When I spoke of the peace agreement in the making and suggested Sihanouk would be returning, people were enthusiastic. Many expressed political preferences, few were afraid to talk to me about the SoC as it then still was. They confirmed travel cost 'fuel and cigarettes', but rejected the notion that they regularly experienced intimidation or harassment. People in the countryside reinforced this, although they were inclined to travel less, they claimed. Many were unaware of the war being fought in the Perm-5 over their country, but all hoped for peace. Policemen and militia joined foreigners at their tables for food and drinks.

Nor were there enforced travel restrictions in place. I could rent self-drive 'motos' without an escort or guide, and I was never stopped or deliberately intimidated or threatened by any provincial border guards. I provided customary cigarettes, which helped facilitate travel to Takeo, Kandal, Kompong Speu, Prey Veng and Kompong Cham over a five-month period that concluded months before the 1991 Paris Agreements was signed. Furthermore, I was far from the only non-diplomat and non-aid worker in the country. Several postgraduate researchers from different countries had taken residence in the Hotel Royale (then US$15 per night), and more than a few back packers could be seen in the open-air restaurant that once existed where the Pailin hotel now stands. None of this is not to suggest dark deeds did not occur. It is to suggest, however, that political harassment and intimidation were not necessarily core characteristics of rural life. It did, I was told, exist more in key cities, especially Phnom Penh, but not to the degree that is insinuated from some sources.[37]

It is important, then, not to lose sight of the effect statements such as Frieson's may have for some. In a sense, there are parallels between the 'distortions' perpetuated by the British Foreign Office in 1979, regarding accessibility to Cambodia and expectations of a violent reception from 'occupying' Viêt Nam, on the one hand; and on the other, the misperceptions prevalent in some of the literature on 'pre-UNTAC' Cambodia.[38] Assumptions about life before UNTAC in Cambodia have the capacity to distort understanding of what Cambodia was like. When a 'culture of violence' took greater root, it was as much a function of the tensions UNTAC's arrival caused, as it was the legacy of Pol Pot, or of the continuity in the arbitrary violence of the 1960s to which Vickery refers (above).

A Critical Overview of the Operation

Early Political Instability

Although the peace agreement had been signed on 23 October 1991 and an expectation existed that the *status quo* would be preserved along with the cease-fire before UNTAC's arrival, Phnom Penh was afflicted by rioting in the two months superseding the covenant. Notable among the causes was the public response to the manifestation of perhaps the most controversial element of the PPA – the inclusion of the Khmer Rouge. The creation of the SNC, central to the political settlement, included Khieu Samphan and Son Sen of the Khmer Rouge, who returned to Phnom Penh for the first time since their ousting in 1978.[39] It may have been the Phnom Penh leadership that took advantage of the emotional outburst that ensued, organising agitation to reinforce their credibility as 'protectors' of the Cambodian people.[40] However, most of the responses to Khieu Samphan's return were genuine. As he was driven the ten kilometres or so from Pochentong Airport into Phnom Penh at the end of November 1991, Pilger reported, people cried out the names of their deceased relatives from the Pol Pot era. The catharsis of emotion reflected the hatred of Pol Pot's lieutenant, as 'the gap between private pain and public fury closed, and the people of Phnom Penh broke their silence'.[41] Samphan was attacked and driven in humiliation almost immediately back to the airport by government troops, his bleeding head ignominiously bandaged with a pair of Y-fronts.[42]

The return of Khieu Samphan and Son Sen clearly evoked something far deeper than day-to-day sadness. On the day that so many Cambodians finally put a face to some of their demons, UNTAC was nowhere to be seen. In a tense political environment, riots also broke out in response to increasingly overt public service corruption. Some representatives of the SoC were seen almost openly selling state property.[43] UNTAC was conspicuous in its absence.

The United Nations Arrives

The post-PPA direction of UNTAC was largely shaped by its lack of preparedness at nearly all levels and the consequent late and poorly organised deployment. The 268-strong United Nations Advanced Mission in Cambodia (UNAMIC) bridging operation began to arrive on 9 November, 1991, with the intention of preserving the cease-fire, setting up communications networks, and liaising with the SNC. The information regarding conditions in Cambodia and the type of response this necessitated, when presented to the UN in New York, was greeted in some cases with incomprehension and incredulity. Furthermore, it is important and useful to note that some NGOs, already long in Cambodia had, according to Farris, 'accurately described the conditions but had not been given much credence'.[44] Such sources could have provided crucially useful data, but were ignored. Few who had not been to Cambodia before the end of the war could have imagined some of the levels of poverty, especially in the rural areas. It is shameful that, eight years after ignoring such a valuable source of information, some key elements of the western military establishment persist in stereotyping such organisations' employees as 'soft liberals' and are prepared more to patronise their views than to embrace them.

The operation was not inaugurated by the Secretariat until 15 March, 1992, five months after its signing.[45] Furthermore, it was not properly marshalled until four months after that. Doyle and Suntharalingum observed that 'even then some important units ... were not fully deployed'.[46] Despite UNAMIC's early deployment, this delay was crucial, as were some aspects of the operational organisation (see chapter four). The general failure to deploy efficiently and effectively had several important effects on the implementation of the operation.

First, it raised in some quarters general doubts about the commitment of the UN to Cambodia. Second, it permitted Cambodian forces on the ground time to consider the arrangement and take action that might compensate for areas of the overall plan over which doubts existed. For example, Jennar argued that the delay 'decreased UNTAC's credibility and gave the Khmer Rouge time to change their minds'.[47] However, as will be seen, it might be more accurate to claim that the delay gave the Khmer Rouge 'reason' to change their minds.

In much the same fashion that the Khmer Rouge considered the ramifications of late deployment, other parties took action to ensure that late arrival was taken advantage of to consolidate positions; or to prevent their marginalisation. Observing this, the *Far Eastern Economic Review* reported that the hesitation in deployment 'created a power vacuum that the Cambodian rivals attempt[ed] to fill ... by resuming their struggle for control of the ... country'.[48] In other words, whilst the planners at UN HQ procrastinated, the Cambodian groups took advantage of the UN's absence to consolidate and advance their positions to as great a degree as possible prior to the peacekeepers'

A Critical Overview of the Operation

deployment. This was a very important development that affected the evolution of the peace process. In the time between the signing of the PPA and UNTAC's deployment, the CPP concealed its bureaucracy and the Khmer Rouge expanded their military control over areas of Cambodia in anticipation of taking advantage of the PPA.

A third effect on implementation was that, according to Jennar, the 'UN ... refused to take into consideration reports ... describing the consequences of [delay because] the dozen quick fact-finding missions sent in 1991 failed to collect information precise and useful enough for implementation of the UNTAC operation'.[49] In a sense, this is understandable, but not excusable. Conditions were indeed difficult and the problems in gathering information would have been compounded by the very conditions they were sent to report on. It did, however, mean that delays were aggravated in the absence of focused and accurate information and assessments.

Fourth, questions regarding the resolve and ability of the UN to implement the agreement in the face of potential opposition were taken advantage of by Khmer Rouge propaganda. Anti-UN rhetoric began early as the Voice of the National Army of Democratic Kampuchea (VONADK) radio station accused the UN of being 'scared' to come to Cambodia; and that the delay 'favoured the Việt Namese lackeys in Phnom Penh'.[50] This was an early expression of Khmer Rouge concerns, as well as propaganda, that the advantage accruing from participating in the Agreement was being eroded by UNTAC's absence; and by the consequences of that absence regarding neutralisation of the CPP's innate advantages.

Fifth, it disappointed Cambodians, who knew of the plan. The high hopes many Khmers felt about UNTAC began to turn to doubts when UNTAC did not begin to deploy after the signing of the PPA. A hotelier in Phnom Penh expressed her concerns in Autumn 1991: 'everyday my sister and I listen[ed] to our radios, to hear the news. But everyday, there [wa]s nothing'.[51] Government troops too were curious and wanted to know when UNTAC would arrive.[52]

Sixth, the delay prompted fears, especially from Prince Sihanouk, that the delicate agreement would unravel in the absence of the body mandated to implement it. Jennar reflected that

> once an agreement, a compromise, an effort of rapprochement between opposing or fighting parties has been reached, the best time for implementation is immediately after the signing of the accord, while the willingness of the parties is high.[53]

A Critical Overview of the Operation

The Force Commander later commented that in future

> there should be an intense effort to reduce the time period between resolution of a negotiation phase and implementation of the agreement.... Delays in implementation of conditions acceptable at one point in time can allow the situation to change.[54]

Indeed, there is a sense that the action taken by the CPP and the Khmer Rouge came as a result of this delay, when with more immediate implementation, they might not have had the opportunity or the need respectively.

Finally, the delay made problematic the chances of the mandate adhering to the timetable.[55] The reliance on the co-operation of the Cambodian parties was considerable; but the delay necessitated accelerating an already frail arrangement that had no contingency plan. This issue caused concern in another sense. UNTAC's capacity to deploy effectively was influenced by Cambodia's monsoon climate. In the wet season, many roads that would otherwise be passable are under water or mud-logged to such an extent as to be passable only by tanks, or by helicopters. The key issue was the availability and capacity of such vehicles to manage such an undertaking as national elections. The delay would therefore alter the logistical requirements of the force and the geographical degree to which it could deploy.

It was not until 19 February 1992 that the secretary-general submitted his official UNTAC plan. He recommended '15,900 troops, 3,600 civilian police monitors, and 1,000 international staff be sent to Cambodia'. In addition to this, '1,400 international election monitors and 56,000 Cambodians recruited locally to work with polling teams would join UNTAC at polling time'.[56] However, even with all this good will, the later the arrival of the necessary forces and support logistics, the closer they would come to the wet season, and this would aggravate deployment. The telescoping of vast resources into a compressed time frame caused by the delay, and the already waning expectations and hopes of many Cambodians, set the scene for some of the earliest problems.

The Khmer Rouge withdrawal

From the outset of UNTAC's arrival in Cambodia, it was abused by the National Army of Democratic Kampuchea (NADK) at different times, in different places and to different degrees. In an early example,

Dutch Marines moved to disarm the NADK in the early stages of UNTAC's deployment, but were instead turned away by a solitary Khmer Rouge boy soldier, in an infamous incident near the Thai border.[57] The Special Representative of the secretary-general (SRSG), Yasushi Akashi, and the Force Commander, General John Sanderson, were prevented from entering one Khmer Rouge zone from another (a process to which the guerrillas had consented through the PPA) by the simple expedient of a bamboo pole across a road.[58] Events such as these demonstrated inconsistencies in Khmer Rouge policy, which reflected debates within their political leadership regarding the utility of the Paris Agreements.[59] As the armed forces of 34 countries filtered into Cambodia to supervise and monitor the cease-fire and undertake their other tasks, the Force Commander prepared on 9 May to begin disarming, demobilising and cantoning of 70% of the armed forces of the three factions and the incumbent leadership.

Phase II was to have begun on 13 June, 1992.[60] However, the Khmer Rouge would not universally comply with this stage of the operation. The first concrete rebuttal on their part found expression in two arguments. First, they claimed that 'Viêtnamese military personnel remained in Cambodia and that, until their withdrawal and non-return had been verified by UNTAC, [they] required that it defer any moves to disarm'.[61] Second, the Khmer Rouge claimed that their CPP opposition in Phnom Penh had not been separated from the state apparatus; and that consequently, UNTAC was not fairly conducting its business which undermined the opportunities for the Khmer Rouge to gain an electoral advantage later.[62] In the first instance, their claims were only valid in the context of the racist paranoia and rhetoric which informed their past history and present dogma. Whilst the presence of Viêt Namese in Cambodia was irrefutable, only by the wildest claims could they fit into the definition of 'foreign forces' to which they had agreed in the PPA.[63] Most were civilians who compensated for the deficit in building labour in the wake of UNTAC's arrival and the increase in demand for hotels; or who had settled in Cambodia, often with Cambodian families of their own. In the second instance, however, there was a great deal of credibility in terms of anticipated advantages accruing from participation in the Paris Agreements.

The *Far Eastern Economic Review* warned at the time that 'the future of the ... Peace Accord [was] in jeopardy as the ... Khmer Rouge ... threaten[ed] to wreck the fragile agreement'.[64] Shortly after came early threats of disruption of the elections if they

A Critical Overview of the Operation

proceeded without their participation.[65] Later, as the elections approached, the guerrillas promised 'that the situation w[ould] get more unstable, more insecure, more confusing.... There w[ould] be more attacks'.[66] In a very real sense, UNTAC's operation was deeply threatened, perhaps not so much by threats of violence, but possibly more by the implications the withdrawal had for the transitional process as a whole. As a consequence of the Khmer Rouge's refusal to comply with UNTAC's mandate, the military component had to give up disarming and regrouping the Cambodian armies. Instead, their role was altered to provide security for the electoral teams in the field, some of which were being intimidated by either the Khmer Rouge or the CPP militia, police and affiliates. They would also provide security at the time of the elections, to underscore individuals' safety and to offer a counterweight to possible attempts at intimidation by any forces so seeking to influence elections in this fashion; and to promote confidence in travelling to the polling stations to vote.

UNTAC's passive response to the Khmer Rouge's position had wider ranging implications. The incapacity, lack of will, or deliberate decision making on the part of Akashi and Sanderson to forcibly disarm the NADK suggested to some that UNTAC had no resolve and was therefore not a credible force for achieving peace in Cambodia. Findlay claims the event 'became a turning point in Cambodians' perceptions of UNTAC's effectiveness' and resolve.[67] Some elements of the Khmer Rouge, according to Ieng Sary, came to the conclusion that they could 'harass and arrest the United Nations because [they would] not fight'.[68] This seemed to have given the guerrillas a sense of impunity, such that their obstructionism was more frequent and with less concern. The *Far Eastern Economic Review* declared that 'having discovered that no-one is about to call its bluff, the Khmers Rouges ... consistently raised the stakes – and won every time'.[69] Furthermore, the *Review* observed that UNTAC's inaction seemed to confirm to the Khmer Rouge that 'there [was] more profit – and no penalty – in defying UN strictures than in obeying them'.[70] Prince Sihanouk reflected with disdain:

> The Khmer Rouge sees that the gentlemen of UNTAC are very kind. If there is a fight somewhere, UNTAC does not intervene. On the contrary, it withdraws. The Khmer Rouge know that the UN will never make war against them. The Cambodian people believed that the UN blue berets were like Jupiter threatening to

unleash lightning against the Khmer Rouge. What do people see? UNTAC pulls back.[71]

UNTAC was facing its first major dilemma, a consequence in large part of its tardy deployment. However, as will be argued later, in conjunction with this were fundamental inadequacies in the prospects for a resolution of the Khmer Rouge's principal concerns regarding the neutralisation of the political environment. Furthermore, failure to resolve these problems led directly and indirectly to the fighting in Phnom Penh four years later, in 1997.

Responses to the Khmer Rouge and the Use of Force

Akashi and the UN more broadly were subjected to an intense debate regarding an appropriate response to the Khmer Rouge. Two views dominated the subject. First was to ensure that any impression the UN might give in the 'new world order' projected the hopes for a more effective organisation that could shed its past image of being a 'watchdog with no teeth'. Therefore, UNTAC should confront the Khmer Rouge. For example, some argued that the Khmer Rouge could have been taken on militarily. By removing their HQ at Pailin, the head would have been removed from the snake, and the problem would be concluded for good. There were several imperatives for this. First, it might have been used to demonstrate UNTAC's resolve and potential threat to non-consent. Second, it might have coerced the belligerent actors to comply with the aspects of the accords they rejected. Third, it might enhance the security conditions in which the Cambodian electorate would vote by stabilising the political environment. Fourth, if it was not applied in such conditions, it might set UNTAC on a slippery slope, whereby respect for the UN was lost more broadly.

The Deputy Force Commander, Michel Loridon, famously stated that he would be prepared to attack the Khmer Rouge to force their compliance.[72] Frustrated at the lack of co-operation he was receiving either from the UN or the Khmer Rouge, he declared that UNTAC was missing its

> chance to deal with the Khmer Rouge, push them to implement the accords they ... signed.... If it came to that, one may lose 200 men – and that would include myself – but the Khmer Rouge problem would be solved for good.[73]

A Critical Overview of the Operation

Heder claims this was in the context of a completely separate operation, which involved the 'parachuting' of UNVs and other administrators into Khmer Rouge controlled areas to facilitate elections.[74] According to Heder, 'Operation Dovetail' was:

> the invasion of Khmer Rouge territory, planning for which continued up until [Autumn] 1992. The actual plan was to establish ... an UNTAC presence in Khmer Rouge zones ... to use UNTAC civilians as a kind of human shield behind which the UNTAC military would stand in case of trouble.... At the heart of it would be UNTAC 12 with its Khmer speakers [who] would make contact with the civilian population under Khmer Rouge control, pursuant to UNTAC's mandate, and if trouble eventuated, then it must have been over to the troops, the Dutch Marines to come in and exfiltrate us. Sihanouk believed that attacking them would not work; and that if they were attacked militarily, that it would end up in the same place that it had in the past, in further deaths and stalemate.

Heder went on to note that the plan 'died because Sihanouk was opposed to it, and because Kofi Anan at UN peacekeeping HQ thought it was harebrained'.[75]

General Sanderson, the Military Component Commander, and the individual least likely not to know about such a proposal, rejects this entirely. Furthermore, no other UN official surveyed admitted to having heard of it. When asked to corroborate such a military undertaking, Sanderson replied that

> in [such] circumstances there are many flights of fantasy about responses to strange and difficult situations. I cannot recall the particular plan.... Heder refers to.... The proposal as Heder describes it would certainly have been harebrained and not militarily feasible.[76]

He also noted that the UN missions in 'his experience' were 'full of amateurs.... Many of these are fresh from academia ... with no experience of the practical realities of the environment in which they find themselves'.[77] He also added that any cancellation of such a 'flight of fantasy' 'could not have been by Kofi Anan as Marrack Goulding was responsible for UN Peacekeeping until late in the year'.[78] General Loridon declared that Heder was 'partial ... [and] had not understood the situation in Cambodia. Nobody ha[d] given me one word about this operation [Dovetail]'.[79]

A Critical Overview of the Operation

Sanderson also refutes Heder's claims regarding the context in which Loridon made open statements about confronting the Khmer Rouge militarily (above). Sanderson believed that Loridon's statements regarding the Khmer Rouge were not rejected because of the fabled 'Operation Dovetail, but rather because they

> were so out of keeping with the mandate, and so at odds with the need to keep the Khmer Rouge engaged, that he became an embarrassment to his own country and had to go. He was withdrawn after a visit by the French Defence Minister Joxe.[80]

Loridon himself refers to copies of his statement, in which he said:

> We have to push the Khmer Rouge to co-operate. We must not hesitate to have a *"bras de fer"* [iron arm] with them. They have killed more than one million Cambodians. If to bring peace for eight million Cambodia people, the UN must risk the lives of 200 soldiers, we must do that.[81]

It would seem Heder's comments are not supported by anyone else. However, the question of what to do with the Khmer Rouge remained. There was a mood for battle in some quarters. However, cautioning the French, Sihanouk reminded Paris that he had 'much admiration for the French army ... but please don't forget Dien Bien Phu'.[82] Akashi maintained that the Khmer Rouge might have been coaxed back into the operation by 'patient diplomacy'. He maintained that the application of armed force would represent 'a failure, a bankruptcy, of peacekeeping'.[83] Few supported this at the time, demanding more but not normally stipulating what might be done as an alternative. There was clearly a continuum, in the Clausewitzian sense, from war to peace. However the position at which a response to the Khmer Rouge was located was unclear. In a period often characterised by calls for 'action' rather than 'appeasement', Akashi was quite clearly correct not to attempt to take on the Khmer Rouge, if only for some of the pragmatic reasons outlined above. Beyond this, the loss of consent, and the implicit recourse the Khmer Rouge would have had to take in their own defence, the rest of the operation would probably have been irretrievably halted.

However, in an attempt to persuade the guerrillas further, the UN underwrote the application of sanctions on petroleum products to the Khmer Rouge, and 'undertook to consider' freezing overseas assets.[84] There was no discernible effect on the Khmer Rouge. Sihanouk censured UNTAC for their response, chiding them tartly: 'Freezing economic assets my foot ... trade ties will just go on underground'.[85] The sanctions were a gesture designed to placate an increasingly vexed media and international community that wanted an election at any cost, regardless of the conditions in which polling might take place so the increasingly tenuous and fragile case could be closed. Observers were also concerned that such a seemingly impecunious group could hold the UN hostage.

Despite the failure of sanctions to coax the Khmer Rouge back to participation, Sanderson has stated clearly that 'enforcement action by the United Nations peacekeepers in Cambodia ... was never an option'.[86] This observation is based on pragmatic and political considerations surrounding applying force in environments like the Cambodian peacekeeping operation. Loridon, on the other hand, still maintains this was an option. Such differences were presented as 'splits' within UNTAC and, more specifically, between the two most senior military officers. Most accounts suggest Loridon was a 'loose cannon', causing problems for Sanderson. His own account, however, is quite different. Loridon argues that he 'could not be incorrect with [Sanderson] for one reason'. He claims that he 'received orders from [his] Chief of Staff to be cool and friends with Sanderson because of [the] nuclear tests ... at Tahiti at that time'.[87] Loridon claimed that many other deputies had a similar, or worse, experience with Sanderson. Therefore any debate regarding military actions against the Khmer Rouge can also be observed through this particular prism.

Completing Implementation

Against a background of passive non-co-operation from the Khmer Rouge, and active but generally non-violent resistance to UNTAC from the CPP, to which UNTAC responded diplomatically rather than militarily, the United Nations Volunteers (UNVs) registered some 4,764, 430 eligible voters.[88] In conjunction with the registration programme, the Human Rights component joined the UNVs in introducing and developing the central meaning of UNTAC's presence in Cambodia. As has been outlined above, there is no tradition of national universal suffrage elections for multi-party candidacies which might in other conditions have provided a template for Khmers to consider the UN process.

Furthermore, a culturally sensitive re-education had to be undertaken if polling was to enjoy a legitimating turn-out. During the Pol

A Critical Overview of the Operation

Pot era, the surrender of personal histories often had deadly consequences. This might range from seemingly plausible requests from Khmer Rouge cadres for people who had a medical practitioners background, to enforced confessions of false pasts in order to disavow the regime of the problems it had created of its own making. Those who identified themselves with a particular belief, or past, or career that was disagreeable to the Khmer Rouge *Angkar Loeu* (literally, high organisation), or who, in the *Angkar's* paranoia, undermined the revolution, were regularly murdered. The taking of personal biographies was associated with investigation by the *Angkar*, and people naturally resisted as far as they could the surrender of such information. Underscoring the fatal view of this process was the awareness that consequences of such 'indiscretions' on the part of an individual could extend quickly to the wider family.

The voter education programme (VEP) had yet more to contend with. Although there is no comparison between the policies and practices of the Khmer Rouge, and those of the government of the 1980s, the severity of socio-economic conditions and the relative limitations upon personal freedom which accompanied some aspects of the PRPK's leadership did not augur well for trust of government officials. This is in no way specific to the SoC/CPP experience. Because of the arbitrary use of power and the limited access for peasants to legal recourse, authority has a much longer tradition of being considered dubious in this sense, especially in the countryside. Vickery reports an illustrative anecdote from 1962. He refers to a village twenty-five kilometres from Thmar Puok. An

> interesting feature of the village was the people's dislike of anyone and anything from the towns of Cambodia.... Officials ... had come to visit.... The villagers hated their pretensions and false promises of aid and development. Most of all they disliked the officials' wives, who minced about ... in high heels with handkerchiefs held to their nose...[89]

The tradition of dislike of authority therefore also has long roots. However, despite such mores, the education programme, conducted by educated 'city folk', be they Khmer or non-Khmer, was accomplished across most of Cambodia, and the message of the secrecy of the vote was put across successfully for the most part. The success of this stage of the operation is well reflected in the comments to a western journalist of a farmer allegedly being harassed by state officials. The farmer recounted that the officials told him that 'if I didn't vote for them, they would kill me'. 'Because of this', the farmer stoically retorted, 'I voted for FUNCINPEC'.[90]

Whilst it was far from perfect, this was a remarkable achievement, and in conjunction with the wider education programme and the commitment with which many UNVs covered even the most inaccessible regions of Cambodia, was critical to the operation. It also demonstrated that elements of the operation could proceed without absolute co-operation from all parties, as the Khmer Rouge were technically withdrawn and the CPP were clearly taking measures to counter-act the values of neutrality and personal freedom of the democracy education programme.

Civil Administration

The PPA determined that free and fair elections necessarily presupposed a neutral political environment. UNTAC was accordingly mandated to separate the various branches of government from the organs of state that might support the executive, for example. This derived from the observation that Socialist states do not generally observe the separation of powers normally characterising liberal constitutional Parliamentary-style democracy. Ashley observes that 'Cambodia has never known separation of powers: the society has rather comprised the all-powerful state (or palace) and the all-powerless rural population with the Chinese traders in between'.[91] The importance of this should not be under-stated. Whilst nominally the country's title had changed in 1989 to the State of Cambodia, its political, bureaucratic and administrative infra- and super-structures clearly reflected a Communist model with an interweaving of departments and political branches. A World Bank report noted that 'a number of organisational features ... arise from (i) the former interventionist role of the state, (ii) persistent centralism, and (iii) the absence of a clear delineation between the public administration, as an instrument of the executive branch, and the other institutions of the state'. The report went on to comment that the various Ministries' structural organisation was complex and over-staffed. For example:

> The supreme authority within each ministry is the minister, who has simultaneously a political role as a member of the central administration and an administrative one as the top member of his own administrative entity.... Each is assisted by one or several vice ministers ... [and] ... has a 'cabinet' and several

departments. This 'cabinet' is in charge of the co-ordination of the ministry and of several other management tasks.... Each ministerial department, headed by a 'general director', comprises several directorates, which in turn comprise several bureaus.[92]

A serious consequence of this was that the PRPK, re-named the Cambodian People's Party (CPP), enjoyed intrusive management of all aspects of state activity, from the army, through the secret police and the foreign office, to low level civil and political organisation in the distant communes. This permitted the party an innate advantage over the opposition, and the key issue of separation of powers had been central in discussions with the Khmer Rouge as the nature of the peace settlement became clearer after early 1990. In a broad study of democratisation in developing countries, Pinkney notes that the general problems of undertaking such a task in single party systems can be observed in many other countries.[93] It was clear to the Khmer Rouge elite that their key advantages lay in leaving the battlefield, on which they were not advancing, and moving to a political arena in which they could compete 'fairly' for the vote. If, however, their main opposition could preserve their influence over domestic politics, the Khmer Rouge's enhanced position would be undermined. The environment would not be therefore politically neutral.

Separating the CPP from the organs of the state entailed UNTAC's civil administration component overseeing the operations of the five core areas that might have an effect on the outcome of the election, as well as other subsidiary and less crucial areas of government. Those core areas included defence, foreign affairs, finance, public security and information. They were complemented by a 'specialized control' group which covered related areas, including health, education, agriculture and transport.[94] Indeed, as Schear further notes,

> by the latter stages of the operation, UNTAC personnel could be found doing such things as probing into the country's penal code, investigating its defence procurement decisions, vetting editorials in state-run media, reviewing regulations on national heritage preservation, scrutinising admissions policies at public educational institutions.[95]

This concept theoretically applied equally to the other parties administering various areas. However, in the same way that disarming the NADK was more problematic than disarming the CPAF, so too was it more difficult to separate the ex-CGDK parties from their political and civil infrastructures. The Khmer Rouge operated far more informal approaches to 'managing' its territory and population which were less identifiable and therefore less penetrable. Compounding this problem was their refusal to permit access to some of the zones under their influence.

In neither instance could civil administration successfully identify and paralyse the political parties' access to their state organs. Furthermore, the majority of civil administrators was employed in Phnom Penh; and all these worked on the CPP (there was no formal or informal state political infrastructure under the control of any other party than the CPP in the capital, for obvious reasons). The inadequacy of civil administration and their failure to complete an impossible task are well illustrated in the campaign period preceding the polls.

The Campaign Period

With the UNHCR, NGOs and UNVs having completed their role in the plan, an electoral campaign could begin with some time to spare. This process ran from 7 April to 19 May 1993, but its brevity was criticised in some quarters. As civil administration failed to render the CPP's innate advantage worthless, that party's control over state organs ensured it could dominate the campaign period to a far greater degree than UNTAC's media vehicles could compensate for. Thus, whilst all parties were guaranteed air time and support for political propaganda by UNTAC electoral law through the UN radio station, Radio UNTAC, the CPP's position ensured this did not match their own capabilities. Furthermore, UNTAC's mandate stated it must supply coverage to all parties irrespective; the CPP took advantage of this, bolstering yet further their capacity to extend party propaganda throughout the country.

The media issue reflected the failure of civil administration to neutralise the CPP; and indeed any of the parties. This lent grist to the mill for the Khmer Rouge, already dissatisfied with UNTAC for their failure to implement what for their leadership was perhaps one of the most important issues of the PPA. Against this background, the Khmer Rouge maintained their position outside the peace process. The cease-fire continued to be violated, with both Cambodian and UNTAC casualties mounting. The elections were to proceed in an atmosphere which, beyond the comfort of capital city offices and security-enhanced rallies, was often insecure.

A Critical Overview of the Operation

This notwithstanding, the staggering cost of UNTAC, estimated at US$ 100 million per month, acted as a steamroller.[96] The Special Representative admitted prior to the elections that the 'neutral political environment' identified in the PPA had not been achieved; and that the outcome of the elections would have to be judged on their 'freeness and fairness'. His change in position reflected a redefining of the grounds upon which the operation would be judged. This in turn reflected recognition that the mandate was not being properly or fully implemented; and that the consequences of this made the outcome yet more unpredictable and unreliable. The further the operation stumbled towards the election, and the more aspects of the PPA it ejected along the path, the more it contributed to the sensation that the polls were less rather than more likely to be successful, in any sense of the word.

The redefining of the litmus test for the polls suggested a paradox: how could elections be free and fair if they were not conducted in a neutral political environment? However, it was no paradox; merely a shift in emphasis from one criteria to another. The 'free and fair' element of the equation was refocused to the actual polling process. This would fit such a criteria if it could be reasonably argued that the vote had been free from front line corruption, perhaps in the form of obvious bullying and intimidation or harassment; free from clear poll fraud; or free from violent attacks from outside. This redefinition would replace the original, which reflected concerns and interests in the political nature of the period preceding the election, in which the political parties' actions were also the focus. Thus, although in the intended sense the elections could not be free and fair because of the absence of a neutral political environment, the actual conduct of the poll itself could be considered free and fair so long as it was not marred on the day by routine or widespread acts of intimidation, harassment or murder. This debate would be echoed in the 1998 elections.

Thus, during and after the campaign period, the most basic preconditions for a free and fair election, as identified by the PPA, were missing. The country was still largely armed; respect for UNTAC had diminished; the neutral political environment was conspicuous in its absence; and one of the major parties had withdrawn, amidst threats of similar retractions by some of the others. Crime was rocketing, violence was the norm, and political intimidation and harassment were unstoppable. The pre-designated 'cooling-off period', between the end of the campaign period and the beginning of the polling, was ignored by many parties. The atmosphere was tense and unpredictable, and was aggravated by the Cambodian 'rumour mill' which had the guerrillas just outside the capital city; and by the western press, which was predicting the possibility of a blood bath.

On the other hand, the UNHCR had returned all the refugees, if somewhat haphazardly, and the UNVs had completed registration in the most severe of conditions. The secrecy of the vote was clear due to Radio UNTAC and the volunteers. The military component was preparing to secure the polling areas; there were no serious infractions of the cease-fire, insofar as there was no widespread civil war; and the campaign period had been relatively peaceful, in the sense that it could have been so dire as to be prevented from continuing.

The Rejection of 'Politics as Usual'

On 23 May, 1993, despite thunderstorms over the north-western province of Siem Reap, the day was largely dry and later very hot. Site 106, not far from the provincial airport, opened only minutes late. For the non-Cambodians, the atmosphere was grim and serious. The expectation of NADK attack was high, because Siem Reap provincial capital had come under a co-ordinated attack by the guerrillas only weeks before, and because it was in the north-west, where the Khmer Rouge were believed by some to be strongest.

But the anticipated attacks never materialised. To the relief of all, 'Cambodians turned out to vote in numbers beyond UNTAC's wildest expectations'.[97] Concerns regarding intimidation appeared to be largely groundless. By 7.30 am, site 106 was packed with Khmers, old and young. Grandmothers carried infants and waited patiently in lines, apparently unconcerned by threats of violence from the NADK. A muffled cheer tickled the air as the first voter presented her registration card to the young Cambodian at the door, who guided her gently through the voting process. She was unafraid of the 'spy satellites' that the CPP had promised would be watching her and the other voters as she ticked her ballot paper in the 'secret room'.[98] Clearly, UNTAC's efforts to promote the secrecy of the ballot and the inviolability of the balloting booth had paid off. Either the Cambodians believed UNTAC; or they did not care about the threats.

As that first old lady swayed across the threshold of the school doorway, and looked around nervously, smiling, the whole process suddenly appeared to have been worthwhile. All the cynicism and scepticism seemed to evaporate in an instant, as if all the horror stories had been imagined. It seemed as if the interminable history of the

Khmers was finally preparing to move on from the time warp that has characterised the last quarter of a century. It seemed that David Chandler's desires for the Cambodians to be empowered to reject the violence of Khmer 'politics as usual' were about to be realised.[99] It seemed that UNTAC had really thrown its hat into the crowd, and kept its promise to the Khmers.

Most of the election was peaceful.[100] There were some outbreaks of violence; but not enough to refute the outstanding 89.56% electoral turnout across the country.[101] This continued as the mobile polling teams began to seek out the physically disenfranchised Khmers who could not come to polling sites, including those in TB wards and jails. A week later, after the amazement at the peaceful procession had given way to relief, Akashi announced the vote count as it was underway. Over 4.7 million out of a total of approximately 5 million cast their votes. They had defied the Khmer Rouge threats and had accepted UNTAC's promise of secrecy. They had completed their part of the 'agreement', making UNTAC's efforts successful. Their defiant response was, as the Special Representative put it, 'a stinging rebuke to the men of violence'. Chandler noted that 'what had happened was very strange and very moving: for the first time in Cambodian history millions of Khmer had voted freely and fairly, and a majority had opposed an armed incumbent regime'.[102] This is a fair comment.

However, Chandler continues by observing that 'in a sense, the vote was a massive statement rejecting politics as usual – the tragedy of Cambodian history'.[103] This is less valid. The campaign run by FUNCINPEC relied very heavily upon their affiliation through history, propaganda and images with Sihanouk, no longer the party leader. At a rally in Takeo in April 1993, Ranariddh told his audience that 'FUNCINPEC was established by Sihanouk and I am his son.... If FUNCINPEC wins [the election], it means that the whole nation wins and Samdech-Euv [Prince Sihanouk] will come back to rule the country as before'.[104] The appeal to tradition and the Monarch reflects an earlier experience. 'Politics as usual' refers to the politics of coercion and minimal choice coupled to limited participation and propaganda. In fact, the vote in 1993 for Sihanouk by proxy reflects a very traditional perspective in Khmer politics. This perspective is further supported by what Frieson refers to as the CPP's vote strategy, whereby individuals were bullied into accepting party membership and told that as a consequence, they must vote for CPP. There were, according to Frieson, other elements to this strategy.[105] Clearly, then, some aspects of 'politics as usual' persisted.

A Critical Overview of the Operation

Against considerable odds, UNTAC had carried off their 'biggest gamble' in the face of obstinacy and terrorism. They had repatriated the refugees, introduced democracy and human rights, and enfranchised the people. It must of course be noted that whilst the UN may justifiably be praised for their role, such verdicts diminish the fact that the actual polling, upon which UNTAC's right to claim an electoral success rested, depended on the day as much on Cambodians as it did on UNTAC. Had the elections failed due to insufficient voters, UNTAC's operation would have been a disaster mitigated only by its refugee repatriation and its electoral registration programme. The first of these two is far from indefensible; a number of grave consequences of the accelerated programme have been highlighted in various sources. The UN Secretariat insensitively described the election as a 'a credit to the men and women of UNTAC'.[106] In contrast to this, Jarat Chopra wrote that 'it is no exaggeration to say that [it was] the courage of Cambodia's voters [which] rescued UNTAC from … a looming disaster, [permitting] Akashi to declare anything short of mayhem a success'.[107] It is important to contrast the somewhat rosy view many have of the Cambodian elections with a different perspective illustrating the fragility of the operation and the transition shortly after.

Akashi stated that Cambodians were 'the true winners in this election'.[108] However, the optimism and cheer were soon overshadowed by doubt, as the CPP, facing defeat, declared that irregularities in the electoral process required fresh polls and recounting in some provinces. They threatened non-acceptance of the results, and shortly after, but not directly connected with this, a secession began on Cambodia's eastern border with Viêt Nam.

Figure 1: 1993 election results by party, seats in the Assembly, and vote count.[109]

	CPP	FUNCINPEC	BLDP	MOLINAKA	Totals
Votes	1,533,471	1,824,188	152,764	55,107	4,011,631
% total	38.23	45.47	3.81	1.37	97.87
Seats	51	58	10	1	120

The CPP's claims, regarding allegations of electoral fraud and irregularities, were rejected by UNTAC. The ensuing, but politically discrete, secession certainly threatened to negate all UNTAC's central

A Critical Overview of the Operation

achievements. The CPP, using the effect of the independently acting secessionists of its own party, negotiated from a position of power which effectively led to the blackmailing of UNTAC with threats of violence against the peacekeepers. When the secession ended, despite their defeat at the polls, the CPP moved into joint equal power sharing with their principal opponents, FUNCINPEC. This, and the US Mission's role in destabilising this stage of political transition, is discussed in greater detail in chapter six.

Thus, despite the tenuous assumptions and foundations implicit in the PPA; the late deployment; the weak command chain in the early stages; the inability of the UN to separate the CPP from the state, or to force the guerrillas and the others to disarm and canton; and the series of cease-fire violations and political harassment and murders, the election was unimaginably successful. An electoral turnout that would embarrass most developed nations led to a choice being clearly stated: Cambodians wanted *santapheap* and *wattanapheap* – peace and development.

A Positive Outcome for the UN

The UN was able to withdraw some months later secure in the knowledge that it had achieved the central point of the operation. Lessons could of course be learned from it, but overall, UNTAC had achieved something extremely difficult, against the odds, and could justifiably congratulate itself. Cambodia had an internationally recognised government, with its rightful place at the UN, once more eligible for development aid and international investment crucial to the country's economic growth. The success seemed to demonstrate how successful and appropriate the application of liberal democratic multi-party power sharing could be.

The elections, undoubtedly, were a magical success for UNTAC and initially succeeded in creating a pleasant illusion of democracy in Cambodia which lent credit and praise to the 'international community', the Perm-5, the UN, UNTAC and Khmer voters. It also further advanced the moral propriety and legitimacy of Young's interpretation of the 'Liberal Project'. However, there was as much a degree of luck as judgement, and in terms of political transition, this particular example was weak from the outset. It is perhaps no coincidence that the volatility of the operation to induce political transition parallels the experiences of Cambodians in the post-UNTAC period in attempting to secure that transition. It is certainly no coincidence

A Critical Overview of the Operation

that one of the key causes of political instability during the transitional operation also lays at the heart of post-UN stability. The following chapter examines the origins of these key problems outlined in the above discussions.

IV
Early Challenges to Transition

The issue of deployment has been briefly introduced in the preceding chapter, and is raised in most of the literature on Cambodia. However, two important questions remain unanswered. First, why did deployment take so long? Second, what were the consequences? These questions are important to understanding political transition in Cambodia, because they illustrate the early links in the chain of events which lead to the Khmer Rouge refusing to accede to the transitional agreements of the PPA. In the longer term, answers to these two questions extend that chain to demonstrate a relationship between UNTAC's deployment, their failure to disarm them because of the civil administration issue, and the July 1997 fighting.

A number of interwoven reasons exist to explain the deployment. At the strategic level, attitudes and understanding in New York, according to the UNTAC Force Commander, contributed in no small part to the tardy departure. In essence, a lack of information and insight, and the incapacity to digest some of the data moving between Cambodia and New York, 'contributed to the long delay in getting UNTAC on the ground'.[1] Furthermore, because of the inability to translate information into meaning, UNHQ often simply did not confirm receipt or analysis of material, or even respond to requests for data or supplies. Jennar observed that in some instances, the field teams were

> obliged to send two liaison officers [back] to New York to follow up messages sent to headquarters ... [and] ... a spectacular failure of planning and logistical abilities [caused] civilian and military personnel to arrive in advance of equipment and ... technical resources.[2]

Furthermore, the absence of what Sanderson refers to as 'integrated planning staffs', and the presence of a 'narrow focus' in relation to the wider political objectives at stake amongst many elements of the UN and the NGO community, further aggravated the delay.[3]

These inadequacies were unfortunately transferred to the United Nations Advance Mission in Cambodia (UNAMIC), which arrived in Cambodia in the second week of November 1991. UNAMIC suffered from a number of logistical deficiencies, but it was further encumbered by a lack of support and planning staff which, according to Sanderson, 'lull[ed] the United Nations bureaucracy into a false sense of security'. Subsequently, New York used the UNAMIC finger to plug the deployment dike. The *Far Eastern Economic Review* complained that 'there was a major screw-up in this whole process – and that is UNAMIC ... UNAMIC was only an afterthought when the peace accord was drawn up...'.[4] Whilst UNAMIC cannot be fairly held to book for its failure to smooth the passage for UNTAC more widely, Mackinlay, Chopra and Minear note that within the advance guard there was 'serious criticism of its lack of investigative rigour, the result of which became apparent during the deployment'.[5] In no small part due to this, Sanderson was prompted to comment that the Advance Mission 'staggered from one crisis to another ... leaving it unable to execute the important task of planning for UNTAC'.[6] Whilst its conduct made inroads into preparing for the main deployment, it was restricted in what it could do by overly optimistic or naive expectations and a work load which was not ameliorated by communications with and directives from the UN HQ in New York. The causes of the deployment delay lay in weak planning and a sense of 'ambush', whereby after a decade of negotiation, the UN was unexpectedly assaulted by the consequences of the sophisticated arrangements signed in its name in 1991.[7]

Schear also posits several reasons for the tardy deployment. First, and in conjunction with Findlay, he argues that shortly after the signing of the PPA, the development of the UNTAC programme and the necessary funding encountered competition from events unfolding in the former Yugoslavia.[8] The peacekeeping department of the UN was 'overwhelmed by the near simultaneous requirements to assemble [and finance] large, multi-component UN operations for Cambodia and Croatia', a problem exacerbated, argues Schear, by the change of UN Secretary-Generals, from Perez de Cuellar to Boutros Boutros-Ghali. The former did not appoint the UNTAC head and that in turn 'delayed other management appointments'.[9] In conjunction with this, the failure of the UN Secretariat to commence negotiations and arrangements with member states during the run up to the signing of the PPA seriously reduced the likelihood of a UN force deploying within any expected or reasonable time frame. All these issues, argues Schear, were then aggravated by the absence of reliable information from the field which might assist in the planning of the operation.[10]

Strategic logistics yet further undermined the deployment. The movement of such large numbers of troops and much of the equipment associated with a large-scale deployment is contracted through the UN secretariat to civil carriers such as the Merchant navies.[11] The progression of such a contract takes approximately three months, before the cargo is shipped.[12] Sanderson comments that

> the undertaking was too ambitious for the UN as it was structured at that time. The Committee processes are too bureaucratic and cumbersome, even though many short cuts were taken to get monies to start the process.[13]

As a result, whilst the UN procrastinated and dithered and attention was focused elsewhere, the operationalization of UNTAC's formation in late February 1992 was further decelerated. From whenever a decision was made, there would be a three month lead time in dealing with contracts, and the decision-making related to this was delayed by five months due to poor appointment planning, the developments in Yugoslavia and the change of the Secretary-Generals.

Looking back yet further, criticism might be levied at those responsible for the PPA as it evolved and took a more recognisable and therefore tangible form than any part of the peace process had before. Despite the general acceptance, by the time of the Pattaya meeting in June 1991, that a large UN peacekeeping force tasked with civil administration as well as military deployment would be underway imminently, 'no anticipatory planning decisions of any value were taken until ... November'. Chopra et al further observed that when UNAMIC's representatives returned from Cambodia aware of the urgency of action, 'there seemed to be no staff available in New York to meet [them] and [there seemed to be] a reluctance to respond to their enquiries'.[14]

Clearly, then, there are many self-reinforcing reasons for the delayed deployment of the UN peacekeeping force in Cambodia. A lack of foresight at an early point later undermined efforts to assess needs. Simultaneously, when the advance party was marshalled, the limitations of staff and their professional experience in some elements were aggravated by a failure of planning and operations staff in New York to understand, assess or react to the incoming information. In turn, this led to a failure to take full advantage of the wealth of source material available from in-country NGOs. Ultimately, UNTAC was not even officially formed until late February 1992, with unreliable out-of-date assessments guiding the contracting of the delivery fleets to Cambodia's harbours, airports and land border points. The logistical consequences of this in terms of soldiers arriving ahead of their equipment and so on have been well documented in many sources.[15] However, this in itself had profound consequences for this stage of the transition.

Clearly, there is little direct link between the PPA itself and the delays in deployment and implementation, other than that the latter undermined the former. But the most important issue arising from the deployment was that the absence of the UNTAC enforcing mechanism at the point of signing, or at least soon thereafter, caused the parties to adjust their positions to accommodate this development. Chopra argues that concerns expressed amongst the Perm-5 were echoed as 'the factions ... began to lose control of forces in the field that feared the consequences of ... loss of power and position' consequent upon the UN implementing the Paris Accords.[16] Chopra's observation referred to obvious 'asset-generating' activities on the ground, but also highlighted the earliest signs since Paris that the politics of exclusion were central to the parties struggling for power. In other words, it was becoming evident to the competing parties and their members that the consequences of marginalisation would exclude them from political power and wealth to an extent they began to recognise as unacceptable. The consequences of political marginalisation ensured that efforts were made by all contestants to alter the power balance as it stood at the signing of the PPA because those terms were not being immediately enforced. In other words, the advantage afforded the Khmer Rouge was eroded, whilst the disadvantage facing the CPP was lessened.

This proved to be the case especially, but not exclusively, with elements of the Khmer Rouge. The conditions to which it agreed, whilst institutionalised in the PPA, were not immediately implemented. Their expectation was that their CPP opponents were to be politically separated from the state. Not only did this not happen, but as a consequence of the failure to start disarmament and political neutralisation in the gap between signing the PPA and arriving, the elites not unexpectedly moved to consolidate their party's and their military's positions to minimise the effects of the absent UN. Sanderson observed that

> it should be realised that parties agree to something because they believe that it is in their own interests at that time and that they can get more from it than they will lose. When an agreement is signed it will create a new set of dynamics as each party tries to use the provisions to its own advantage.[17]

Equally, once the dynamics are created they must be guarded to preserve the conditions agreed to, to prevent parties from stepping outside the boundaries of the contract whilst no oversight exists to prevent this 'slippage'. The absence of the UN 'guardians' represented a deficiency in the restrictions which should have served to impede further advantage-seeking or activities which might compensate for disadvantages accruing from one or the other side's abuse of that vacuum. That abuse was a direct product of a desire to minimise conditions that would lead to defeat, and the severity of the consequences of exclusion from elite power.

The delay accentuated the degree of difficulty in implementing the terms of the PPA, and made the job both harder and less possible as the results of the political and military manoeuvring subsequent upon the delay changed the effect the PPA could have on providing what each side sought. The delay, and the compensatory jockeying through until July 1992 (and after), altered the balance of power equation that the PPA had been designed to assuage such that the PPA could no longer have the effect anticipated by the manoeuvring parties which had occasioned it in October 1991. As Findlay noted, 'UNAMIC's prolonged tenure and the hiatus in power resulting from the delay ... led to a serious disintegration of the situation in Cambodia...'.[18] Sanderson argues that the UN 'lost an opportunity to get the SoC under control and to commit a substantial part of the Khmer Rouge to the process. All the damage had been done before the UN had sufficient presence to be credible'.[19] The 'molasses-like' military deployment and subsequent implementation of the rest of the operation was compounded by the innate impracticalities lent to the intervention by the nature and content of the Paris mandate.[20] Whilst this assumes the air of a very critical attack on UNAMIC, it would be unwise to blame that body for all the ills noted by Sanderson and Findlay.

Disarmament and demobilisation

The relationship between the consequences of delayed deployment, and the refusal of the Khmer Rouge to disarm, is another example of the consequences of political exclusion. The delays were, for Sanderson, 'a major cause of many of the difficulties which followed'.[21] UNTAC had arrived late and been unable to achieve disarmament of the Khmer Rouge, after which the CPP began to halt its military cantonment. The combined total of surrendered weapons came to 50,000 amongst all parties. Of these, 42,368 came from the CPP.[22]

The consequences of the delayed deployment, then, extended to demobilisation and disarmament. This arrested development undermined the opportunity to capitalise on the cessation of hostilities and the preservation of the cease-fire that loosely ensued. The Khmer Rouge elite concluded that the delay would minimise the capacity of UNTAC to separate the CPP from the state and thus create a neutral environment in which they could compete politically. It would also encourage the CPP to conceal or disguise the connections between state and party in order to prevent their own political marginalisation through the empowerment of political opposition through the vote. The failure of UNTAC to disarm the four groups cannot be divorced from its failure to secure a neutral political environment; and this has its origins in the impropriety and solecism of the Paris Peace Agreements.

The Politics of the Neutral Political Environment (NPE)

The provision of an NPE necessitated UNTAC's Civilian Administration component to supervise nine areas (not ministries) of the state in Phnom Penh, five of which were considered to be potentially particularly influential in an election.[23] Clearly, these rules applied to the neutralisation of the CPP; little effort was made to apply the same approach to Khmer Rouge or FUNCINPEC administration elsewhere in the country. It was envisioned that direct supervision of these five areas by UNTAC personnel would disempower the CPP and satisfy the requirements of the 'neutral political environment'. This in turn would both even the political contest and satisfy the worries of the Cambodian parties that had voiced concern over the CPP's advantageous position derived from their long-standing ownership of the state apparatus.

Several substantive issues determined the failure of civil administration to satisfy the terms of the PPA, and to create the conditions central to the Khmer Rouge's participation. First, some sources within UNTAC claimed they were 'inside the [state] system to an incredible degree'.[24] However, the CPP undoubtedly exercised its natural prerogative, retaining completely control 'of all government structures and all government workers ... [resulting in] no separation of party and state'. This source went on to observe that 'despite the UN efforts, the power of the CPP state apparatus remain[ed] intact'.[25]

This penetrative capacity ensured intimidation of civil administration could be utilised to undermine UNTAC's efforts in this area. Of the 818 representatives of civilian administration present by August 1992, 599 were Cambodians.[26] Chea Sim, President of the National Assembly, warned that 'the majority of Cambodians working for UNTAC were from the refugee camps and ... capitalist countries'. This then assumed an anti-CPP perspective, as few overseas Khmers have much sympathy with the formerly Communist CPP after residing in western/capitalist states. With this potential threat to the security of the party, CPP police forces 'at every level' were encouraged to 'push to keep a firm grip on the enemies that are hidden within the ranks of [UNTAC]'.[27] Whilst there is clear evidence that elements of the CPP acted in a way that would make UNTAC's job more difficult, especially after disarmament was halted, there seem few references to individual UNTAC operatives having been bullied or harassed as Frieson suggests. The document is the only evidence Frieson presents of such events.

To imagine that the UNTAC operatives, Khmer or non-Khmer, could penetrate such a secret, swollen and clandestine organisation is little more than fantasy. The claim that 219 non-Khmer speaking aliens had penetrated the State of Cambodia across at least nine ministries is erroneous to the point of disingenuity. One UN official exaggerated for effect that to properly carry out the task in hand would require not 500, but 500,000 civil administrators.[28]

The task was impossible. As the *NATO Review* observed, the problem lay largely with 'the mandate being overly ambitious and in some respects clearly not achievable, given the UN's stretched resources...'.[29] A FUNCINPEC representative in Siem Reap argued that 'UNTAC had an impossible task.... CPP would permit to happen only what CPP wanted to happen'.[30] Official sources later confirmed this view.[31] A UN District Electoral Supervisor (DES) considered the notion absurd, noting that Civil Administration 'couldn't speak the language or read Khmer documents ... they couldn't even decide between French and English as the UN language'.[32] Finally, a civil administration representative with four years previous experience of Cambodia objected that it was in some ways 'doomed from the start'.[33]

The political settlement signed by the superpowers with Cambodia in tow completely disregarded the

> inherent impossibility of a handful of foreigners, in the space of less than a year, monitoring and imposing neutral behaviour upon an authoritarian bureaucracy determined to resist control [when there was] inadequate or inappropriate staffing and a passivity that in some cases has bordered on incompetence.[34]

UNTAC's civil administration component was further impeded because 'the UN bureaucrats began their work without ... knowledge of the country or its ancient culture and customs and, worst of all, without any proper planning. This is perhaps unsurprising, and was exacerbated by the painfully slow recruitment and delayed deployment of the civil administration body.[35] Doyle and Suntharalingum further note that by the time UNTAC had arrived and all its administrators were in place. As a result,

> much of the SoC administration had collapsed and effective control had slipped to provincial governors and generals, so that 'controlling' ministries that themselves did not control their nominal areas of responsibility meant very little ... in the areas of policy-making where a central administrative apparatus was still functioning, the SoC administered around UNTAC. Moreover, when the factions wished to be controlled, they allowed themselves to be 'controlled'. But usually, the actual chain of policy bypassed UNTAC control, as the UNTAC officer was kept busy controlling an official without function and the real ... mechanism flowed elsewhere, diverted out of UNTAC's sight.[36]

The majority of oversight took place in Phnom Penh, where much of the labour and resources were concentrated in this context. The situation was serious in the capital, but in the Provinces, it was even more difficult. 123 UNTAC representatives dispersed throughout twenty Provinces, notes one observer, 'faced entrenched, labyrinthine local administration backed by all the resources of the party-state: foreign officials with no experience of the country, denied direct contact by the language barrier, found it impossible' to implement their mandate.³⁷ This was a result of 'over a decade of single-party rule [which] has given the CPP the opportunity to build a solid party structure (largely indistinguishable from the government bureaucracy) at the provincial, district, communal and village levels'.³⁸ The nature of the relationship between party and state is well documented and, whilst the CPP was not in any meaningful way Leninist, some elements of a socialist bureaucracy unsurprisingly pervaded the system. This, coupled to traditional networks of government/bureaucracy patronage and commune and village clientelism, ensured that even the few administrators deployed outside the capital had almost no chance at all of ensuring the provision of a neutral political environment.

UNTAC did not finish deployment of their administrators until September 1992, by which time the Phnom Penh government had taken action to ensure they retained the necessary services. UNTAC's responses could not satisfy the Khmer Rouge. In the end:

> UNTAC had no choice.... Control of SoC was a laughing game. They had no idea of the depth of SoC power, except for a few experts.... The main problem was that we could never admit this [at the time]. The credibility of the whole thing would have come down around our ears. If we were seen as impotent from the beginning, what effect would this have on our ability to finish the job? So the problems were ignored, and we put on a brave face.³⁹

This clearly made a mockery of the notion of an NPE. Although UNTAC, by way of deploying, appeared to be implementing its mandate, Hippler observed that 'in practice ... the [Phnom Penh] government remained in control'.⁴⁰ Several years before UNTAC deployed, *The Economist* had observed that 'the main question for a [peace] deal ... was whether the [UN] would be enough to break [the CPP's] control of the country'.⁴¹ The UN secretary-general conceded that the inability of the Civil Administration component to carry out its mandate ensured that 'widespread and persistent use of the SoC state apparatus to conduct political campaign activities ... in which state employees – police, armed forces and civil servants – [could be] mobilised for CPP electioneering'.⁴²

Accordingly, a UN Progress report candidly noted that 'the Khmers Rouges could ... claim that the government ... was surviving [the PPA] almost intact'.⁴³ The CPP remained in control of the levers of influence within the state infrastructure, which in turn permitted them an electoral advantage unintended in the PPA. Furthermore, the advantage to the CPP was particularly demonstrable and significant because the opposition parties wielded limited administrative or bureaucratic influence in the regions they nominally controlled. The Khmer Rouge were perhaps worst affected as a consequence of the ancillary and unintended empowerment enjoyed by the CPP through the state infrastructure. The BLDP could draw voters through their venerable political leader Son Sann and the emphasis on the Buddhist culture. FUNCINPEC could clearly campaign on the halcyonic Royalist platform. However, the Khmer Rouge were limited in the way they could garner sufficient legitimate mass support to confront their advantaged arch-opponents the CPP in any meaningful sense.

The evidence demonstrating that UNTAC neither could nor did separate the CPP from the state is increasingly important, because it re-contextualises the debate regarding the challenge to political transition engendered by the Khmer Rouge withdrawal. The following chapter will demonstrate that UNTAC's inherent inability to fulfil the PPA's conditions, which the Khmer Rouge viewed as favourable, prevented the first stage of transition from taking place in June 1992. It also created conditions by which the still-armed Khmer Rouge offered value to a divided coalition in 1997, when the ultimate challenge to political transition set Phnom Penh alight. The following chapter also identifies a key concept in the broader process of transition as it relates to the Cambodian experience: that of the consequences of defeat and the absence of institutions capable of ameliorating such defeats.

V

Elite Challenges to Transition – the Khmer Rouge

The gradual escalation of political instability at the end of 1991 clearly began with the delays in deployment discussed in the preceding chapter. This was a portent of political evolution and transition for several years to come. The early transitional period was first marred seriously by the Khmer Rouge refusal to participate in the disarmament phase, which was then viewed as essential. Furthermore, for longer-term political stability, non-disarmament in the context of the quickly developing power struggle in the elected coalition after UNTAC left aggravated the post-UN stage of transition. The importance of the following discussion is that it identifies an underlying tenor of Khmer politics that found repeated expression in the years that followed the UN intervention.

The withdrawal of the Khmer Rouge is not best explained as 'intransigence'. Instead, it was due to concerns that they would be marginalised or excluded from government by elections that would be conducted in a political environment predisposed to their principle opponents, the CPP. Defeat would be exacerbated by their ultimate de-legitimisation at the United Nations. The issue more widely was one of a tension between two forces. The first was political transition from a position of relative strength to one of relative weakness. The second was the consequence of political marginalisation or exclusion where that exclusion is rendered absolute or extreme by the absence of institutionalised opposition; that is, the absence of a role and place for the losers.

Until recently, the Khmer Rouge refusal to disarm has been laid at the door of the 'intransigent' guerrillas themselves. To many it was clear that UNTAC's civil administration was not going to be able to separate state from party. However, the myth persisted that the Khmer Rouge claims to this effect were a pretext, the product of an untrustworthy group that never intended to abide by the plan they signed in October 1991.[1] The Khmer Rouge's acceptance of the PPA had depended significantly on this aspect of the settlement, for it meant their own elevation and simultaneously the disempowerment of their opposition.

Evidence gathered shortly after the July 1997 fighting in Phnom Penh suggests strongly this is not the case, and that the key concerns advanced by Khieu Samphan, Mak Ben and others regarding UNTAC's futile efforts to separate the CPP from its state organs have validity. The evidence strongly suggests that the Khmer Rouge had every intention of co-operating with UNTAC and embracing the peace process in order to gain a foothold, directly or indirectly, to 'legitimate' political power in Cambodia. Furthermore, they did so because the PPA offered them much politically that they had failed to achieve on the battlefield. In other words, 'Pol Pot had agreed to the accords with the hope that their provisions for the neutralisation of the [CPP] and the demobilisation of its army by UNTAC could ... sweep aside his enemies and thus allow [his] regime to advance politically'.[2]

Two schools of thought dominate the limited discussion of the reasons for the Khmer Rouge's withdrawal. The first relies predominantly on western diplomats and analysts, who were then cited in both media and academic studies of the peacekeeping operation. These sources assert that the Khmer Rouge had never intended to co-operate with UNTAC, or that their actions were merely a pretext to increase their influence and even return to military confrontation as the peace settlement appeared not to offer them much of value. This is the most popular and broadly accepted view. However, a second school, which relies on detailed primary field research examining the evidence from senior Khmer Rouge political and military cadre, generates a very different conclusion

The Khmer Rouge Position

The publicly stated position of the Khmer Rouge throughout the operation identified two key aspects of the operation with which it was unhappy. The first referred to the alleged presence of Viêt Namese remaining in Cambodia when UNTAC's military component should have overseen their departure under the terms of the Paris Accords. The Khmer Rouge claimed, for example, that 'almost a

Elite Challenges to Transition – the Khmer Rouge

million Viêtnamese ha[d] been given ID cards by Phnom Penh', supported by some eleven Consulates throughout the country.[3] The second referred to the inability of UNTAC to underscore a free and fair atmosphere for elections by separating the incumbent CPP from the organs of state which threatened to advantage it over the other 19 parties.[4]

Some sources within the Khmer Rouge, and others outside the organisation, have recognised that the issue of the Viêt Namese was a product of xenophobia and paranoia, and of a tendency for the Khmer Rouge to believe their own propaganda. There is little evidence to suggest that this was a meaningful concern in the context of the operation itself. It does, of course, take on greater significance in the context of Cambodian racism towards Viêt Nam more generally, appealing to quite recent historical animosity and racial tension. The issue of the Viêt Namese was also exploited by the Khmer Rouge as a political platform to gain legitimacy and support. However, in no meaningful sense was it a valid ground technically for non-co-operation with UNTAC. Furthermore, in no way were the existing Viêt Namese a threat electorally to the Khmer Rouge because of a lack of enfranchisement in numbers large enough to make a difference in favour of the CPP.

The Khmer Rouge admitted the difference between political policy and public rhetoric and propaganda in their diplomatic manoeuvres. During 1992, they demonstrated the level of significance of this issue in the context of the peacekeeping operation, and perhaps more importantly, in the context of the election, and 'backed away from all their demands on the Viêt Namese'. The Khmer Rouge 'essentially agreed by September [1992] ... that the problem of the Viêt Namese civilians [would] be resolved by the elected government'.[5] Evidently, the main role of the declarations and actions against the Viêt Namese revolved around an often violent and racist rhetorical, propagandistic pretext, devoid of meaningful or justifiable grounds, in some ways similar to the approach adopted by Sam Rainsy and Norodom Ranariddh in the 1998 elections.[6] It was, therefore, 'much less important than the issue of the power of [the CPP]'.[7] This said, however, whilst appearing to drop the issue, the Khmer Rouge restarted, at an institutional level and approach, their policy of genocide against the Viêt Namese in Cambodia, a fact which Heder contends UNTAC concealed at the time.[8] Clearly, whilst conceding the lesser of the two planks upon which they built their case, a vicious reaction to the Viêt Namese 'presence' was still forthcoming. The issue of the failure of UNTAC to separate the CPP from the state was a valid one, and the strategy for dealing with it explains well the Khmer Rouge's responses to the UN after July 1992, when they withdrew from the disarmament phase.

The Khmer Rouge's activities were framed mainly by the thoughts, speeches and writings of Pol Pot, whether supporters and dissenters agreed or disagreed with those views. In contrast with received wisdom, Pol Pot was both very much in direct charge at the time, and was in fact in favour of the PPA. He declared openly in documents recording internal speeches in February 1992, that 'the Paris Agreements are the fruit of a struggle waged for 13 years'; and that they were 'the weapon that [they] must use to defeat' their political enemies. He elaborated further that they 'were talking only in terms of diplomacy'.[9] Stephen Heder has referred to other internal Khmer Rouge documents from the late 1980s which 'show that Pol Pot and other top leaders believed the Khmer Rouge not only could and should but must participate in parliamentary struggle'.[10] Other sources also claimed that 'internal Khmer Rouge documents show clearly that the faction planned to comply with the main components of the Paris peace plan at the time it was signed'.[11]

According to the February 1992 documents the PPA was, at the time it was signed, seen as 'an advantage'.[12] A senior United Nations representative in Cambodia considered that the Khmer Rouge saw the provision of UNTAC as a passage to an end state whereby they would re-enter the Cambodian political arena. Their participation in the peacekeeping operation and, ultimately, the elections, gave them access to the political arena in Cambodia whereas before, their participation could be only military in nature.[13] According to Ieng Sary, Pol Pot's former Foreign Minister, 'Brother Number One' was waiting impatiently for UNTAC to arrive and set in motion the vehicle by which his party would politically counter their arch-enemies in Phnom Penh.[14]

Indeed, Pol Pot was worried that the period after the signing of the PPA was too 'cozy'. He was also worried that 'since the childbirth [of the political settlement] has been easy, there's no need [for the UN] to worry about caesareans or other emergency procedures, and so there's no need for UNTAC to come'. In other words, it may have been necessary to incite riot to hasten the dilatory despatch of peacekeepers. Pol Pot continued that in order to prompt UNTAC in the face of its tardy deployment, the NADK might have to 'launch attacks that create panic'.[15] It was clear therefore that the Khmer Rouge

Elite Challenges to Transition – the Khmer Rouge

anticipated keenly the implementation of the peace process at the time it was signed; and indeed, for some months after.

The political interest in participation was reflected in the machinations of the military wing of the Khmer Rouge, the National Army of Democratic Kampuchea (NADK). From the beginning, one particular strategy revolved around the preservation of access to Route 12, which divides parts of Cambodia east and west. When the Khmer Rouge was planning co-operation and participation in the future elections, NADK operations around Route 12 served the objective of 'maintaining a supply corridor ... in preparation for the elections, pursuant to a policy not of a resumption of armed struggle ... but of keeping open ... lines of communications so they could move people along that front as part of their preparations for the election...'.[16] In fact, the efforts of the Khmer Rouge 'up until 30th April 1992' revolved around 'attempts to move politically into contested or [CPP] administered areas'.[17] Ieng Sary remarked that 'Pol Pot saw it as important, vital, that we have access to other parts of the country for political work with political cadre. Without this, political campaigning would be limited'.[18]

Some of the NADK interviewed claimed that prior to the intended demobilisation process in June 1992, 'their units initially respected the main provisions of Phase One of the cease-fire ... [and] stressed that they were under instructions from higher up within the NADK to cease all offensive operations and to restrict themselves to self-defence'.[19] In much later interviews, Colonel Saing Rin, who claimed to have been with the 415th Division based at the Khmer Rouge stronghold of Pailin in north-western Cambodia, declared that 'most of us wanted reconciliation. We wanted this very much. The war has been going on for so long. We wanted an end to this. That's why we agreed to abide by the Paris Agreement'.[20] Major-General Nuon Bunno, military advisor to the Khmer Rouge leaders in the SNC, concurred: 'At the time of the Paris Agreements, everybody was very happy because everybody wanted peace after the fighting'.[21] Furthermore, others reported that 'they were told they were no longer to receive arms or ammunition'.[22] Soldiers across a wide geographical dispersion stated that they 'were told to prepare for cantonment'. They 'constructed barracks that could have been used for cantonment'. Others declared that 'after the Paris Agreements, we were prepared to undergo full demobilisation'; and that 'in the period immediately following the Paris Agreements, NADK units made preparations to accommodate UNTAC personnel in their zones...'.[23]

Such interviews also demonstrated that in April 1992, 'NADK troops [had been] instructed by [Khmer Rouge] cadre to gather the people there to welcome UNTAC'. This was corroborated by Ieng Sary, Pol Pot's former colleague and by a western specialist in human rights and the Khmer Rouge. According to Ieng Sary, there was an almost uniform view regarding the positive aspects of the PPA within the Khmer Rouge. Ieng stated that he, 'Pol Pot, Khieu Samphan, Son Sen, Nuon Chea and Tep Kunnal were all in favour of the settlement,' and that 'the political and military cadres were to act in a manner appropriate to this view'.[24]

In a series of interviews conducted in 1990, however, Roger Normand claimed that all the Khmer Rouge elite were conspiring to manipulate the peace process to take advantage of the breathing space the PPA would give them. Ultimately, he contended, the organisation would apply force to the situation in order to win political power. The evidence presented more recently suggests that if this were the case, Pol Pot began to realise the advantages a political settlement offered as the nature of the evolving settlement became clearer, and that force would not have to be applied unless the settlement broke down. It must be recalled that there was over a year between Normand's report and the signing of the PPA, during which time much of the detail of the Perm-5 solution altered significantly as it metamorphosed into the Accords.[25]

Christophe Peschoux reminded that in many areas, the Khmer Rouge and NADK had already begun the construction or refurbishment of buildings that would serve as offices and accommodation for UNTAC representatives and troops. There was 'much evidence', he claimed. The Khmer Rouge:

> decided to play the game.... There was active preparation for receiving UNTAC. They were building things to provide them with housing and offices, delivering furniture. They also were organising the [political] campaign slogans. They were quite open about all this at the beginning. They were making preparations in all provinces: in Anlong Veng, Banteay Meanchey Province, Phnom Chhat, from Samlaut and Pailin. They were clearly getting ready to receive the UN.[26]

Heder maintains that the Khmer Rouge was planning to hand over their areas in stages to UNTAC's inspection. Whilst some were keener than others, such debates reflected 'harder and softer lines but a unified position in the sense that the Khmer Rouge would proceed to

Elite Challenges to Transition – the Khmer Rouge

try to open [compliant] areas first and then to proceed to areas controlled by harder liners such as Ta Mok'.[27]

Political planning and work began almost immediately, further suggesting desire to participate politically in the peace process. Pol Pot declared that his strategy was to 'conduct a strategic political offensive in the countryside and to open up a [political] battlefield in Phnom Penh in order to capture political strength'. He went on to claim that the groups would 'capture it politically'.[28] Some of Heder's military interviewees corroborated the political approach. They stated that once they had disarmed, their work took on a subversive political character. Amongst other activities, they attempted to 'propagandize and agitate [for] small-scale grassroots renditions of the quadripartite Supreme National Council (SNC)'.[29] This was a fairly constant theme in Khmer Rouge negotiations with UNTAC from the point at which they realised the CPP would retain a significant advantage in terms of power distribution both in Phnom Penh and in the communes and districts.[30] Heder argued that 'the general agreed policy [at this stage was] to switch over from political struggle backed by military struggle ... to political struggle'. This change was based on the assumption 'that with the demobilisation of the [opposition], the Khmer Rouge's ... political activists would be able to walk right into villages and do political organisation and take full advantage of the political support'.[31] The emphasis lay, according to Pol Pot, on the 'dissolution of the [incumbent's] political administration in the villages and sub-districts' in order that their innate advantage as incumbents be neutralised in the manner that the PPA proposed.[32]

The objective was clear: the SoC administrative process in the countryside had not been separated from the CPP, which remained a key issue for the Khmer Rouge in their withdrawal of consent. The elements of the NADK, as well as political cadre, were seeking to eliminate the imbalance caused by SoC's influential penetration of rural society and replace it with four party oversight similar to that engaged in the SNC in Phnom Penh. Clearly, the choice of such an activity was political, and indicates that rather than political rhetoric on the part of the Khmer Rouge, not only were the concerns genuine, but that the Party took action to redress the situation of its own accord. Political participatory activity had been pre-planned, according to the documents; but when

> it became clear that UNTAC was not going to arrive immediately, we realised that our activists would have to

undertake the task that UNTAC was failing in, or there would have been no contest.... The stronger the CPP became as it abused the [PPA], the weaker we became relatively.[33]

Clearly, the Khmer Rouge 'was preparing politically for participation and was instructing and co-ordinating its military to do likewise'.[34] With one or two significant exceptions, most of the military, as well as the political leadership, seemed convinced that there was potentially much to gain from the PPA.

Resisting Transition

The fact that Khmer Rouge cadre were having to conduct such a strategy merely to create a level political playing field starkly illustrated UNTAC's failure to either arrive in time, or, when they did, to fulfil their obligations to neutralise the political environment. As Pol Pot became more aware of the significance and possible consequences of this situation, by February 1992 he was prompted to declare that his Party must not 'allow [the opposition] to bury the Agreements ... if the Agreements are incorrectly implemented, then we are dead'.[35] Pol Pot clearly recognised the fragility of his position, and relied heavily on a fair implementation – this, according to his senior advisors and colleagues, was what he sought. He told some of his closest followers that under these conditions, the Party

> could not allow a situation which [was] evolving in this manner to evolve further... If this is the way things are going to be, then it is our conclusion that it will be impossible to implement the Agreements.[36]

Pol Pot went on to stress that the intention was 'not [to] wreck the agreements'.[37]

His naiveté and over-optimism regarding the fair and complete implementation of the PPA made him vulnerable to the influences of those within the Party. Throughout the 1980s, the Khmer Rouge, like most political parties, experienced cleavages, primarily of an ideological nature. Pol Pot has to a degree been a *relative* 'moderate' within his Party's ranks. To his left lay Ieng Sary and Son Sen, the military commander. To his right was Ta Mok.[38] At these extremes, Ieng Sary had advocated a more pragmatic and peaceful approach since 1985; Ta Mok had been firmly against a peaceful settlement, preferring to wage war in Clausewitzian fashion for absolute victory.[39] Not long after it had been recognised as 'futile' to expect a change in the implementation of the PPA, Pol Pot moved right and swung into Ta Mok's orbit.[40] The outcome was a hardening of the Khmer Rouge's position.[41]

By July 1992, Pol Pot had come to the conclusion that, although his interests would have been better served by full implementation of the mandate, his earlier concerns, voiced in the narrative of February 1992 speeches and documentation, proved to be coming true. Pol Pot had been prepared to wait and see if the situation could be ameliorated and rectified, in the hope the Accords could be implemented the way he desired. However, it seems that he calculated a cut-off point on the basis of diminishing returns, after which the decision had been made not to participate in what was widely regarded as an unfair political process that was dominated by the Khmer Rouge's archenemies.[42]

In much the same way that the NADK's military policy shifted to reflect a positive adjustment of the political perspective in 1991 in favour of consenting to the PPA, so too did military developments in mid-1992 reflect the negative changes in political doctrine regarding co-operation with the Paris mandate. Whereas once the NADK had been carefully instructed not to confront UNTAC or its predecessor UNAMIC, some regimental commanders were saying that:

> The fighting had to resume because the two key points [of the PPA] ... had not been implemented ... if there was a positive resolution with regard to the two key points, the fighting would stop and the Khmer Rouge would participate in the elections.[43]

Another source claimed that 'the higher ups said that because the situation had not progressed, there had to be a new military plan. [Because the Khmer Rouge leadership] didn't think the elections could work, the NADK was to advance things politically by using military power again' to force UNTAC's hand.[44] Although these comments derive from the intensification of confrontation after November 1992, they clearly reflect the relationship between implementation of the accords on the one hand, and the parallels in policy direction between the political and military wings of the Khmer Rouge.

However, the military still had to ensure their political credibility was not affected in adverse ways internationally more than it had to be. Accordingly, the order was passed that 'UNTAC was not to be attacked, because it was said this would bring down international condemnation on the Khmer Rouge'.[45] In fact, the nature of discrimination in Pol Pot's orders reflected a reversion to ideological

Elite Challenges to Transition – the Khmer Rouge

dogma. UNTAC troops, if they were to be targeted and attacked, were racially and ideologically discriminated between. Thus, according to Heder, Chinese, Nigerian and Ghanaian troops, for example, were to be spared, but western Europeans were preferred subjects of possible attacks.

The Khmer Rouge quite clearly viewed the PPA as positive, in the sense that it empowered them in a political fashion previously denied by the *de facto* leadership in opposition in Phnom Penh. Furthermore, Pol Pot encouraged his party cadres and military to actively support UNTAC. Ultimately, however, the Party position changed as a consequence not of pretext, but of the realisation that a central proviso crucial to the way the Khmer Rouge viewed a free and fair election was not to be met by UNTAC's civil administration component. For these reasons, the PPA was no longer a vehicle that might create the politically neutral environment envisaged both in the PPA itself and in the minds of the Khmer Rouge leadership. The conditions to which the Khmer Rouge and, indeed, the other parties had agreed, were not met.

It seems clear Pol Pot, as the driving force behind the diplomatic face of Khieu Samphan, sought involvement from the outset. This was because, pragmatically, the PPA represented an opportunity to achieve a key objective of the Khmer Rouge that remained unfulfilled in the twelve years of fighting preceding the October 1991 settlement. The administrative and bureaucratic disempowerment of the CPP by UNTAC would, theoretically, have partially removed one of the main foundations of its national political support base, without which popular support would have been eroded, and without which the Khmer Rouge's opportunities to campaign would have been enhanced. This, as Pol Pot has explained, was one of the main reasons for signing the PPA. Without that aspect of the mandate being implemented, the opportunity for a roughly even election was denied.

Despite the constant attention of the United Nations, UNTAC and the many interested states, on 13 April 1993, the Khmer Rouge left Phnom Penh. At this stage, there was no longer any chance that the guerrillas would participate in the elections; indeed, efforts were focused on the possibility that the Khmer Rouge might deliberately disrupt the polling. All attempts to persuade them to maintain the co-operation with which they had clearly begun the operation failed to convince them that they should participate in the larger process. They left the city, reminding those still listening that the Paris Agreements had not been fulfilled fairly, and that as a result there was no 'neutral

Elite Challenges to Transition – the Khmer Rouge

political environment' essential for a 'free and fair' election. International efforts to return the Khmer Rouge to the political contest failed.[46]

The Khmer Rouge was clearly concerned that the political environment denied them opportunities that they had anticipated at the signing of the PPA. Their consequent political marginalisation exacerbated their exclusion from political participation and access to power and the associated privileges.

This stage of Cambodia's political transition was clearly challenged by the absence of the Khmer Rouge on the justifiable grounds that the PPA was not being implemented in the manner that they had been led to believe it would. However, it is also important to note that the consequences of non-participation, which included disarmament and withdrawal from diplomacy, greatly affected the evolution of the deeply divided post-electoral coalition of Hun Sen and Ranariddh. The contest fought by these two leaders for the Khmer Rouge elite and military's loyalty was a direct function of the guerrillas' exclusion from participatory politics.

VI

Elite Challenges to Transition – the CPP

This chapter examines, as a core element of political transition, the first power transfer in Cambodia which occurred under conditions of multi-party pluralism coupled to universal suffrage, from what was the sole ruling elite to what would be a quadripartite coalition. It represents the third stage of the political transition beginning with the signing of the Paris Agreements in 1991 and continuing with the UNTAC-managed elections. It focuses initially on the refusal of the CPP to accept a political defeat that threatened to marginalise their position in the National Assembly as it evolved after the May 1993 elections. It also examines this problem in the context of the conditions created by the Paris Peace Agreement and the absence of a culturally sophisticated consideration of the period in which power would be transferred.

Most observers agree that during the May 1993 elections, Cambodians 'were able to make a free and fair choice'. They are also inclined to agree with the observation that 'the UNTAC polling operation was unimaginably successful – technically and politically...'.[1] Despite its many travails, the operation had concluded with its electoral credibility intact. As this was the cornerstone of the operation, the overall view taken was positive. However, although the electoral turnout was staggering, post-electoral transition was quickly undermined and destabilised. The events of June 1993 have not received the critical attention they warrant; UNTAC was unable to manage the developing crisis after the poll results were announced.[2] In a very real sense, the first transfer of power – of political transition within the elites in a democratic sense – was underway. It met with great obstruction.

Elite Challenges to Transition – the CPP

Early signs of CPP anxiety and resistance to what might be a negative outcome for them appeared on the first and second days of the election that began on 23 May, 1993. The party, used to ruling Cambodia in an uncontested fashion since 1979, declared their dissatisfaction at the manner in which some aspects of the polls were being conducted. Their complaints initially revolved around accusations of almost nation-wide irregularities ranging from ballot switching, through UN-led fraud, to a lack of suitable overnight ballot box security.

Such allegations during the polling preceded demands for a second poll in some provinces, and for recounts in others, as polling closed and counting began.[3] The potential consequences of not pandering to the party were made quite clear. The CPP, claimed the *Bangkok Post*, 'predicted bloodshed ... unless its demand for an inquiry into alleged poll fraud was granted'.[4] Furthermore, they would not 'hand over power until the UN investigate[d] the allegations' of malpractice'.[5] By 1 June 1993, after polling had closed, the CPP had challenged the elections in four Provinces, referring to procedural violations and irregularities.[6] It became increasingly clear as partial results were announced that the CPP was going to come in second to the FUNCINPEC party, and that because neither would achieve a clear 66 percent majority necessary for unilateral leadership, there would be a powersharing coalition.

The CPP's case, and the manner in which it was presented, escalated over the two-and-a-half weeks which divided the start of the election and the declaration of a discrete secessionist movement. The CPP was aware that they would be relegated to an unsatisfactory, but electorally representative, second place in the developing coalition. They intensified their claims of irregularities, their calls for recounts and their demands for fresh polls in some Provinces.[7] The party also announced that it would not 'hand over power until the UN investigate[d] the allegations of malpractice'.[8] The CPP made a case for victimisation. Western observers joined some of its members in declaring, for example, that elements of UNTAC, most specifically the Information/Education division, were partisan, and 'hardly ill-disposed to seeing the CPP defeated'.[9] They were also described as 'leading a campaign hostile to the State of Cambodia';[10] 'directing propaganda to the Cambodian people to malign CPP';[11] or disseminating 'very anti-[CPP] propaganda'.[12] Such concerns were far from incredulous, in some cases.

The UN electoral component responded to the claims of irregularities enunciated by the party, but rejected their validity in all but a very few cases. The dearth of foreign interest in this stands in marked contrast to international support for the Royalists and Sam Rainsy Party losers of the 1998 elections, who also complained of irregularities, but whose concerns were taken more seriously than those of the CPP in 1993. The CPP then commenced secret negotiations with Sihanouk, whose son led their political opposition, FUNCINPEC, to 're-engineer' the poll outcome. The Prince met with Chea Sim of the CPP and Norodom Ranariddh of FUNCINPEC on 31 May, when Sihanouk 'mooted the idea of forging a government of national reconciliation'.[13] Sihanouk heard at this meeting that 'unless a deal was struck it remained possible that powerful figures within the ruling regime might not accept a real transfer of power'.[14] Clearly, this unveiled threat was designed to push Sihanouk towards persuading important figures who would resist such a formula, such as Ranariddh, to accept the deal or face the threatened consequences (similar to what he would have to do after the 1998 elections). The interim arrangement sought by the CPP would provide for both FUNCINPEC and the CPP to share power as Deputy Ministers overseen by Sihanouk as final adjudicator.

As this ominous portent of violence developed hinting at trouble ahead, the volatility and fragility of this situation prompted Sihanouk to accede to the CPP's proposals.[15] To head off armed confrontation between UNTAC, the CPP and the other major political parties in Cambodia, he announced on 3 June 1993 'the formation of a new government with him as the Head of State and Hun Sen and Ranariddh as vice ministers'.[16] Sihanouk would assume the powers of Chief of State, President of the Council of Ministers and Commandant of the Armed Forces and the Police; and the CPP and FUNCINPEC would share power on a fifty-fifty basis.

In a sense, this strategy – to intimidate participants into accepting an alternative political outcome – succeeded. Sihanouk was aware of the growing instability, and launched his 'interim government' in order 'to avoid the threat of military intervention by the CPP losers, unhappy with the prospect of relinquishing power'.[17] This did not reflect the statistical outcome of the election, but it did stave off any further escalation of the developing crisis.[18] Hun Sen observed several years later that he owed then a debt of gratitude to 'the King's wisdom', through which the CPP 'reached a compromise to keep what it had'.[19] He continued that

> the situation was explosive in Phnom Penh at that time. This problem ... was like a buried corpse. As I said, however, there

was a tornado in the heart of Phnom Penh that blew off the cover to expose the corpse'.[20]

Others concurred with this pragmatic analysis. The fifty-fifty system Sihanouk proposed, although clearly not reflecting FUNCINPEC's electoral victory, would have avoided almost inevitable 'conflict between the two parties, and the danger of a new civil war, and insured the collaboration of the two larger parties, without which Cambodia [could] not be governed'.[21] Vickery further argues that although this arrangement represented 'a negation of the election, it was nevertheless a positive move'.[22] Without such a course of action, it is difficult to imagine how external actors could have peacefully managed the crisis, with virtually no influence over the CPP. Doyle and Suzuki note that the character of such an arrangement 'accurately reflected Cambodian realities'.[23] In other words, the only option for any form of peace and stability was political inclusion of the CPP in the proportion they sought.

Sihanouk's proposal was not received favourably anywhere outside the CPP. The US Mission released, at 5.30pm on the same day, a so called 'non-paper' rejecting Sihanouk's proposal, and requesting that the outcome of the election be rigorously adhered too. Sihanouk withdrew his offer to manage the interim government, noting the 'great difficulties impeding [the new coalition's] formation'.[24] The following day, it was noted in *the Bangkok Post* that this 'non-paper' had 'played a role in the break-up of the coalition just hours after it was formed'.[25] Prince Sihanouk withdrew his offer, accusing 'some Cambodian politicians, certain members of UNTAC, the United States and some other countries of having "meanly attacked" him over the plan'.[26] He was forced to respond to 'reservations by not only FUNCINPEC, but UN officials and key big powers'.[27] He further stated angrily that he had 'learned his lesson' and must in the future 'avoid constitutional coups'.[28]

On the morning of 4 June, then, Sihanouk 'issued another statement announcing that he had cancelled the new government due to legal objections [from the US] ... and disagreement with some UNTAC officials'.[29] The CPP's position within the Sihanouk framework was crippled by US obstruction, coupled with UNTAC's hostility, and underscored by a reluctant Ranariddh who performed a *volte face* on his original, if reticent, agreement with his father to abide by the inevitable necessity of the fifty-fifty solution. The CPP's attempt to manage a crisis in transition that disempowered them and their clients had been thwarted. The coalition crumbled, denying the CPP the opportunity they had engineered to keep them in proportionate power, and the US Mission achieved the goal of its 'non-paper' – temporarily.

Negotiations between Sihanouk, FUNCINPEC and the CPP continued over the following days to re-order the transition. Simultaneously, the political situation deteriorated rapidly as CPP militia, and 'rent-a-mob' groups allegedly organised by the CPP, terrorised UNTAC in a number of provinces. For example, according to an NGO journalist, in Kompong Cham:

> A crowd of maybe 500 gathered.... Shepherded by [CPP] soldiers, the group of civilians – all [government] employees ... carried signs reading, "we reject the results of the election and demand new elections".... A man with a loudspeaker led the demonstration, announcing that the CPP would not accept the results of the elections [and] that a new government headed by Sihanouk must be formed....[30]

Some of those involved were undoubtedly acting under orders. However, the nature of the patron-client networks makes it reasonable to argue that much of the activity was de-centralised and independent of the party elite. It was in the interests of those CPP rural leaders and government workers to protest the decision because they would also lose their positions of power if the transition resulted in a share of power for FUNCINPEC. The process was clearly designed both to intimidate UNTAC, which was being told to leave the country at this demonstration, and to stipulate the type of political arrangement favourable to the CPP and its beneficiaries.

The CPP continued to press for a fifty-fifty arrangement similar to that advocated on 3 June by Sihanouk. In an obvious attempt to demonstrate the extent and nature of CPP power and military influence, 'about 40 top military and police officers, including Defence Minister General Tea Banh, arrived at Sihanouk's palace in a 36-strong convoy' to convince Sihanouk of the need for reconciliation and unity.[31] Julio Jeldres notes that 'the CPP began a carefully orchestrated campaign to convince Prince Sihanouk ... that it should remain in power'.[32] (In fact, that process had begun earlier). The intentions were made clear when Khieu Kanharith hinted at a deal, suggesting that 'the CPP would drop the matter [of irregularities] and accept the results if the coalition [was] allowed to form'.[33] CPP would achieve this, Jennar argues, by 'putting pressure on FUNCINPEC to make it accept an equal sharing of [political] influence'.[34]

Elite Challenges to Transition – the CPP

These events are quite distinct from the secession that occurred after. It is normally considered that in order to regain the fifty-fifty position advocated by Sihanouk but over-ruled by the objections of the US Mission in Phnom Penh, the CPP orchestrated the secession. It is also often argued that the CPP's strategy included the resignation of a significant number of CPP representatives from the Constituent Assembly. These two sets of events are also discrete, however. On 10 June 1993, General Sin Song and Prince Norodom Chakrapong, both CPP party members, declared publicly the existence of an autonomous breakaway zone, occupying seven provinces east of the Mekong river along the Viêt Namese border.[35] At roughly the same time, 32 CPP candidates to the Constituent Assembly resigned their positions.[36] Although the timing of the events was close, there is little logic in any connection.

Heder contends there is.[37] A report he wrote for UNTAC's Information and Education division (UNTAC 12) in response to the secession maintained it represented 'the implementation of a longstanding CPP contingency plan for dealing with a situation in which its hold on national power [was] threatened or lost'. The document characterised and explained the above events as a relatively typical communist 'fall back to base area' strategy, pre-planned in the event of an unexpected defeat at the polls. It thus represented 'an overall CPP plan'.[38] The report further contended that 'the establishment of such bases [east of the Mekong] is an integral part of the routine strategic thinking of the Cambodian communists imbued in the political culture of Mao Zedong Thought and ... [which] reflected a long tradition within the Cambodian communist movement'.[39]

The document also connected the resignation of CPP Assembly members to the secession. Heder maintained the resignations were effected 'to keep some elected members of the CPP in the Assembly as "legal cadre" ... [and to] ... withdraw other CPP members and assign them to "semi-legal" or "illegal" work outside the Assembly'.[40] Various members of the party would thus resign in order 'to conduct "illegal" activities outside the Assembly context', some of whom would possibly be involved in undermining national stability to force conditions suitable to the CPP re-acquiring political power.[41] The two would link together, Heder maintained, giving the CPP the 'possibility of participating in a government based out of the Assembly at the same time as it controls an illegal "countergovernment" based in Cambodia east of the Mekong'. Furthermore, this plan 'reportedly also included negotiations and arrangements with

Viêt Nam for the provision of support for the fall-back base'.[42] No evidence was presented to authenticate the allegations, either in terms of empirical fact or qualitative argument.

Heder's paper is hard to support for several reasons. Leaving aside the empty theorising and the lack of substantiating evidence, the most obvious issue to note is that of all the secessionists, only one was an Assembly member. General Sin Song, Minister of National Security and a member of the Party Standing Committee was the only individual to have resigned from that body. Even Chakrapong, a son of Sihanouk and half brother to FUNCINPEC's Ranariddh as well as being Vice Chairman of the Council of Ministers, was not a member, having been barred from political participation by UNTAC prior to the elections after having broken UN electoral law.[43] Therefore, to claim the resignations were based on a planned and pre-conceived strategy of destabilisation is nonsense. The resignees were not resigning because they were planning to become law-breakers and secessionist. Only one secessionist had resigned from the Assembly.

Second, the resignations took place before the secession began, and reflected rational pragmatism. Jennar records the date of announcement of departure as 9 June, 1993.[44] This was some time after it had become clear how many seats the CPP would lose to FUNCINPEC and the BLDP in the Constituent Assembly. More importantly, however, the UN Electoral Chief, Reginald Austin, told one scholar that the letters of resignation had been sent before the election results were made official. There were clear indications from early polling that the CPP would not achieve the sixty percent it had anticipated; action was then taken to accommodate such changes. This permitted 'the replacements for the 32 to be named when the results were officially announced'.[45]

Third, the resignations can be more pragmatically explained as a separate issue altogether, with far less sinister motives. Like most of the parties involved in the elections, the CPP submitted more candidates' names to each Province for the Proportional Representation ballot than they actually won. In other words, there were more candidates available than seats. The purpose of the resignations, then, was

> to permit the most capable CPP people to enter the Assembly, when it became clear they couldn't get the seats they expected. That is, many of the most capable people were low on their provincial election lists, below old party hacks who would have been higher for reasons of status and hierarchy.[46]

Fourth, a thorough analysis of the qualifications of the resignees and their replacements both supports the arguments (above) and suggests two pragmatic themes. First, older, harder-line cadres were being replaced with more technocratically competent young people. Second, those most likely to cause problems in any reconciliation with FUNCINPEC, with some exceptions, were dropped.[47] In fact, Heder noted that amongst those retaining their positions in the Assembly were 'almost all the intellectuals and ... "econocrats" and "technocrats", the party's propagandists and educational and cultural workers, and its legal experts'.[48] The most obvious question to pose must be, 'why would they not?'. As Vickery notes, 'those are precisely the types of people which any rational western party would put into a Parliament'.[49]

Fifth, the secession itself also is discretely explicable. Rather than an intricate, pre-conceived plan concerning illegal operations and 'fall back to base' theory, Vickery maintained that the break-away movement could be

> better explained as an unexpected, *ad hoc* action by a few hotheads in protest against the election, perhaps also in protest at being dropped from the Assembly, and it was encouraged by Sihanouk both in protest against UNTAC, and to create an opportunity to gain credit by exerting his moral authority to put down the autonomy movement.[50]

However, if he did attempt to use this jostling as a means of 'exerting his moral authority to put down' the secession, he was not allowed to. Hun Sen's personal actions and his diplomacy primarily with his brother, Hun Nheng, ended the autonomy movement, although it would be reasonable to assume that Sihanouk supported such a move.

Sixth, Viêt Nam immediately distanced itself from the secession, despite allegations that Hanoi supported the breakaway movement. Several statements over the period from Viêt Namese sources in Cambodia or Hanoi requested conciliation and co-operation. Furthermore, when the secession was declared over, its core elements, including Chakrapong, Sin Song, Bou Thang and Phok Samoeurn, were halted in their bid to escape to Viêt Nam. Border guards at UN checkpoint 4 (CV4) 'turned back five of the [20] vehicles and their occupants after detaining them for two hours'. The Foreign Ministry declared that 'Viêt Nam was "unable to prevent" Prince Chakrapong from crossing because the neighbouring countries "have an agreement exempting holders of diplomatic and official passports from visa requirements".⁵¹ This does little to suggest co-operation on Hanoi's part with the secessionists.

Seventh, the secession was put down by Hun Sen with the co-operation of other members of the CPP. It was widely reported that Hun Nheng, Hun Sen's brother and outgoing Governor of Kompong Cham, had co-operated in marginalising the secessionists. If the goal had been to retain individuals outside the Assembly, there is no logical reason to have halted it. If the CPP were as deviously-orientated as Heder suggests, there would have been greater utility derived from maintaining instability and keeping such 'illegal' and 'clandestine' forces in a position where they might have been useful.

The political marginalisation inherent in the election result was unacceptable to the CPP primarily because there exists no institutionalisation of opposition in Khmer elite politics. Their defeat, and the possible transfer of power, were not options to the leadership. The Sihanouk coalition represented an opportunity to take back through blackmail and intimidation what they had lost in the election. CPP was 'jockeying to force a powersharing agreement ... in order to give them more power than was accorded them through popular polls'.⁵² The Minister of Information declared that the party was 'pleased that Sihanouk had arranged the interim [government]' because 'everybody respects Sihanouk, so he can manage the situation, and the parties are reconciled'.⁵³

The tension lasted until the 20 June, when the CPP accepted a second offer of a fifty-fifty solution comparable, if not almost identical to, the original arrangement proposed by Sihanouk on 3 June. The CPP's announcement declared that they recognised 'the results of the May elections ... based on four criteria'.⁵⁴ These were that they were following the lead of Sihanouk, in whose fifty-fifty coalition the CPP were now located; and that they were 'pleased UNTAC ... acknowledge[d] that irregularities did occur during the election'. They would also suspend judgement on those problems until the internal UNTAC audit had been completed; and would accept the results in the name of 'national reconciliation'.⁵⁵

The US Mission withdrew its resistance to the coalition and reluctantly accepted the political propriety of this body. All parties were eventually made aware that without a satisfied CPP in a position of strength, UNTAC and Cambodia could be held hostage. Sihanouk observed that 'we have to share power equally otherwise the violence can not end'.⁵⁶ The external agents who had sought to influence the interim government's composition were forced to accept that their authority was meaningless in the face of the CPP's challenge, at grass-roots level.

The situation settled down precisely as the CPP and Sihanouk predicted. The resignations were pragmatically effected in order to ensure appropriate and proficient members of the party were in place instead of ideologues with less capacity to conduct modern international government. The secession was self-serving and drew upon disaffected groups and clients loyal to the main individuals.

The US Mission's Role

As has been noted in detail above, the Mission's so-called 'non-paper' acted as the catalyst and precipitant for the escalation in tension and confrontation between the CPP and FUNCINPEC. Without that particular intervention, the coalition initially advanced by Sihanouk would have been endorsed, whether Ranariddh was happy with it or not. Jennar concurs in this view, noting that whilst the CPP must 'bear responsibility for [the secession] ... they are not alone. Those who sought to torpedo the Sihanouk initiative by calling it a "constitutional coup" helped to push matters to this extreme situation'.[57] He adds that the US-led, UNTAC-backed intervention 'was the reason for the fluctuations which characterised the period from 3 to 16 June'. He also claimed to have heard a senior US official stating that

> In order to do what we want to do in Cambodia, we can do without Prince Sihanouk. We can do without the CPP. We have ninety million dollars to keep the officials and soldiers of the SoC and to buy the CPP Deputies necessary to get the 2/3 [majority] and then put in place the coalition of our choice.[58]

This has not been substantiated with documentary evidence from other sources as yet. Were it to be found accurate, it would be unsurprising, in that it would merely reflect continuity in the proven and substantiated anti-CPP US foreign policy towards the CPP and Hun Sen. Clearly, US policy in Phnom Penh was aimed at restraining the CPP using close adherence to the PPA as a pretext.

A number of observers have commented on the reason for the US intervention, and a discussion of these helps contextualise the position taken by the US Mission in Phnom Penh. The Mission itself, in denouncing Sihanouk's 3 June proposal, argued that it represented 'a violation of the Paris Accords and the spirit of the successful election

... [which] would undermine the entire electoral process and the transition to democracy'.[59]

Criticism of the Mission came from a variety of sources, including independent NGOs in country; independent academics researching peacekeeping; from some diplomats; from scholars specialising in Khmer studies; and from the CPP. An independently-funded NGO information service, for example, claimed that the US Mission 'non-paper', and the resistance Sihanouk referred to from elements of UNTAC, was the product of a desire to 'promote the formation of a government without CPP in it', and to minimise any advantage accruing to the CPP.[60] The Mission could appear to do this under the mantle of electoral law and democracy by insisting on the letter of the PPA being strictly adhered to. However, the Agreements had already been breached prior to this on numerous occasions with little or no resistance appearing from the US Mission. Certainly, the Mission had advanced nothing of this scale before. Adherence to the PPA was only a fig leaf of respectability permitting a more partisan intervention. The 'non-paper', claimed the information service, 'appeared not to favour any arrangement which include[d] SoC [CPP]'.[61]

Randall, an academic surveying the peacekeeping operation, was of the view that past history was informing current policy as the reasons for the 'non-paper' were discussed. He observed that 'the United States ... would have preferred the total elimination of the pro-Viêtnamese faction from the new government'.[62] By this he was referring to the CPP and Hun Sen, installed more than a decade earlier and long-since divorced ideologically from Hanoi. Furthermore, as the Cold War drew to a close, any form of political and economic dependence correspondingly diminished. Despite this, Randall and others were concerned that Cold War policy was being extended into the UN peacekeeping forum.

This has precedent. A senior British Foreign Office official, John Pedler, was informed specifically by the US State Department that before the operation, the US 'President w[ould] not accept the Hun Sen government', and that Washington was 'working for a messy sort of situation with a non-Hun Sen government, but without the Khmer Rouge'.[63] There was therefore some good reason to suspect, given such statements, that the 'non-paper' was an attempt to facilitate such an eventuality.

The Khmer scholar Michael Vickery is noted for his observations regarding US foreign policy in Cambodia. He argues that it was the intention of the Mission 'non-paper', as far as possible, to establish a government with the CPP either absent or marginalised. He takes the position that the fifty-fifty solution 'certainly irritate[d] Washington' at the time, given their backing of FUNCINPEC and the KPNLF both throughout the 1980s and during the peace formulation and implementation.[64] Others, such as Kiernan, have enunciated similar views with regard to past US foreign policy and its continuity.[65]

Internal US documentation and commentary seems to confirm such views. The actual poll outcome, whereby FUNCINPEC would dominate the coalition, had been the stated goal of US interests. A General Accounting Office (GAO) communication, obtained in Phnom Penh at the time of the elections, noted that the US Administration had 'achieved their goal ... [which was to] ... support the non-Communists in their effort to reunify and lead Cambodia after the peace settlements, *as evidenced by the results of the May 1993 election for the Constituent Assembly*' (emphasis added).[66] This would suggest an extension of the policies that had characterised the Cold War and the formulation of the PPA, which sought as far as possible to ensure the CPP did not fare well in the Cambodian elections. When the CPP's jockeying undermined the desired outcome, a US representative dismally complained that a coalition with CPP represented was 'not quite what we had in mind ... it doesn't work for us'.[67]

Elite Political Culture

Whilst these various explanations were generated primarily at the time of the secession, others have developed over time. It is the argument of this text that the pre-secession political jockeying, which manifested itself in intimidation and a degree of violence, represented the provisional response to the consequences of political transition in the context of indigenous elite political culture. In other words, the political culture of the single party Communist state, brooking no opposition, was confronted for the first time in recent Khmer history with opposition legitimised by an imported system of elite selection, the consequences of which were powersharing.

The issue was compounded yet further. Whilst some scholars argue that Hun Sen himself is imbued in the political culture of the single party communist state, in fact his leadership seems to reflect an approach more specific to Cambodian history than styles of Communism.[68] For example, whilst his parents were peasants, and whilst he served the Khmer Rouge until defecting in 1977, he is a proto-typical 'King of the People'. Like Sihanouk, he lost family to the Khmer Rouge. Sihanouk presents himself as the father of the people and the nation. Hun Sen claims similarly to be 'entrusted with the task of the bigger brother, who has to gather all the younger brothers and sisters' to co-operate.[69] He, like many political leaders in Cambodia, seeks legitimacy through impersonating the respected King Sihanouk, in whose absence Hun Sen dominated his country's politics. Like Sihanouk, he nurtures the image of a leader of the people; he sits with them and listens and enjoins them, to rise above them after offering his wisdom. His credibility and a degree of legitimacy are thus derived from the manner in which he presents himself to Cambodian people, which itself is reminiscent of the Cambodian royalty.[70]

The two perspectives, of Communism and Khmer tradition, share the commonality of absolutism. Sihanouk's period of political control was characterised by some of the same approaches as Hun Sen's. For example, at the height of their respective power, both tolerated opposition poorly. Sihanouk's treatment of the Far Left is well documented, and the parties that stood in opposition to him were primarily of his own creation and control. Hun Sen's domination of the party and the limitations his party placed on various activities in Cambodia, whilst nowhere near as restrictive as Sihanouk's, are representative of an approach reluctant to tolerate opposition. The pre-secession jockeying was an instance of this.

It was also a rejection of powersharing more fundamentally. This concept is as oxymoronic and inappropriate to the former ruling party of the 1980s as it is to Khmer royalty. It is also alien to the other leaders vying for power, including Sam Rainsy and Prince Ranariddh. Simone and Feraru have generalised more broadly regarding political authority in Eastern Asia that 'majority rule [is] a threat to continued elite dominance'.[71] Hun Sen made it clear that powersharing could be discussed in other countries, but to do so in Cambodia was inappropriate.[72] The 'masters' of Cambodia are traditionally appointed out of their origins and their location within society. It has been their duty to rule, not govern democratically. Their demise has given way to their replacement with groups known as *neak ta-sou* (people of struggle). Their authority, once in place, is the same, however.[73]

As a consequence of the election results, the CPP anticipated not only being in a weakened position politically; but also having to share power from a minority perspective. The assumption, then, that multi-party, pluralistic elections under a PR system were anything other than anathema to Cambodia was a simplistic attempt at restoring peace to Cambodia for the Perm-5. They ignored both the historical evidence and the realities of Cambodian politics, and their intervention resulted in a very shaky political transition impeded by the relegation of an elite used to absolutism to a seriously undermined and relatively powerless position in Khmer politics.

This itself had further consequences which contributed to the priority the CPP placed on retaining at least a fifty percent share of power, through the Ministries, within the Council of Ministers, and in the Assembly as it was to be created. Complex pyramids of patron-clientelism in a two-way dependency relationship underpin political power in Cambodia. Those at the top of the pyramid, such as the various heads of Ministries, depend on support through the bureaucracy and through less centralised networks which administer the Provinces through Governors and so on. The loyalty of those Ministers, who support various interests in the Ministries and elsewhere, is in turn repaid by favours granted in the upper echelons of government. Ashley notes that

> patrons ... considered the need to protect their clients to be more important than justice. Any wrongdoing, from incompetence and laziness to murder and drug trafficking ... was considered subordinate to building up and protecting one's party and personal networks.[74]

This applies to the opposition to a degree limited by their absence from national politics over the last two decades. Their propensity to recreate such networks for their own power bases is not disputed.[75] In this way, each preserves the other's position and each gains politically at the top, and more broadly as the network fans out.

The defeat of a key party such as the CPP had consequences far beyond its own immediate concerns. The networks that underpin political parties also suffer a loss of patronage, which in turn undermines client support, thus reinforcing the problem of preserving political power for the elites. This is far from unique to Cambodia; such systems have been recognised and classified in the scholarly literature.[76] In essence, the problem can in part be characterised as a lack of the institutionalisation of political opposition. When removed from power, rather than facing the victor from the relatively stable socio-economic position of a 'loyal opposition', a form of economic exile is pursuant. Implicit in the absence of formal opposition as part of a parliamentary system is under-employment. Whilst some might continue to enjoy a government post through patronage, many do not;

and the consequences for dependants, in either a family sense or in the sense of clients, can be extreme in Cambodia. As Ashley maintains, 'neither Hun Sen nor Ranariddh was prepared to rely on elections to determine the next government. The political and financial stakes were too high.... The only way to protect one's wealth was to hold onto power'.[77] Thus, the pre-secession jockeying, aggravated by the US intervention into a violent breakaway movement, was also caused by the aggravation of the consequences of political and economic impoverishment.

The Paris Accords and Political Transition

The immediate power transfer problems have other origins at another level. The net consequence of the struggle for power, both during the elections and throughout the transitional phase immediately superseding the polling, was the reinforcement of traditional confrontation between those competing for power in a form of political organisation institutionalised and 'legitimised' by western interests. It had no basis in Khmer political thought, and, equally important in this context, had no vehicle for its passage.

The key problem at the end of the elections with a vote that diluted power into a broader range of parties was that the switch from single party to coalition – or indeed any form of transfer – had not been considered or provided for. Reginald Austin, head of the UN Electoral Component, observed that 'the Paris Peace Agreements are completely vacuous on the post election environment'.[78] Sanderson concurred, noting that:

> one particularly glaring omission of the Paris Agreements ... was the arrangements for the politically ambiguous period between the election and the end of the mandate. The difficulties of the period ... were probably predictable enough, but it was only just before the elections had started that they were seriously addressed by UNTAC political staff.[79]

No mechanism existed to manage the power transition that should have taken place as a consequence of the structure of the vote. In some western liberal democracies, which this electoral process sought to duplicate and create, after 'hung' elections, it is not unusual for an apolitical representative of state, such as a President or a monarch, to take a central role as mediator (a duty often constitutionally-enshrined) and ask the winning parties to form the new government.

Elite Challenges to Transition – the CPP

Other times, in the absence of a clear majority, the main party is asked to form a coalition government. Sihanouk was arguably that representative for two reasons. First, he occupies a position of great prestige, if not power, amongst mass and elite Khmer society due to his Monarchical status. Second, the PPA recognised this seniority when it welcomed 'the unanimous election ... of HRH Prince Norodom Sihanouk as the President of the Supreme National Council', a body which the Accord describes as 'the unique legitimate body and source of authority in ... Cambodia'.[80]

Sihanouk asked the CPP and FUNCINPEC to share power in an interim, temporary government of reconciliation, mirroring western tradition.[81] In a sense, then, the absence of a clearly stated legal position in the PPA, in which 'there is nothing about how coalitions should be formed', left room for uncontroversial precedent.[82] Thus, some form of democratic process was indeed followed, if precedent is to go by. Furthermore, this approach was paralleled by political pragmatism; the CPP appeared unlikely to relinquish power completely peacefully, thus casting doubts over the immediate durability of the operation. It is indeed ironic that Sihanouk's act to stave off violence, which also would have ensured no secession took place (had it not been torpedoed by the US Mission), finds precedent internationally. It is also ironic that his rejected attempt to reconcile the two parties compensated for a critical weakness in the Paris Accords.

The tensions created at this point set in train Cambodian political development over the course of the next five years, and limited and defined the directions in which it could move. The issue of powersharing was unresolved, and yet forced upon the Khmer actors. The issue of allocation of elite positions was only tolerated with the greatest reluctance. Clients still supported patrons, with the least representatively powerful CPP the greatest benefactor. Contrarily, FUNCINPEC's electoral victory could not be underscored at grassroots level, and the issue of the Khmer Rouge remained unmanaged. It was not long before these tensions combined to create an escalation of violence culminating in the July 1997 fighting. Lizée argues eloquently that

> 'the tension between the pressure for democratisation generated by the elections and the efforts by the elites in power to contain any direct challenge to the social and political structures on which their authority rest[ed] set the trajectory of subsequent political developments in Cambodia'.[83]

Elite Challenges to Transition – the CPP

Political confrontation between FUNCINPEC and the CPP was reinstitutionalised in the disputed coalition framework in a context where political survival was absolute, and where power was defined and sought in more absolute terms. The imported democratisation ensured that confrontation would characterise political development in Cambodia for the foreseeable future. Furthermore, in order to negate the problem of the lack of institutionalised opposition, all four parties were enshrined in the coalition body to maximise political control over potential dissenters. This improved conditions for the core elite of FUNCINPEC and the CPP which might have existed had the remaining two parties, BLDP and Molinaka, moved into parliamentary opposition as opposed to their submersion in the coalition framework.

Political transition, in the sense of a shift from one system of organisation to another, was not achieved. Whilst a multi-party coalition offered the illusion of a democratic system, this was a superficial veneer imposed externally on a reluctant elite, all elements of which sought dominance and rejected shared power. Ashley notes that the coalition 'represented extreme distrust and an inability to compromise'.[84] More specifically, it represented not equalitarian multi-party powersharing, but the insertion of three powerful extra patrons with competing client bases, representing not a co-operative body to work in conjunction with Hun Sen, but a direct challenge to him and his party's interests. If a transition occurred, it was only in the sense that the front line of war had shifted to an artificial construct flawed conceptually in Khmer political culture and bearing within it the seeds of implosion.

VII

From 'Coalition' to Confrontation, 1993 to 1997

This chapter examines political transition in Cambodia between the end of the secession in 1993 and the violent changes of July 1997. It identifies two linked themes which characterise transitional politics and which have some of their origins in the Paris Peace Agreement. This, it will be argued, contributed to the destabilisation of an already fragile political order in Cambodia. Orbiting these two core themes are other, related, ancillary themes which have acted in parallel to challenge or reinforce the 'order' established through the United Nations transitional force, and which will be pursued in the following chapter.

The first theme is the consequences of the failure to enjoin the Khmer Rouge in the electoral process and in the Phnom Penh government coalition. This did not occur because the guerrillas refused to accept that the PPA was correctly implemented with regard to the separation of the CPP from the state.

The second theme is the failure of powersharing. Central to this was the CPP's unwillingness to surrender elite power generally, after the election, and then more specifically at grass-roots level; and FUNCINPEC's incapacity to absorb such responsibilities as might have been devolved to them. McAuliff observed that of that party's National Council, '75 percent came from the refugee camps on the border, 5 percent were returnees from overseas, and only 20 percent had been resident inside the country, principally in Phnom Penh'.[1] The BLDP were in a similar situation. Curtis notes that in contrast, 'all the CPP's ministers and vice ministers had long experience with the Cambodian bureaucracy.... CPP politicians were more rooted in the realities of Cambodia'.[2]

The distribution of political power after Sihanouk's brokered deal theoretically followed a fifty-fifty arrangement. For example, each Ministry would have Ministers from both parties; and there would be a first Prime Minister (Prince Ranariddh) and a second Prime Minister (Hun Sen). Nominally, Ranariddh outranked Hun Sen. More precisely, each Ministry received a new vice-minister, appointed from the ranks of whichever party was not represented at top level. Below this, two new under secretary of state positions were created, with one from FUNCINPEC and one from the CPP. Curtis notes this model, although swelling the bureaucracy and minimising efficiency, was extended to Provincial level as well. Here, there would be 'the appointment of a governor, a first vice governor from the competing party, and two additional vice governors'.[3] This mirrored the under secretary of state positions in the Ministries.

This did not translate in practice. Although FUNCINPEC took more seats in the National Assembly, this was counterbalanced by the preponderance of the CPP's political power distributed throughout the country at lower levels. Thus, whilst there may have been some potential for marginalising the CPP in the Assembly, that party's power and reach, deeply entrenched since 1979, ensured that policy choices made in Phnom Penh would by no means necessarily be reflected in policy implementation at the local level. Brown observed that 'FUNCINPEC ... [was] all but subsumed by the CPP at policy level ... the 21 provincial and special zone administrations [were] dominated by CPP cadres'.[4] Thayer reported in November 1993 that 'the provincial political structures which control police, armed forces, tax collection, and civil service ... remain under the control of the CPP and respond to political loyalties before central authority'.[5] Sam Rainsy, then Economics and Finance Minister for FUNCINPEC, admitted that his party had 'neither the time nor the political means to bring the provinces under central control ... [FUNCINPEC] central control has very little knowledge – not even to speak of control – but knowledge of the provinces'.[6] This view was held widely, including within the party. FUNCINPEC's secretary-general, Prince Norodom Sirivudh, admitted that 'the party's substructure remained weak ... [it] has suffered from a lack of experience in running administration since it joined the coalition'.[7]

This problem is largely accounted for by FUNCINPEC's absence from local politics during their opposition from exile, and thus by a relative lack of experience of commune-level issues and power distribution.[8] This short-fall in skills and knowledge is well reflected in an anecdote cited in an English language daily report. Whilst FUNCINPEC officials in Sihanoukville claimed a commitment to rural 'development', they were asked to expand. 'You know', said one, 'for farmers and so on'. When asked to expand further, the daily reported, 'they argued over the word in Khmer for a few minutes, then hit upon it, proudly, in English: "Fertilisers!"'.[9] When prompted with the suggestion of tourism, in relation to Cambodia's finest beaches, they responded, 'every company can invest money! Everything is open for investment in Sihanoukville!'.[10] Such naiveté was not restricted to those FUNCINPEC officials alone, and is unsurprising given the length of time they have spent outside Cambodia.

The issue of access to power was exacerbated as tensions only superficially below the surface in 1993 erupted at various points and to varying degrees as the search for positions of strength on the part of FUNCINPEC and the CPP were exacerbated by the disintegration of the Khmer Rouge. The extra-parliamentary presence of the guerrilla group outside the government and the National Assembly, and the fracturing of its elite, coupled to a steady stream of defections enticed by both main elements of the government, offered to those elements an opportunity to increase their political power bases. In other words, both FUNCINPEC and the CPP fought for 'ownership' of the fragmenting Khmer Rouge to increase their power.

An example of this was the contest for Ieng Sary. For the CPP, the 'capture' of Ieng's loyalty offered a counterbalance to Ranariddh's position as First Prime Minister. For Ranariddh, the potential gains derived from negotiations designed to 'capture' the loyalty of the Khieu Samphan faction of the Khmer Rouge offered a counter balance to his innate incapacity to match Hun Sen politically and militarily. The failure of the Paris Agreements and UNTAC to create conditions which either integrated the Khmer Rouge into political opposition, or disarmed their military, created a 'prize' over which the Cambodian leaders fought. The consequences of this were altered balances of power in Phnom Penh, in the context of a weak and artificial coalition the members of which vied less to co-operate with one another, and more to compete with each other for political survival and party unity and enhancement.

The cohesion of the coalition in Phnom Penh was further undermined by other thematic challenges to its unity and its legitimacy from various sources. For example, in the western democratic tradition, one of the roles of the media is to act as an impartial check and balance on arbitrary abuse of power and corruption within the government of the day. Its role is not to represent a political challenge to government authority. In Cambodia, however, the indigenous media is not so far generally imbued in such traditions, and whilst the notion of an independent media arose quite quickly after UNTAC's arrival, it did not necessarily, in many instances, fulfil the role impartially. In such a form, many elements of the media and its invective represented a form of extra-parliamentary opposition that could not be countered in the Assembly. The ebb and flow of the treatment of the media by the elites reflected its uneven path between fulfilling the traditional western model, on the one hand, and the indigenous weapon it became to damn various elements of the elites, on the other. In an already inherently weak coalition, it exacerbated rivalry and undermined stability and the passage of political transition to a form of democracy.

Another thematic challenge to political stability and successful democratic transition is the fragmentation of various parties in this period. For example, the splits that developed within the coalition's third party, the Buddhist Liberal Democratic Party (BLDP), and the spoils to be collected by the two main parties, created similar competition to that produced by the fragmentation of the Khmer Rouge. The CPP and FUNCINPEC, rather than engaging in accommodation and conciliation among themselves, fought to bring over elements of fragmenting parties to increase their political power base. In this manner, although without the violence of the final confrontation in July 1997, was FUNCINPEC and CPP unity and cohesion undermined and progressive political development arrested. According to the *Phnom Penh Post*, such internal divides 'promised months, if not years, of further low level [political] conflict'.[11] Khmer Rouge sources considered that 'the new government will collapse under the pressure of internal conflicts'.[12] The end of the period 1993–1997 is characterised not merely by armed inter-group conflict; but also by political conflict within the parties of the coalition. This included, as will be demonstrated later, within FUNCINPEC, the Khmer Rouge and to a lesser degree the CPP.

Another theme of the period between 1993 and 1997 was the increasing commitment of Khmer society to the principal of democracy invoked via UNTAC. Their embracing of choice, whether culturally normal or not in the appointment of the country's leaders, suggested a strong commitment to leadership change (or continuity) which was repeated in 1998 with a similarly high voter turn-out. Underpinning Khmer involvement in this process was significant foreign support for the creation of institutions, values and processes that are designed to facilitate political transition. For example, indigenous human rights groups which flowered under UNTAC have received support from organisations such as the National Democratic Institute for International Affairs (NDI), and the International Republican Institute (IRI), as well as Human Rights Watch Asia and the United Nations Commission for Human Rights (UNCHR). The NDI and IRI have supported in the past brutal right wing death squad parties, such as the ARENA party in El Salvador. IRI also supported the retention of Raoul Garcia Prieto, inspired protégé of Major Roberto D'Aubuisson, the leader of the Salvadoran Death Squads, to come to Cambodia to oversee human rights and democratic transition in 1993.[13] When the US Embassy, USAID and IRI were approached in 1993 regarding this issue, the Embassy representative, David Miller, declared that IRI acted independently of USAID, although the latter's constitution states it should be fully appraised of such issues. The 'democracy' section of US Agency for International Development (USAID) declined to be interviewed when the content of the interview was made known through his secretary.[14] Anne Bradley, then Assistant Program Officer for IRI, stated that they had 'no knowledge' of this.[15] However, Prieto was working with IRI and when the issue was raised with the UN, it raised 'not a peep of objection'. Despite these paradoxes, however, the process of incorporating the rights of individuals to chose their governors has been taken up to a degree which would probably not have happened in the absence of both UNTAC and western rights organisations. Many indigenous rights groups now co-exist with international institutions in Cambodia.

The success of various organisations in creating such changes at the grass roots level is clearly distinct from the limitations that have become self-evident when pressure to bear for change is brought on the ruling elites. This is aggravated by the way in which some who occupy positions of power undermine the role of mass society in political decision-making. For example, Prince Ranariddh declared in 1995 that for Khmers, democracy was less important than more fundamental issues of survival. He declared that 'discipline was more essential for the population than democracy, though both were needed'.[16]

In a sense it was easy for them to do this in the rural areas. For example, the *Cambodia Daily* surveyed individuals around the country to elicit expectations of the people. One farmer commented that farmers 'never hope for anything other than the rice field.... I don't know exactly what democracy is, we just think about whether we have rice to eat'.[17] Another, Nham Soeung, defined democracy as 'a fresh life' in which 'religion is free from government', a notion related with, but by no means necessarily specific to, democracy. Yet another, Hem Sorom, said she was unsure 'about democracy and politics', and that 'people here ... focus on business. They don't think much about politics'. Ty Khan equated democracy not with precepts such as the rule of law or universal suffrage, but with peace, so he could 'start a business and make a little money'. The use of such examples is not intended to imply a broader generalisation necessarily; nor do they necessarily reflect values in the largest cities. Some views in Phnom Penh are somewhat different, reflecting a more cosmopolitan and politically mature grouping. However, the experiences and views of Phnom Penh rarely reflect the broader rural make up of Cambodia. Government spokesperson Khieu Kanharith reminded that 'Phnom Penh is not Cambodia'.[18] The distinction reflects Ranariddh's parochial statements regarding the 'needs' of the rural majority (see above). The absence from such statements of implicit recognition of values underpinning democracy, argued Dr. Lao Mong Hay, of the Khmer Institute for Democracy, means Cambodians 'need to internalise the concepts'.[19] While this debate holds some currency in the academic debate regarding the role of democracy in development, however, those who, like Ranariddh, declare themselves to be democrats in very poor societies do not normally espouse it.[20]

At issue, then, was a multi-faceted resistance to and rejection of power sharing in an environment lacking a framework capable of responding to the concept of co-operative and 'loyal' opposition. However, the same period was also characterised by an increased movement towards and experience of participatory democracy at grass-roots level. In the search for strategic and tactical counterbalances to the usurpation of power, on the part of the CPP, or efforts to bolster and substantiate their position in relation to their actual enfranchisement, on the part of FUNCINPEC, both 'sides' of the same coalition sought alliances with external bodies, including other parliamentary parties such as the BLDP, or extra-parliamentary forces such as the Khmer Rouge. Simultaneously, other institutions, such as the media, challenged the already fragile political order, adding at some points to the growing instability.

After the Elections

By July 1993, a form of relative political stability in Cambodia appeared to have replaced the violence, intimidation and harassment of the immediate post-electoral trauma. Such conditions, despite not reflecting the technical mandate of the peacekeepers, or the actual outcome of the poll, served to inspire not a little hope that Cambodia would from this point be released from the externally-applied political bonds that had arrested its development opportunities in the wake of the Pol Pot disaster.

Whilst the system of government emplaced after the UNTAC election bears no comparison with that employed during the Pol Pot regime, it was far from healthy, by most standards. A highly inefficient system of dual-managed ministries throughout the Executive reflected and reinforced the ambiguities of powersharing and clientelism in such a deeply cleaved political culture. As a response to the CPP's refusal to surrender its positions, and to FUNCINPEC's natural desire to assert itself in government and administration, as well as Ranariddh's tendency to regal absolutism, FUNCINPEC brought its own representatives to match those employed by the CPP. In the absence of such a strategy, political power would have resided even more obviously in the hands of the CPP. Ranariddh would have been limited in the manner in which he could disburse to his clients what little he effectively had.

However, this was not the only motivation for FUNCINPEC. The denial of access to 'rewarding' jobs in government undermined Ranariddh's capacity to act as patron and distribute largesse for loyalty. In return for support of the party, the elite had promised positions of authority and privilege to its activists and its financiers as a reward for party loyalty. This process has precedent and tradition in Cambodia. Although the formal system of reward for people of status died out during the period of the French protectorate, Vickery argues that 'the mentality that accompanied it persisted. All state employment ... was still ranked on a scale of desirability according to the opportunity it provided for private benefits...'.[21] A little over a century after the beginning of the French experience, Veng Sereyvudh, a senior member of FUNCINPEC, stated that 'the price list quoted by FUNCINPEC officials for jobs in the administration ranges from 200 USD to 3,000 USD, depending on how good the position will be for extracting bribes'. He added that this was 'bound to happen [as] ... FUNCINPEC is more vulnerable to corruption because they come with empty hands and they need houses'.[22] CPP President Chea Sim stated that FUNCINPEC members were all competing for posts in the National Assembly.[23] Lao Mong Hay confirms this system. He notes that the Royalist party got their houses and villas. Whoever got closest to Ranariddh gets more favours. Strong organisation is lacking. They wanted power and then they became drunk with it and neglected the necessary consolidation of their already fragmented and inexperienced party.[24]

Frieson noted that this system was 'abundantly clear after the election, when huge crowds of *khsae* members formed outside the offices of the FUNCINPEC party in Phnom Penh to try to cash in on their support by gaining a job in the new government'.[25] Curtis observes a similar phenomenon with regard to the BLDP. He notes that in their attempts to reward their followers, they mismanaged the sole Ministry they had been awarded in the government. He observed that

> the Secretariat of State for Women's Affairs, headed by a BLDP member, hired scores of BLDP supporters without regard to qualifications. Many of the new recruits performed no real function other than filling a party-based position, a sinecure that, while not paying very much, at least provided a regular income, ample opportunity for outside employment, and a claim to status.[26]

Ashley observes that the integration of FUNCINPEC representatives 'was formally justified as a post-conflict "unification of existing administrative structures"'. This, he continues, 'involved integrating small numbers of existing and large numbers of newly recruited civil servants, police, and military into the already bloated apparatus of the former CPP-controlled state of Cambodia'.[27] The administration, rather than becoming streamlined and more efficient, expanded and stagnated as each department struggled to come to terms with the challenges to its unique authority and as the newcomers struggled to gain a foot-hold. The allocation of bureaucratic and executive representation was yet another facet in the struggle to achieve, and then assert, political power in Cambodia. In a fragile and vulnerable political system resistant to powersharing, one side struggled to enter the arena of state management without having a reasonable capacity to absorb the responsibilities attached to the inherent duties.

Simultaneously, the other side, used to absolute and largely unchallenged authority and through it, control of the state, sought to limit the effects of this breech of their political security. Cambodia's system of patronage and clientelism ensured that CPP members were provided for through access to self-aggrandising positions of power and authority. Whilst the CPP enjoyed it, FUNCINPEC coveted it. Jennar observes that this is one of the most striking aspects of Cambodian society: 'protection of a party or a clan takes precedence over respect for the law'.[28] Kao Kim Hourn maintains that this 'tradition was still very much alive, with the powerful patron/passive client relationship a hallmark of Cambodian political culture'.[29] Instead of halving the number of CPP representatives to accommodate the FUNCINPEC arrivals, the CPP sought to preserve their positions and their clients who help keep them there. This was in order to continue the reward system and simultaneously maintain positions of influence and act as a brake on FUNCINPEC policies that would inevitably affect the CPP.

There were a number of consequences attached to this arrangement. First, struggles within ministries and Provinces subsumed the development agenda that should have flowed from the conclusion of the UNTAC operation. Second, the wage bill for civil servants, for example, has increased, rather than decreased through rationalisation and modernisation. Third, much of this remained unpaid, or only periodically paid, exposing government workers to the temptations of bribery and corruption, which again limits the development agenda. Fourth, where work is conducted, it may be grossly inefficient in cost and labour.

Perhaps most important, however, is the concern that the battle for political domination between the elites is also conducted within the Ministries, and loyalties to reward-givers subsumes the execution of the tasks and responsibilities of many departments. Ashley summarises the outcome:

> rather than depoliticizing a one-party state (controlled by the CPP), powersharing ... created two separate and competing party states operating within every ministry, province, military command and police commissariat. Instead of working with their counterparts from the other party, officials from the prime ministers' level down conducted business with their party clients and colleagues. [This has] served to weaken the state by building and reinforcing parallel structures of personal and party authority, operating both within and outside the state. Hierarchical patron-client networks ... have expanded and subsumed the formal state structure.[30]

Competition of this nature served to reflect political party divides, as one party's representatives vied for privilege in opposition to the other. This was a mirror image of the deeper confrontation within the elite. The former reinforced the latter while the latter necessitated the former. Rather than ministry-sharing acting as a potential vehicle for conciliation, it reinforced cleavages which underpinned political conflict whilst simultaneously undermining the creation of non-partisan institutions which might be used to build relationships rather than aggravate enmity and malice. Prior to the creation of the Senate at the end of 1998, little institutionalisation of conflict management systems has appeared in the Cambodian political structure.

Such divisions characterised the early evolution of Cambodia's post-UNTAC political transition. At the elite level, the CPP resisted FUNCINPEC's advances towards government and state administration while FUNCINPEC's arrival doubled the civil administrative infrastructure and made real and visible confrontation within ministries, departments and Provinces. This arrangement was an inevitable outcome in a society where power sharing is oxymoronic and where the institutionalisation of opposition is non-existent. It was also in part predetermined by the consequences of marginalisation or, worse still exclusion. Furthermore, resistance to transition was entrenched in a hierarchically ordered patronage and clientelism system that preserved a traditional distribution of power that served and rewarded personal and filial financial interests in an extremely impoverished country. This reinforced the political divide, running counter to external attempts at reconciliation.

The attendant prioritisations of the new parties reflected the way in which the state and privilege is viewed by some. Shawcross catalogues a series of high-level decisions, most of which can be easily verified, made shortly after the coalition came into being. He notes that an expensive beauty pageant was staged at roughly the time Cambodia's Constituent Assembly was transforming into the first universally elected pluralist government. He also observes that 'leading members of the coalition showed more interest in foreign travel or fripperies than in setting an agenda for the country'.[31] The latter reflected reward for party loyalty, and for some in both parties, free overseas flights were taken in part for novelty value. It was, and to a large degree remains, reflective of underlying concerns in Cambodian politicians that over-ride other issues and set the tenor of the direction political relationships would begin to move in.

From 'Coalition' to Confrontation, 1993 to 1997

Early Warnings

This system appeared to some 'to be designed to encourage power struggles'.[32] Indeed it did. However, this concept was not new. In fact, it represented an extension of the conflict which, fought between and among essentially the same people, had characterised the 1980s. While a memorandum of understanding was signed to facilitate the transition from single party state to coalition, the event was little more than gesture politics.[33] No framework for sharing responsibilities or workloads was established, and few meetings took place thereafter. The Cabinet barely met, and the progress of resolutions and laws through the Assembly and Courts was slothful. For example, by April 1994, only budget and investment laws had been dealt with by the Assembly, but 'no press law had been accepted, no penal code, no criminal procedure law, no immigration law, no citizenship law, and no property law' had found its way to the Assembly's debating arena.[34] In areas which clearly would have been dangerous to debate, such as appropriate treatment of Prince Chakrapong and General Sin Song, the secession leaders, and, later, the leaders of an alleged 'coup' in mid-1994, no movement was made for some time.[35] The absence of debate on such topics probably contributed to non-confrontation, in the early days, between Assembly members. The initial stage of the government's development did not produce stand-offs and intolerance in any wider sense than day-to-day management of ministries, departments and Provinces. As the *Far Eastern Economic Review* noted, 'these faltering steps indicate there is some hope the ... country can be steered into a new era.... However [some] are doubtful that national stability can withstand a complex governing coalition...'.[36]

Although no dramatic confrontation threatened renewed war within the coalition at that time, by February 1994 observers spoke of 'internal power struggles' which had 'paralyzed the fledgling government' and which were 'keeping it from tackling the problems facing Cambodia'. *The Nation* continued that 'cosmetic changes have been made, such as adopting a new flag and anthem, but there [was] little evidence that the lives of ordinary people [had] improved'.[37] In a sense, this reflected the developing crisis. Although not manifesting itself at the time as such, these events represented a refusal to engage in inflammatory issues. The National Assembly rarely met to discuss any form of change which might cause confrontation, and the decorative changes made to Cambodia were a form of denial which permitted the members of the coalition to ignore the fact that they were not engaging in substantive debates or issues. 'The fear of confrontation', argued *The Nation*, 'has resulted in a rubber-stamp Assembly'.[38] Ashley observes that 'the government ... worked so long and insofar as Prince Ranariddh [and FUNCINPEC] agreed not to threaten the CPP's interests'.[39] In the light of this, many Assembly members saw little utility in attending meetings which were relatively few and far between, and the spiral downwards became self-reinforcing.

Sharing Power

However, these were indeed signs of problems to come. Hun Sen confirmed that a facade was in place, and admitted that although he and Ranariddh 'hug and kiss each other, we do not love each other. In fact, we barely speak. We do not have regular scheduled meetings because we have little to discuss'.[40] An example of this lackadaisical relationship occurred when an interview with Hun Sen in his Phnom Penh residence was interrupted by a telephone call from Ranariddh. An assistant to Hun Sen answered the phone and told him who was calling. Hun Sen ignored this and continued with the interview. Nodding towards the phone he told me, 'it doesn't matter, it's only Ranariddh'.[41] A similar modus operandi took effect when Ung Huot replaced Ranariddh in 1997 (see below).

Ranariddh's reluctance to confront Hun Sen over his inferior position to the second Prime Minister led to a number of problems for the Prince. The denial of such positions undermined his capacity to reward his supporters for their loyalty before and during the elections. As a consequence of this, a second challenge he faced was growing unrest within his party, exacerbated by his own personality and regal dogma. Party members and affiliates increasingly became aware of the limitations of Ranariddh's political astuteness and courage, and worried for the effect this would have on the future of their party and its capacity to take representative power. They claimed, for example, that they had 'already made too many concessions'.[42] Jeldres observes that as early as July 1993, 'newly appointed FUNCINPEC Ministers were starting to complain that they were unable to implement even the smallest changes at the Ministries allocated to them because of resistance from CPP officials'.[43] Jeldres did not add that some were technocratically incapable of undertaking such tasks. Ahmad Yahya, a FUNCINPEC representative, dismally added that 'after we win, we are like the losers'.[44]

Despite the transition induced by UNTAC, then, little other than a superficial veneer had been grafted on to the extant systems of power distribution. An election had suggested a transition away from a dominant elite towards a multi-party coalition, but the transition itself was far from complete. In a very real sense, UNTAC withdrew before the real transition had been even identified, much less commenced. The CPP remained in control of almost all aspects of the state, but although this suggests they were unreasonably intransigent in transferring power lost through a genuinely democratic process, they were also concerned at the consequences. Party loyalists and clients had to be maintained as they had been in the past; but it was also recognised that FUNCINPEC was incompetent to satisfy the terms of such an enormous undertaking. As Shawcross notes, 'FUNCINPEC had a basic problem: lack of its own personnel. Indeed ... without its coalition partners, it would have been quite unable to function at all. The process of governing depended completely on CPP personnel'.[45] In other words, FUNCINPEC could not have filled the government posts and, even if it had, the majority of its newcomers were incapable of fulfilling the routine management of a state.

These problems did not go away. By April 1994, the *Phnom Penh Post* observed that 'despite having a majority in the National Assembly ... the government apparatus, for the most part, [was] still controlled by the CPP'.[46] However, they did not become particularly worse in any meaningful way until the following year. As a pattern in post-UNTAC transition, the struggle for representative power continued to ebb and flow without either party taking a specifically confrontational position. Only when it became clear that the issue had to be publicly addressed were the consequences of such demands realised.

Thus, by March 1995, the situation became significantly more tenuous when Kompong Som's FUNCINPEC Governor Thoam (Thiem) Bun Sron 'hit out against the effective stranglehold' that the CPP held 'over rural Cambodia'.[47] Thiem claimed 'he couldn't even get a letter signed without CPP approval in his Province', despite him holding the Governorship. It was his Deputy Governor, the former CPP governor, who authorised policy decisions. Furthermore, Thiem claimed, local CPP civil servants 'actively ignored his orders in deference to their former CPP leaders who have, in practice, retained all power'; and that 'most FUNCINPEC-led Provinces suffered similarly'.[48] In effect, the position of the Deputy Governor as a former CPP leader guaranteed the system of patronage persisted in favour of the CPP. Brown notes that

> FUNCINPEC governors ... where the Provincial political structure remains loyal and indebted to the former CPP governor, understand clearly the cost of not being able to establish their own patronage system.... Patronage explains why cutting Cambodia's bloated bureaucracy is almost impossible without paying-off those let go.[49]

In many areas, this was undoubtedly true. Even in Phnom Penh, such omission and disdain were not uncommon. There, Ranariddh complained that CPP deputies did not liase with him or his colleagues over events and issues that should have employed joint participation.[50]

Such incidents were partially representative of the degree to which the CPP had not surrendered power at commune and Province level, much less in urban areas such as Phnom Penh. Jennar illustrates that

> in 4 provinces where FUNCINPEC won, the governor remained a member of the CPP. In 5 provinces where the CPP won, the post of governor is held by a FUNCINPEC member [through pre-ordained deals]. Three of the four Provinces where the election results were not respected, to the detriment of FUNCINPEC, are among the 5 most important provinces in the country, while of the 5 provinces lost by the CPP to FUNCINPEC although the CPP won, three are among the four least important provinces in the country.[51]

Loy Sim Chheang, later to split from FUNCINPEC and lead the *Sangkum Thmei* (New Society) party, stated that FUNCINPEC held 'less than 20 percent of the district and local positions that CPP agreed in 1993 to hand over'.[52]

The constant complaints by FUNCINPEC representatives eventually had an effect. In October 1995, Prince Norodom Sirivudh, a half-brother of Sihanouk and long an opponent of Hun Sen's denial of FUNCINPEC's political access to the rural areas, demanded that they 'must finalize absolutely how to share the districts between FUNCINPEC and the CPP ... our grassroots cannot wait any longer'.[53] That same month, according to FUNCINPEC at the time, a deal was struck that would enable such a provision and which would represent 'the first upheaval in the balance of power since provincial governorships were divided between the two parties after the 1993 elections'.[54] Not long after, Ranariddh's strategy of mute acceptance of the CPP's control was forced to alter to active confrontation as a consequence of the calls of some of his disaffected party members.

The heightened October 1995 impetus derived from at least two sources and arguments. First, Ranariddh was under pressure to demand action because without control of the rural areas, his leadership was made a mockery of by the CPP. One aide claimed that the Prince was ever more agitated that the CPP would not permit him his victory, and that as a result, he looked an 'important fool'.[55] He was concerned that respect for him in his party was declining, which lead to the second source of concern for the FUNCINPEC elite. Without equal sharing of the Provinces, the rewards sworn prior to the elections for party loyalty could not be disbursed. The many positions that should have been FUNCINPEC's to allocate through patronage would not become available as long as the CPP retained them. Thus, the issue was as much about party cohesion, reward and internal stability as it was about a call to have the democratic outcome of the elections respected.

The CPP initially conceded, as Jennar has noted (above), some less important provincial governorships. However, whilst this re-allocation of rural representation appeared to appease FUNCINPEC, in reality, the redistribution of power did not necessarily equate to increased influence for Ranariddh's party. The CPP did not permit FUNCINPEC to effectively permeate commune-level politics. Although some power was redistributed at higher, district and provincial levels, the problem of patronage and loyalty persisted for the Royalists. In the same way that Governor Thiem's orders were disobeyed by the CPP Deputy Governor at Provincial level in Kompong Som, so too could CPP commune and village level chiefs ignore the policies and decisions of the FUNCINPEC district level leaders. In a sense, then, while a redistribution of power appeared to have taken place formally, informally significant limitations existed to restrict the capacity for those superficial changes to be meaningful. Little, then, had really changed.

The recognition of this forced Ranariddh's hand and escalated the crisis between the two Prime Ministers. Elements of his party had decided as early as March 1995 that less than fifty percent of the district positions was unacceptable.[56] This had not been respected by the CPP and by conditions such as the lack of personnel capable of undertaking such a commitment. At the elite level, by October 1995 Ranariddh had 'for the first time publicly questioned the CPP's dominance of the justice system'.[57] The Prince complained that 'it was not fair' that FUNCINPEC had not appointed any judges to the judiciary. He went on to say that 'as a Prime Minister,

I am not happy with our justice system. What justice is running today is not satisfactory to me, maybe satisfactory to others, but not to me'.[58]

Clearly, Ranariddh's position within his own party, and his credibility to Cambodians and the international community alike, were compromised by his repeated inability to wrest significant power from the CPP and execute the mandate granted through the election. One observer claims that 'Ranariddh ... had failed to establish a clear sense of direction.... By Spring 1994 ... the party and its leaders had already lost enormous good will'.[59] Ranariddh appears to have left himself with little choice but to escalate the situation, and in so doing, confront the CPP. In March 1996, FUNCINPEC held its first party Congress since the elections. This in itself is unusual, and suggests weak leadership and a lack of awareness of the levels of resentment extant within his party. Shortly after, senior FUNCINPEC representatives declared the party was 'ready to withdraw from the coalition government if the CPP continued to ignore powersharing arrangements made after the 1993 elections'.[60] Ranariddh perhaps learned some lessons from this. Three years later, in 1999, as some district power was ceded from CPP to FUNCINPEC, Ranariddh reminded his party that he did not want 'to talk too much about district chiefs because, during the 1996 party Congress, problems occurred because of this'.[61]

This move represented a sea change in FUNCINPEC strategy and policies. The Congress, held in March, pushed for a harder line against the CPP, in which Ranariddh 'finally expressed his party's frustration at the unequal nature of the coalition'.[62] CPP sources, as well as some scholars, claim that FUNCINPEC commenced a 'Strategy of Provocation' at this point in time with, the party alleged, the intention of pushing CPP leaders into a corner and forcing them to make mistakes. In a government '*White Paper*' released after the fighting in July 1997, a number of claims were made by the CPP, some of which were substantiated from other sources. The *White Paper* claimed that the rationale behind the FUNCINPEC Congress was to 'gain lost political ground by creating a crisis in which [Hun Sen] would make a fatal mistake that would then benefit Prince Ranariddh'.[63] It is not stated that Ranariddh almost certainly expected international sympathy for his beleaguered party to help this strategy.

The manifestation of the FUNCINPEC strategy came in the demand for fair political participation coupled to a threat to leave government. Loy Sim Chheang warned that 'if the CPP does not want to solve this problem, which concerns the constitution and district chiefs and district members, maybe FUNCINPEC will retire from every level of government'.[64] In a clear allusion to the effect of the failure to develop adequate powersharing for FUNCINPEC's needs, Loy Sim Chheang made it clear that escalation to this point was irrevocably linked to the inability of the party to broker representative power distribution in the Provinces.

Furthermore, and for the first time since the coalition's inauguration, Ranariddh raised the Viêt Namese issue in what was clearly, as Ashley notes, a return 'to the populist, anti-CPP rhetoric of pre-1993'.[65] This was a reference to the CPP's alleged continuing subjugation to the Communist Party in Hanoi, and reflected the historical fight against the CPP's forerunner in the 1980s. As such, it was a FUNCINPEC-instigated war-cry. The very notion of fighting the Viêt Namese 'invaders' had in the 1980s underpinned the conflict in Cambodia and between the various governments and factions and their foreign supporters, as well as defining the character and content of the settlement which purported to end that struggle.

It therefore presented a major setback to coalition politics and the relations between the two Premiers that inflamed relations and accelerated the drive among both parties to seek allies elsewhere. Hun Sen responded by nurturing an anti-Ranariddh faction of FUNCINPEC led by Siem Reap Governor Toan Chhay.[66] Any form of transition, however superficial, was arrested and reversed at this point. The powersharing system inevitably consequent upon the terms of the PPA had re-created and reinforced traditional tensions that reignited as open competition for power manifested itself through the challenge to the old order and the predominance of the CPP and its clients. The UN-imposed transition, rather than installing a shift from confrontation to mutual powersharing, created conditions that would destabilise the country's fragile political order by intensifying competition for limited resources.

Clearly, none of these developments represented the political transition invoked in the calming words of various UN statements, or in the conditions of the PPA, or in the manifestation of the elections. In the structure of government and in its procedures and the constitutional separation of powers, a clear characteristic became yet more visible. The dominant CPP, with so much to lose before FUNCINPEC in terms of prestige and access to privilege, as well as the support of its political clans and clients, resisted subjugation to FUNCINPEC. The nature of absolutism in the CPP elite may have been inspired originally by the dictates and structures of the socialist single party state, or by Hun Sen's search for legitimacy through his adaptation to 'peasant-King', or by the hierarchical and patronage structures. Either way, absolutism did not permit a surrender to the consequences of the actual election outcome. Democratic transition was quite clearly impeded by resistance from elite political culture. This applies equally to the challenger. Ranariddh's objectives were less motivated by a desire for adherence to western democratic principles, and more by a desire to undermine the CPP's position in order to create for himself a degree of power which would not be characteristic of a democratic system. As an absolutist himself, he shares an equal amount of blame for attempting to alter the *status quo* in the full and certain knowledge of the resistance it would engender.

Until this point, however, the challenge to unilateral absolutism had found expression through relatively peaceful and new institutional mechanisms such as the joint Premiership, or through opposition to various policies in the Assembly. Whilst there was a number of allegations of political killings, some of which might be explained as such and some of which were turf wars, little real conflict had occurred. The decisions taken at the March 1996 FUNCINPEC Party Congress marked the beginning of the end of this phase, and the escalation of confrontation at this point was only an acceleration of the procedures already underway as soon as the 1993 election results were known. They were also continued from the point at which the PPA institutionalised the approach which would mandate multi-party, proportional representation polls in Cambodia's context.

The Congress also demonstrated Ranariddh's denial of the consequences of such a strategy. The Prince said 'he did not expect it would lead to more civil war'.[67] However, his choices were limited from the outset by a combination of the CPP's resistance in the context of its elite's political culture; and the pressure that would be brought to bear on those interests if they were politically marginalised. Ashley notes that the only options open to FUNCINPEC from 1993 were to form 'a coalition with the CPP and accept limited access to state power or try to assert its electoral mandate and face renewed civil war'.[68] Ranariddh, in his drive for power, picked the latter without accepting the consequences.

Relations between the two Prime Ministers quickly began to deteriorate amidst name-calling and accusation. Although Ranariddh precipitated the downturn, Hun Sen also responded in a way unlikely to soothe fears. As Ashley states, Ranariddh's activities 'triggered a fierce reaction from Hun Sen, and the personal relationship that had [before] sought security was transformed into a major source of insecurity'.[69] Any notional stability and cohesion between the two parties, competing for institutional power bases as well as for more grass-roots support, was quickly consigned to a vague memory of what had always been a myth.

Hun Sen's position quickly hardened. At a meeting in Kandal Province in May 1996, he warned Ranariddh to 'stop talking about the powersharing game; otherwise [he] would dump it completely'. He continued to warn FUNCINPEC that 'while the situation [had been] proceeding very smoothly, they brought up something out of tune. They threatened to walk out of government'. Referring to Ranariddh's threat to withdraw from the government, Hun Sen declared that 'if they really want to get out, I gladly invite them to do so. If you want to stay, stay; if you want to leave, leave. If you opt to stay, we will work together again'.[70] A little under three months later, Hun Sen reiterated his threat: 'If you don't walk out, you're a real dog'. *The Economist* declared that this amounted to a 'virtual declaration of war'.[71]

However, in contrast to the reporting and commentary on Hun Sen's response, little was made of the incitement and invective of Ranariddh's party. It is highly unlikely that Hun Sen or the CPP would have taken the position they did without Ranariddh inciting such riot. In a very real sense, the trouble at this stage was started by Ranariddh's stance, taken because the CPP refused to allow him to try to do something that his own party admits it was ill-equipped for in resources and experience. Doyle confirms that 'FUNCINPEC failed to provide a plausible, comprehensive list of candidates' for district level management.[72] Furthermore, Hun Sen declared publicly this was a serious consideration, and that he had never received any such list and therefore the CPP 'cannot accept wrong charges'. He continued that the party had 'not been slack', and that he had 'never received a list of nominated district governors'.[73] FUNCINPEC was incapable of fulfilling the positions to which they wished to apply themselves. Hun Sen declared that FUNCINPEC had 'asked to shelve the district level powersharing'.[74] They failed to submit plausible candidates, and concluded by blaming Hun Sen for not surrendering district-level power. Despite this, the government's *White Paper* published after the July fighting claimed accurately that CPP had 'agreed to integrate more than 11,000 persons from FUNCINPEC [and] more than 15,000 FUNCINPEC ... personnel were taken into' the police.[75]

Ranariddh's efforts to emulate the position his father had held in the 1960s were significant drivers of the confrontation.[76] This is not to claim the CPP acted legally or fairly in the context of the election results. However, each party was pursuing its own power consolidation agenda in the context of its elite leadership's political culture. To blame one or the other for poor gamesmanship in a democratic context is both an over-simplification and inaccurate.

The Khmer Rouge, the general elections and the fracturing of the coalition

If the FUNCINPEC-CPP confrontation was a tinderbox, the split within the Khmer Rouge elite provided the flint. The increased competition and enmity between the two Prime Ministers also has to be considered in the context of the run up to the anticipated 1998 general elections. The exchange of words noted above preceded the next stage of Cambodia's political transition from the uncontested single party state to a multi-party democracy. Furthermore, by this stage, the remaining Khmer Rouge elite were beginning to demonstrate more visibly what many already recognised from analyses: that their elite was further splitting. In this context, and as part of similar pre-election strategies on the part of both Hun Sen and Ranariddh, each of these sides sought to generate political and military support of the different 'cliques' of the remnants of the Khmer Rouge leadership.

Simultaneously, some members of the CPP began to claim that Ranariddh was already in secret collusion with the guerrillas at the time.[77] Whilst ostensibly part of the government coalition in Phnom Penh allied with Hun Sen, Ranariddh appeared to many to be manoeuvring 'to create a broad opposition front by resurrecting, with defectors, FUNCINPEC's pre-1990 alliance with the Khmer Rouge'.[78] Ashley corroborates such a view after translating the 'Khmer Rouge papers'.[79] The *Far Eastern Economic Review* claimed that it had been agreed in June 1998 that 'the Khmer Rouge ... could join the ... coalition of anti-Hun Sen parties led by FUNCINPEC' whilst Ranariddh still shared power with Hun Sen in the ruling coalition.[80] There was no doubt, then, that Ranariddh by late 1996 was plotting to engage in exactly what the CPP had accused them of, and which they had denied.

Ranariddh and FUNCINPEC were not the only ones who were involved in seducing defectors from the Khmer Rouge. In late 1996, Ieng Sary, a former foreign minister in the Khmer Rouge period, defected to the government under Hun Sen's aegis.[81] Ieng Sary explained that he had moved to wards Hun Sen in part because he 'did not want to be on the side of the losers'.[82] Despite Ranariddh's negotiators having done some of the legwork, Ieng immediately declared neutrality whilst assuring Hun Sen of his discreet support. Many declare this to have been a function of a quite recent split within the Khmer Rouge. However, Ieng claimed that he had been ostracised from the party and sent into exile in Pailin in 1986. Others support this. He has been at odds with Pol Pot, Khieu Samphan, Nuon Chea, Ta Mok and Chan Youran since then; and as they favoured Ranariddh above Hun Sen, Ieng Sary would get a better deal from Hun Sen.[83]

The move had implications for Ranariddh's ongoing attempts to expand his power base. In a sense, it forced him to consider efforts to woo other elements of the Khmer Rouge with whom he had been allied in the 1980s, but who had departed from the process of elections and democratic transition before the 1993 elections could be held (see chapter five). He failed to gain access at grass-roots level and he failed to gain Ieng Sary's support. Thus, despite his best efforts and his altered strategy, Ranariddh was, by August 1996, perhaps even more marginalised than he had been before he shifted from begrudging co-operation to belligerent confrontation. The Prince's secret and denied strategy of alignment with anti-CPP Khmer Rouge forces prompted Hun Sen to utilise emerging schisms in the Khmer Rouge to his own advantage; this in turn upped the ante for Ranariddh. As Ashley maintains, 'the rivalry between Ranariddh and Hun Sen led both to court the Khmer Rouge dissidents and hard-liners, before and after the revolt' already threatening to split the Khmer Rouge elite over a number of other issues.[84] This problem caused each to search for a counter-weight to the shifting balance of power.

The rivalry sparked debates in many quarters. Some took the position that Ranariddh was entitled to pursue such a path because Hun Sen left him with no choice. Advocates of this view also often argue that what he did in courting the Khieu Samphan/Ta Mok Khmer Rouge groups was no different from Hun Sen's negotiations with Ieng Sary.[85] Others, however, argue that Ranariddh created the conditions for his own demise. Furthermore, he undermined himself by embarking on a series of clandestine meetings with various leaders with whom he plotted the overthrow of Hun Sen by re-creating the agenda of the 1980s CGDK alliance-in-exile.[86] Quite clearly, Ranariddh's negotiations with Khieu Samphan became less and less transparent and more and more unilateral. Whilst this was visible to many observers, it raised no objection or comment from the 'concerned' international media, which focused on demonising Hun Sen for the moral questions raised by his attempts to unify the country through the undermining of the Khmer Rouge. Curtis argues rightly that 'had Hun Sen and the CPP attempted such "secret" negotiations, it is certain that the international press would have seized on such dealings as proof of [their] Khmer Rouge origins'.[87]

However, distinctions were made, not least of all by Sihanouk, regarding the two parties' different approaches to the Khmer Rouge. For example, all sides to the coalition were involved at most, or made aware of at least, the process of wooing Ieng Sary and splitting the Khmer Rouge in order to undermine it. In other words, 'each group [was] competing to gain the support of rival factions of Pol Pot's Khmer Rouge...'.[88] This was part of a national strategy of eliminating the Khmer Rouge as an extra-parliamentary force. However, Ranariddh's policy with regard to Khieu Samphan and Ta Mok was undertaken not with the intention of splitting the Khmer Rouge with a view to their elimination, but rather to create a force aligned with him which would challenge, politically and militarily, the CPP. Furthermore, Ranariddh continued to deny that this was his course of action. The *White Paper* declared accurately that 'there was a unified government policy at the time to encourage [Khmer Rouge] defections in the Northwest'.[89] However, the same cannot be said with regard to Ranariddh's strategy and communications with the Anlong Veng Khmer Rouge.[90] Hun Sen declared that 'anyone who helps the Khmer Rouge or brings them to Phnom Penh [is] breaking the law'. He viewed these efforts as attempts 'to bring [the Khmer Rouge] back to life politically'.[91] Finally, he gave Ranariddh 'a few days to decide whether to carry on to work in the coalition government or to go to work with the Khmer Rouge', adding that this 'betrayal ... cannot be accepted'.[92] Even Sihanouk criticised Ranariddh's behaviour as 'immoral'.[93]

Insofar as one side sought to expand its power base and the other sought to prevent the reduction of its own support, the developing tensions found expression in emerging splits within a potentially powerful extra-parliamentary force. Both key sides of the coalition sought to embellish their political positions through various machinations, but one did it with the intention of overthrowing the other by building power outside the coalition, as opposed to developing allies within a parliamentary framework. Curtis notes that

> on July 3, 1997, Prince Ranariddh ... signed an agreement with Khieu Samphan.... This political ... alliance ... essentially recreated the Coalition Government of Democratic Kampuchea in clear opposition to the CPP.[94]

Furthermore, that side denied this was the case, and illegally smuggled arms whilst lying about the contents of the packaging. It is well known that Royal Government officials 'found weapons and ammunition instead of [the] spare parts' listed on the container coming in to the port at Sihanoukville.[95] It is also well known that Ranariddh, who rightly claimed it was legal to import arms to Cambodia, could not respond when asked why he had deliberately disguised the contents. The government raised the obvious question: 'If it was legal for [Ranariddh] to bring weapons into the country, why did he hide them? If bringing weapons into Cambodia is a normal activity, why did he lie about the shipment of arms?'.[96] Ranariddh had no reasonable defence, especially as three tons of the equipment was made up of anti-tank weapons, and the CPP clearly dominated the armoured cavalry sector of the military.

The coalition schism aggravated

The 'loss' of Ieng Sary and his troops to Hun Sen undermined Ranariddh's already fragile position. Simultaneously, as schisms within the Khmer Rouge elite opened wider in response to this defection, and in response to Pol Pot's reversal of 'new liberal' ideology invoked for the UNTAC period, a movement towards the overthrow of Pol Pot developed.[97] By 6 June, 1997, Ranariddh, in a rapidly escalating search for allies splintering from the Khmer Rouge fall-out, 'negotiated the defection of more Khmer Rouge troops'. He also 'attempted to bolster his position by building ties to the Khmer Rouge ... [over] several months of negotiations, resulting in a political military alliance' coupling FUNCINPEC to the Khmer Rouge and two other parties opposed to Hun Sen and the CPP.[98]

On 17 June, in an early indication of problems between the disintegrating government coalition and the evolving Khmer Rouge/

FUNCINPEC alliance, fighting broke out between the police headquarters of the CPP and FUNCINPEC. This element of the conflict undoubtedly reflected not merely the wider contest conducted at party and coalition level, but also a personality clash, between the respective heads of party police. The creation of dual heads of department across most government structures and within political loyalties not unsurprisingly aggravated inter-party tension. In particular, the heads of police, Ho Sok of FUNCINPEC and Hok Lundi for the CPP, were directly opposed and equally loyal to their parties and their positions of power. Increasing tensions between the two, noted by many diplomats at the time and suggestive of worse things to come, can be viewed in the wider context of the political tinderbox developing over the negotiations with the Khmer Rouge elite.

Khieu Samphan, the apparent Khmer Rouge leader, prepared 'to lead [his party] into an alliance with FUNCINPEC ... to fight against the CPP'.[99] It is not clear what form of fighting was inferred in the report; however, the presence of extra-parliamentary alliances against the CPP cannot be ignored. The fighting was concluded quickly, but a great deal of bad blood was fostered at personality level. Ho Sok died after the fighting in CPP police custody; the direct causes are still disputed in some quarters.

What made it difficult to accept for the CPP was that instead of building support for themselves with the Khmer Rouge as part of an 'opposition' in a parliamentary sense, Ranariddh and his negotiators were creating an alliance targeted against the CPP, whilst simultaneously sharing power with them in the government coalition. Few accepted this position, because it supported the CPP's analysis and discredited Ranariddh's claims of innocence in the matter of government loyalty and anti-CPP scheming. Indeed, Curtis notes that 'the somewhat biased western media rarely noted ... charges against Prince Ranariddh, focusing instead on the bloody coup d'etat [sic] which deposed him'.[100]

Complex and clandestine negotiations continued to attempt to forge a relationship between Ranariddh and Khieu Samphan. Whilst these included nominal representation from the CPP, the Khmer Rouge leadership insisted on referring to them as representatives of the 'Viêt Namese'. This issue, as ever, held up negotiations until Khieu conceded the point and prepared to sign a deal with Ranariddh to join the government, but simultaneously operate as a force to confront the CPP in conjunction with FUNCINPEC and other disaffected groups from Phnom Penh politics. Before a final deal between Ranariddh and the remnants of the Khmer Rouge could be cemented, the fighting broke out in Phnom Penh and Ranariddh's fate was sealed. It appears, argued the *Far Eastern Economic Review,* that his secret ties to the Khmer Rouge and a hidden agenda 'proved to be the trigger for Hun Sen's actions'.[101] This school of thought, however, infers from such a statement that Hun Sen started the July fighting. Many refute this.

A great deal has been written about the origins of the so-called 'coup', insofar as the questions asked have revolved around whom started it.[102] That question itself is yet further complicated by the loose definition applied to the event. Nowhere in political science definitions, for example, is a 'coup d'etat' normally followed by a democratically elected, Assembly-ratified replacement for an individual who, whilst democratically elected himself, broke the rules of his own constitution.[103] Nor, for that matter, does a 'coup d'etat' normally take place without a replacement of government and Ministry figures; it rarely ever preserves the role of the party belonging to the 'ousted' leader. Nor was the radio station taken over, as ubiquitous an event as any in coups. Chea Sim stated in a speech that the CPP's actions

> bear no characteristics of a coup d'etat. It was not an armed confrontation between political parties. The operation was the Royal Government's effort to enforce the law against the illegal force.... It was within the domain of the government's responsibility to prevent and put a check on illegal armed elements and to act against the clandestine outlawed elements of the Khmer Rouge.[104]

Finally, the so-called 'ouster' of Ranariddh attempted not once to co-opt the Constitution, or to take power himself to any degree greater than that which he already enjoyed. Imagawa observed 'the military action taken by Hun Sen ... was not a coup d'etat in the sense that the nation was completely overthrown or the government toppled'; and that Hun Sen did not 'change the constitutional monarchy, king, constitution, government or coalition framework'.[105] No real change took place, other than the departure of the individual who pre-empted the fighting by provoking the CPP via an anti-constitutional and aggressive policy pursued naively.

The Royal Government *White Paper,* published shortly after the fighting stopped, points to inconsistencies in the arguments which implied that Hun Sen led a staged 'coup' to rid himself of Ranariddh without justification. It is clear now, as it was to some then, that Ranariddh forced Hun Sen's hand whilst the latter was out of the country on a well publicised holiday in Viêt Nam. The *White Paper* argued that 'one faction of the government wants to ally itself with the Khmer Rouge outlaws. It could not be for the sake of reconciliation because the hard-liners at Anlong Veng have never accepted the principle of national reconciliation'.[106] Curtis moves to add that on the one hand, the *White Paper* and its timing, so soon after the fighting, 'presented a convincing, if convenient, justification for military action'. He added, however, that it

> is to be noted that neither Prince Ranariddh nor FUNCINPEC refuted either the succession of events outlined in the [government] White Paper or the specific charges relating to the importation of weapons, the non-authorised redeployment of troops, or secret negotiations with the Anlong Veng-based Khmer Rouge.[107]

Opinion continued to be divided on this issue, and until May 1998, limited evidence existed which would strongly corroborate a Khmer Rouge role in Ranariddh's attempts to undermine Hun Sen and create an opposition whilst within the coalition. However, the documents recovered from the fall of Anlong Veng, one of the final redoubts of the Khmer Rouge, confirm not only that Ranariddh was negotiating with just such duplicity in mind; but that the Khmer Rouge were still using Ranariddh in much the same way as they had in the 1980s. These documents, referred to in some sources as the 'KR papers', reveal that

> the Khmer Rouge viewed FUNCINPEC's offer to join the coalition of anti-Hun Sen parties, the National United Front (NUF), in precisely the same way as it had viewed similar alliances with the Royalists in 1970-1975 and 1982-1991.[108]

Ashley notes that the papers continue to 'prove Hun Sen correct about the Khmer Rouge objective in joining the NUF and correct in alleging that Khmer Rouge fought alongside the FUNCINPEC resistance'.[109] They also reflect the utility this offered the Khmer Rouge to continue their war against the CPP/Viêt Nam, rather than to settle the conflict and share power peacefully. However, he further notes that there is no reference to military planning between the Khmer Rouge and FUNCINPEC regarding the presence of armed forces attacking Phnom Penh in July 1997. Curtis surmised that it was a 'strong likelihood that the July "coup" was less a planned attack by the CPP against FUNCINPEC than an escalating series of events precipitated by FUNCINPEC which then spun out of control'.[110] This, on the other hand, does not detract from the notion that Ranariddh's actions were illegal and inflammatory. Had as many forces as accused Ranariddh of unconstitutional behaviour accused a politician of his position in a European country, he would almost certainly have faced a judicial enquiry. With the evidence available against Ranariddh, he would almost certainly have been arrested and indicted.

There is no longer any doubt that Ranariddh was attempting to expand the NUF to embrace the Khmer Rouge in direct contradiction of his role as a member of the Royal Government coalition, aggravating tensions between himself and the CPP. However, whilst the debate regarding the origins of the fighting continues, what seems more clear is that this stage of Cambodia's transition to democracy emerged as a function of the failure of the Paris Accords, and of the paradox of powersharing it inappropriately created.

The third stage of Cambodia's political transition from conditions characterised by entrenched elitist absolutism, a sometimes relatively passive population, and foreign domination and intervention, to a first attempt at multi-party liberalism appears to have been as troubled as the two which preceded it. In many ways, the evolution of political development after UNTAC departed reflects the impediments to peaceful transition experienced in the preceding stages. In the first, during the 1980s and up to the signing of the PPA, the concept of powersharing, in its form and content, stymied the conclusion of the conflict. In the second stage, during UNTAC's tenancy, the demand for equal access to state organs characterised much of the problems Cambodians and the UN faced. In the third, post-UNTAC stage up to 1997, that period may be characterised, in the context of political transition, as one party fighting for access while the other sought to deny such ingress.

The nature this contest took, and the defining elements thereof, are interwoven in a complex meld of the ebb and flow of political power. That contest was also a part of the actions taken to redress or enhance alliances that would counter the effect, at any time and for either of the main parties, of political marginalisation. The problem began with the assumptions of the PPA which, it will be recalled, limited the options for political settlement in Cambodia by first insisting on power-sharing; and then ensuring that a coalition would be formed through the use of a voting system that dilutes power.

From 'Coalition' to Confrontation, 1993 to 1997

The issue of power sharing was aggravated by three events that at the time appeared to have no long term effect on the transition to democratic government in Cambodia. First, UNTAC failed to militarily disarm the Khmer Rouge. It left the organisation fully armed and outside the peace process. This was a consequence of the second event, whereby UNTAC failed to politically disarm the CPP, such that Hun Sen's party retained control of state organs such as the judiciary, the military, the Ministries, Provinces, districts and communes. All of these should have been neutralised; but UNTAC was not provided with the skills or the time to do this. Finally, the PPA dramatically failed to ensure that the first major transitional period, between the vote being announced and the formation of a new government, was prepared for.

Thus, at the end of the UNTAC period, there existed in Cambodia a fully armed guerrilla force which exhibited major fault-lines within its elite but which retained its violent racist dogma and denounced the 'two-headed, three-eyed' government in Phnom Penh.[111] The conditions which led to this also led to the immediate marginalisation of the FUNCINPEC electoral winner, as FUNCINPEC's margin was cancelled by the CPP's control of the state arms apparatus. The Khmer Rouge rejection of the UNTAC peace process, and the inability of Ranariddh to take the power he won, are both symptoms of the same two problems: the CPP's domination of the political system in Cambodia, and the PPA's incongruity with conditions in Cambodia. In turn, that incongruity ignored the CPP's grasp on power and even tried to neutralise it, without considering that this would not happen as long as there was so much to be lost and so little to be gained, if Opposition did not exist as an accepted, mature institution.

The coalition outcome of the 1993 election, long since inevitable from the point at which it was adopted with glee by some and with anxiety by others, was antithetical to conditions in the Cambodian elite. This arrangement did what it set out to do in 1991, which was to create a political order agreeable to the superpowers and permit them to disengage and reinforce international rapprochement and economic integration. It did not create conditions that found acceptance for Khmers, either dogmatically or practically. It is quite clear, as Lizée claims, that the 'idea of rooting political power in Cambodia in the concept of popular representation rather than in the complex of factional allegiances that have traditionally dominated the nation's political landscape was seen by the factional elites as inherently

From 'Coalition' to Confrontation, 1993 to 1997

threatening to their authority'.[112] From the very outset, the enforced powersharing system created competition. The coalition constituted nothing more (inside Cambodia) than a new arena in which to continue the fight on the one hand to usurp power from the entrenched elite, and on the other to protect that entrenchment from assault, whilst simultaneously seeking to consolidate whatever power base existed for each. 'It was', argued Dr. Lao Mong Hay, 'the politics of exclusion rather than accommodation'.[113]

The new conflict differed principally, although not absolutely, in weaponry. Until July 1997, and with some political killings along the route, the main weapons were words, threats, insults, and provocation from both sides. The issues remained the same, and involved a rejection of a system that undermined the manner in which power was derived traditionally and which marginalised groups to an extreme exacerbated by the absence of liberal opposition that ensures political and financial continuity and survival.

VIII

Peripheral Challenges to Transition, 1993 to 1997

Cambodia's third stage of transition between 1993 and 1997 was deeply influenced by the two interwoven themes discussed in the preceding chapter. The failure of UNTAC to create conditions whereby the Khmer Rouge would accept disarmament (by politically neutralising their CPP opposition) and participate in a parliamentary context, and the paradox of creating a powersharing environment between arch enemies imbued in a political culture of absolutism and intolerance of difference, established the tenor of the inter-party contest for power in Cambodia.

However, these two themes were not the only characteristics of this stage of political development and transition. A great number of unique individual and interconnected events took place in the four years between the UN elections and the violence of July 1997. However, there was also a series of discernible themes that linked these events, including the internal disintegration and reconstruction of opposition parties, and the role of mass society, which are readily identifiable with this stage of political transition.

Internal disintegration took a number of forms including, for example, hostility between the two key parties, already addressed in chapter seven. However, these two, and the third key party (the BLDP) also suffered from dissent within their elite. Various examples of this demonstrate the nature of change in the post-UNTAC period, and the manner in which it constrained the process of political transition.

The CPP

Although the most obvious points of tension arose almost immediately after the May 1993 election, between the CPP and FUNCINPEC and the respective personality politics associated with each party, another source of strife quickly became evident within the CPP itself. The party has, historically, experienced a divide which does not necessarily represent a 'split', but which is in some contexts little more than a variegation or classification, essentially between Chea Sim, party President, and Hun Sen, its Vice-President. This classification was complicated by the 1993 elections, in the sense that many of the older party representatives and members of the Standing, and later Central, Committees were replaced by younger, more technocratically competent cadres.[1] McAuliff notes the February 1997 expansion of the CPP Central Committee, for example, which 'indicated a continuing balance of political tendencies and the infusion of non-ideological technocratic leaders', following the pattern established in 1993.[2] These tensions represent one aspect of resistance to the consequences of transition.

Indeed, this was one of the issues behind the 32 CPP resignations from the Assembly that preceded the secession (see chapter six). It may be recalled that the CPP could not provide for its party members the seats it had expected or hoped to take, and the positions of privilege which accrue from such disposition. The CPP share of the Assembly was subject to many new, younger names that broke with the past and simultaneously influenced the balance of power within the party. In essence, the intra-party struggle in the CPP subsequent upon the shift from older ideologues to younger facilitators is as much an example of the challenge to transition from the old order to the new as were the inter-party challenges that arose in response to the imposed democratisation. Vickery argues that in this context, 'the Chea Sim faction ... lost status, that of Hun Sen ... gained, and the changes ... in ... CPP ... Assembly and government reveal a passing from one generation to another'.[3]

By September 1993, as the structure of government was adjusted and a number of positions eliminated, the *Cambodia Daily* warned of 'an internal power struggle' between 'moderates and hardliners' in the CPP 'over who should have the greater role in Cambodia's new government'.[4] *The Daily* is not recognised as an especially neutral paper, and it has demonstrated a number of inconsistencies in argument and position over the recent years. However, given the limited number of daily sources with some degree of internal contacts, it is cited where it can be corroborated as far as is possible. The struggle, then, arose in response to a number of problems. First, a CPP representative was cited in the *Cambodia Daily* as claiming that 'Chea

Sim and [his] followers [were] not happy because they [did] not have a role in the government'.[5] This was incorrect. Clearly, Chea Sim's involvement was codified in the Constitutional acceptance of his chairing of the National Assembly. However, equally clearly, that role was relative to the group more loyal to Hun Sen. It seemed at the time, and research has since concluded, that the Chea Sim group was marginalised in this debate but not excluded.[6]

There were implications attached to such marginalisation, however. For example, the removal of a number of the Chea Sim 'old guard' had the effect of both enhancing Hun Sen's allies, and of limiting access to structures for the Chea Sim clan. In this context, the loss of political position and the ensuing reduction of 'gifts' downwards would aggravate the Chea Sim brigade's already diminishing support base. One consequence was the undermining by degrees of some members of the Chea Sim clan. The vacancies created by this were filled with pro-Hun Sen individuals who then came to enjoy the very benefits stripped of the Chea Sim-ists.

Another implication of this change was that, while it was accepted that a two-Prime Minister system should continue to prevail, Chea Sim advocated to Hun Sen that Sar Kheng, ally and former Interior Minister, should be the country's Vice Prime Minister. Indeed, in the chosen government, Sar Kheng was appointed Vice Prime Minister.[7] This was a clear challenge to Hun Sen's position, but one aimed at warning him of concern over other issues, rather than a threat of a 'putsch'. Following this, the Chea Sim group criticised Hun Sen's Cabinet on the grounds that many of then 'had never made any great sacrifices for the party'.[8] This is an oblique reference to the traditional elements of the party who had either communist, or non-communist but revolutionary, experience in Cambodia's political development since the formation of the Communist party in 1951. The appointment of Chea Sim to the Head of the National Assembly, the post he had occupied when it was solely a CPP forum, was a method of resolving this problem.[9]

This illustrated that even the CPP, seemingly solid by comparison with other parties, had divisions which arose from issues related to the benefits of patronage and clientelism which flow more from greater positions of authority. When no external threat had existed to the party elite, and when internal power bases were secure and unchallenged, conflict tended to be over issues of ideological correctness. This was especially the case before 1985, but also thereafter as the 'hard-line' elements sought adherence to older values as their primacy was challenged more and more. The 'new' divisions arose more from competition for access to privilege and power than from the degree to which Leninism was adhered to in 1980s Cambodia, but was still a consequence of the changes heralded by transition and the threat it came to represent.

The reallocation of Assembly seats, and the similar reduction in party privileges as Ministry positions were surrendered, if not to opposition groups then to other party members, contained the possibility that the 'victims' would be rendered vulnerable. If unable to 'pay' the clans, support would diminish and a downward spiral would commence. Such systems of kinship and clans are not unique to Cambodia; a 'pattern' of traditional loyalty and cash relations is clearly identified and recognised as an alternative to capitalism on its own.[10] The introduction of a new political system of powersharing undermined traditionally secure positions and forced responses that appeared to destabilise Phnom Penh. These systemic challenges both fractured a fragile order, and simultaneously provided no system of recourse to alternative revenue and political support generation. These concerns were exacerbated directly as wealth and resource access often depended on such systems and had far-reaching consequences not merely for the elite, but equally importantly for all those dependent on such patronage. In other words, whilst undoing the old system, no account was taken of the need to compensate for political and economic injuries sustained in this transition and transformation. Such issues were not specific to the CPP.

Chea Sim's early and indirect 'challenge' to Hun Sen's party primacy was superseded by a second, superficially dramatic threat to Hun Sen from within the CPP in mid-1994. On 2 July, pro-CPP military forces intercepted and turned around a group of 'rebels' at Neak Luong, the Mekong ferry crossing that supports national route one between Phnom Penh and Ho Chi Minh City. Forces loyal to the CPP challenged a body of some 300 men and armoured vehicles.[11] Shortly thereafter, Prince Norodom Chakrapong was identified as the culprit behind the move and, after a brief attempt to hide in a hotel, his release and exile were secured. Almost simultaneously his alleged accomplice, General Sin Song, was arrested but later escaped. These two names will be familiar from their role in the June 1993 secession (see chapter six).

The issue raised a number of questions regarding the possible complicity of other highly placed officials of the CPP. General Sin Sen of the CPP was promoted quickly to secretary of state for the Interior for his role in identifying various individuals and processes in what became known as an attempted coup.[12] He was then arrested two days later as he prepared to board a pre-scheduled business flight bound for Malaysia, to where Chakrapong had already fled. The Ministry of the Interior was implicated through the passes issued for the mobilisation and despatch of the initial 'coup' forces crossing Neak Luong. However, Minister of the Interior Sar Kheng claimed that this was not the case and that the orders and passes had been issued from east of the Mekong.[13] He too fell under suspicion immediately, partly because he was allied with Chea Sim.

Awareness of the event was raised slightly earlier. An anti-Hun Sen secretary of state for Defence, Chhay Sung Yung, attempted to have arrested three senior officers in the Defence Ministry who would oppose the 'coup' militarily. The Military Court smelled a rat and Chhay Sung Yung 'confessed' to the plot. It was then that the group had been turned back; the confession implicated both Sin Song and Chakrapong.[14]

A number of explanations of this event have been offered. Some suggested Chakrapong sought power, but only to hand over to the King. This came in the light of comments made in preceding months by Sihanouk, who had earlier urged that he felt the need to re-take power 'if the situation is one of anarchy'. He qualified this by referring to the constitutional limitations on such a course of action and requested, effectively, an invite from the two Prime Ministers.[15]

Another, higher explanatory connection was made. Sin Song, under interrogation, threatened to reveal highly placed names within the CPP. It has also been noted that all those arrested were linked with the Chea Sim/Sar Kheng 'faction' of the CPP. Indeed, even Sar Kheng was not above suspicion, as he was not informed of the 'coup' attempt by CPP sources until several hours after it had folded.[16] Furthermore, Shawcross alleges, but without furnishing any evidence, FUNCINPEC had been 'courting such alleged "hardliners" as Sar Kheng and Chea Sim' to reinforce their position, knowing they were unhappy with Hun Sen's primacy.[17] Without reference to other sources for such a claim, it cannot as yet be substantiated reliably. However, given FUNCINPEC's behaviour regarding the Khmer Rouge, it is not necessarily unlikely.

Alternatively, it was posited that Chakrapong and Sin Song were still disappointed at their lack of access to government posts or other positions of power and influence from which they could enrich themselves, and therefore agitated accordingly. The 'coup' attempt, according to such a theory, was therefore attention seeking and intended to generate access to political power and privileges for Chakrapong and Sin Song. Vickery observes with reference to traditions of rebellion especially prior to the 1970s that 'the potential rebel wished to be bought off, not to change the system'.[18] He also notes that during the 1940s at the French political prison at Pulou Condore in Viêt Nam, the 'trusties, police spies, and torturers were all Khmers currying favour for individual special treatment' and reward.[19]

While there will continue to be disagreement over these, and other, explanations, the *Phnom Penh Post* noted that what was not in doubt was that the event reflected 'an internal CPP matter'.[20] Similarly, *the Bangkok Post* characterised the issue as 'an expression of the intensity of rivalries within the CPP'.[21] Such instabilities were certainly present in the CPP prior to its attempted transition from an unchallenged single party state to a partner in a fractured coalition. However, they did not find such physical expression then. Since the party's marginalisation through the elections and the broader transitional process, the divides within have been aggravated by the challenges to the breadth and depth of the party's power base and the undermining of traditional networks which have supported and preserved each element of the bipartisan political classification. As a consequence, such tensions find more physical expression. The July 1994 'coup' is a clear example of this.

FUNCINPEC

As was noted earlier, the CPP was not unique in facing contests for political power, privilege or authority within its own ranks.[22] Only a matter of weeks before the July 1994 CPP 'coup', Finance Minister Sam Rainsy and Foreign Minister Prince Norodom Sirivudh were known to have reached a point where they could no longer agree on fundamental issues with party leader Prince Norodom Ranariddh. By mid-1994, broader concerns regarding Ranariddh's competence as a leader capable of challenging the CPP's grip on powersharing and development direction had grown to the point that that party looked increasingly unstable. Shawcross notes that by this stage, 'people complained almost as much about FUNCINPEC as they did about' anyone else; 'the party had already lost enormous good will'.[23] These challenges to FUNCINPEC central authority characterised the party's decline up to the July 1997 fighting, but became more apparent in the weeks immediately superseding that summer's transition.

The sacking of the 'popular' Finance Minister Sam Rainsy in October 1994 exacerbated the problem between Ranariddh and FUNCINPEC.[24] It also prompted the resignation of Prince Sirivudh, another well-known figure in the party, from party office (but not yet from his Assembly seat).[25] Rainsy had begun to centralise tax revenue and popularised himself by leading 'heroic' crusades such as one against the seemingly endemic Khmer illness, in Rainsy's view, of corruption. As he continued to denounce the government, he was also expelled from the National Assembly. Many argued this was wrong because 'it was never put to an assembly vote [it] was illegal, a very sad day for Cambodia, and a turning point after which criticism of the government was no longer possible'.[26] Heder argues such instances reflect 'the general refusal of elite culture to recognize the legitimacy of difference and opposition'.[27] This applies, of course, to each group of elites, and is appropriate as much to Rainsy and Ranariddh as it is to Hun Sen.

Rainsy was also outspoken regarding Ranariddh's compromises over the CPP and his lack of direction and policy drift. He managed therefore to alienate himself from both the CPP and FUNCINPEC. On the one hand, he threatened Ranariddh's position and questioned his competence, undermining his regal status. On the other, he alleged CPP involvement in both corruption and tax revenue mismanagement. Heder argues that the elimination of Rainsy, and others, represented the 'purge ... of voices that were critical of [Ranariddh's and Hun Sen's] joint actions...'.[28] Ashley argues that the expulsion of Rainsy from FUNCINPEC, and later from the National Assembly 'symbolized Ranariddh's willingness to eliminate any challenge to his decision to compromise with the CPP'.[29] Heder further argues that, in the context of the ruling coalition, political transition to democracy was

> being reversed and delayed by a political elite subscribing to a stated or unstated neoauthoritarianism that constitutes a middle ground on which leaders who were previously at war with one another have now met and are attempting to consolidate power.[30]

The splits within FUNCINPEC that continued to develop prior to the July 1997 fighting were a product of at least three forces. First, Ranariddh's inability to fulfil FUNCINPEC's mandate granted by the electorate undermined his authority in the eyes of an increasing number of party loyalists. Early internal party dissent was obvious from the outset. Vickery notes, for example, that with regard to Assembly debates over the formation of the 1993 government, 'Ranariddh complained that not all FUNCINPEC members voted for his proposals...'.[31] Vickery also argues that there existed 'a faction within FUNCINPEC that is lukewarm towards Monarchy, especially of the Sihanouk variety, and this faction [was] probably headed by Sam Rainsy'.[32] Given Ranariddh's aspirations to emulate his father's position in Khmer society, and his regal and often pompous behaviour around his party faithful, dissent is unsurprising. Others have made similar observations.[33]

Second, his decision, before March 1996, not to meaningfully challenge Hun Sen over powersharing, left many of those loyalists without the jobs they had been promised in the Cambodian tradition as a reward for their support. It further left them fully aware that Ranariddh would acquiesce to Hun Sen's wishes each time at the expense of his party, about which he was not overly concerned before the pre-Congress problems threatened to blow up, wreck the party, and in so doing undermine his power and client bases. Lao Mong Hay observed that

> Ranariddh kept yielding to requests from the CPP. For most of his time in power, Ranariddh gave in to Hun Sen, which in part accounts for the splits within his party. Every time Hun Sen set the rules, Ranariddh accepted meekly, except for the district level powersharing, when he opposed Hun Sen.[34]

Lao Mong Hay cites a particular example early on which caused great upset because of its historical context and meaning, and over which Ranariddh was quickly defeated. In Cambodia, 7 January is celebrated by some as national salvation or liberation day. It marks the date, in 1979, when the Viêt Namese and the Kampuchean Salvation Front liberated Phnom Penh from Pol Pot and instituted the PRC and the PRPK. It also marks the beginning of the war between the FUNCINPEC/Khmer Rouge/BLDP coalition against Phnom Penh. 'Ranariddh', Lao reminded, 'didn't want [the] 7 January holiday'. He then narrated that Hun Sen had said, 'maybe he would prefer to celebrate 17 April [1975; the date of the Khmer Rouge take-over]. And the holiday stayed'.[35]

A third cause of the splits is to be found in Ranariddh's ultimate desires for the absolutism enjoyed by his father.[36] This reflected the notion that the party was, Ashley notes, 'less a political party with a clear political programme than a Royal court'.[37] Ranariddh sought to dominate the party in the same way as Sihanouk had dominated both the *Sangkum Reastr Niyum* and the Cambodian government during the 1960s before his toppling at the hands of the 'Republican' Lon Nol in 1970. Only the most dedicated were concerned with politics; but far more were concerned with wealth distribution either in the form of direct pay or through access to positions of authority from which bribes could be elicited.[38] Shawcross also notes the presence of corruption within the FUNCINPEC elite.[39]

In a very real sense, before March 1996, the persistent theme running through accounts of internal opposition to both Ranariddh and Hun Sen from within their own parties is the elimination or undermining of any opposition which challenged either political direction or the flows of patronage and clientelism. Until then, Ranariddh had accepted his 'lower' position in relation to Hun Sen, knowing that he had few palatable alternatives. In a mainly partisan and anti-CPP documentary filmed by a British television team, Ranariddh admitted, with some considerable discomfort, that 'Mr. Hun Sen has outmanoeuvred us all again'.[40] Hun Sen, on the other hand, could 'accept' Ranariddh because the opposition he represented was weak.

In other words, a main threat to the fledgling *status quo*, which itself had been imposed from outside, came not only from the expected parliamentary opposition, but also from within the two parties sharing power in the elected coalition. Sirivudh's arrest confirmed for some that an effort to 'marginalize opponents of the government' – that is, Hun Sen and Ranariddh's coalition – was underway with the complicity of both actors.[41]

Ranariddh's ruthlessness in betraying Sirivudh reflected the degree to which he was prepared to compromise his party's broad position in order to ensure his own locus in the coalition. When Prince Sirivudh was accused of plotting to kill Hun Sen, 'Ranariddh not only acquiesced in the arrest ... but denounced him for plotting to assassinate [Hun Sen] on the flimsiest of evidence'.[42] That arrest, argues Lizée, 'appeared to a large number of observers to have been based more on an attempt to silence him than on the reality of his actions'.[43] Thus were threats to Ranariddh's security in the coalition managed.

While such splits were a clear manifestation of internal dissent, the efforts to manage them clearly suggested a control ideology was in place to preserve the conditions under which elite access to power and the associated advantages could be enjoyed by both Ranariddh and Hun Sen. This in turn would succour their clients. It has been argued earlier that both leaders reflect differing forms of absolutism and intolerance to opposition, whether that opposition takes the form of dissent over policy choices, or whether it represents a challenge to the mechanisms which preserve privilege, as in the case of Sam Rainsy.[44] This attitude towards power is corroborated by responses to intra-party challenges to leadership, for both FUNCINPEC and the CPP.

The false veneer of political stability engendered by such acquiescence and surrender on the part of Ranariddh was challenged by a shift in his policy towards Hun Sen, the CPP, and the notion of his political authority as he viewed it. Two forces combined to generate this shift which, because it altered a *status quo* favourable to the ruling elite, caused the ongoing Khmer political transition (as distinct from the one envisaged in the PPA) to stagger and, ultimately, collapse in July 1997.

Ranariddh's ineffectual challenge to the CPP's domination of political control at grass-roots and intermediary level, in the Ministries and Departmental offices of the bureaucracy and administration, demonstrated his degree of political impotence before Hun Sen. It has been noted earlier that for many good reasons, FUNCINPEC was incapable of assuming effective authority at the grass roots level. Kanharith forcefully argued that

> there was no-one capable of doing the task. We did not want to say, "yes, you can have equal representation at all levels, and then take our people out and have no-one replace them and not do the job that needs to be done"'.[45]

The second force derived from this. Because this conflicted with both Ranariddh's own ambitions for power, and with his party membership's desire for something a little less ambitious but politically representative and capable of creating some degree of wealth and leadership, the *status quo* had to be altered

These concerns found expression at FUNCINPEC's March 1996 Congress. The Congress permitted both concerns noted above to be ventilated. Both Ranariddh, on the one hand, and the party, on the other, could no longer permit such conditions to continue with regard to the CPP.[46] The splits within FUNCINPEC were internally destabilising and externally embarrassing. The control of this problem, and the necessary reintegration of the dissidents, 'was at the cost', argues McAuliff, 'of Ranariddh's adopting a provocative strategy against the CPP'.[47] The March Congress, it was hoped, would unite FUNCINPEC around a campaign through a strategy which involved secret negotiations with the Khmer Rouge, the provocation of the CPP through verbal confrontation, and the simultaneous development of a political and military coalition with Khmer Rouge forces. FUNCINPEC created, in order to compensate its comparative weaknesses with the CPP, the National United Front (NUF: see chapter seven) with the Son Sann faction of the BLDP. This functioned in parallel with their former enemy Sam Rainsy, who started his own Khmer Nation Party (KNP), despite their having been no laws yet passed on new political parties since the National Assembly had been promulgated. In fact, the government declared this illegal in the context of the emerging constitution. To this were added the ranks of the Anlong Veng Khmer Rouge in an anti-CPP coalition.[48]

This was in a sense perhaps the greatest provocation of all (see chapter seven). Ranariddh continuously denied this, even continuing to claim after the July 1997 fighting that he did 'not have any interest to flirt with the Khmer Rouge'.[49] The captured documents from Anlong Veng confirmed the protracted nature of his relations with the constitutionally outlawed guerrillas. The evolution of the NUF, with Ranariddh and FUNCINPEC at the helm, clearly represented clandestine and extra-parliamentary opposition to the CPP and, for that matter, to the BLDP.

However, its creation temporarily sealed some of the leaks within FUNCINPEC and offered it a new sense of unity, hope and direction. This was to be short-lived. In essence, the NUF, with its origins in both internal party dissent and external feebleness before the CPP, attempted to shore up the Royalist Party.

Their various loyalties were well illustrated in the days and weeks following their leader's involuntary exile. The party secretary-general who replaced Sirivudh after the latter resigned, Loy Sim Chheang, took no time in refuting the lack of credibility of resistance to the CPP, and soon thereafter formed the *Sangkum Thmei* party. Provincial Governor Toan Chhay, who had already seen the writing on the wall, escalated internal problems by leading a factional split in FUNCINPEC in April 1997 and creating the National Unity Party.[50] In May 1997, Ranariddh denounced his former ally, 'delivering a fiery oration in Siem Reap, demanding the replacement of ... Toan Chhay as the Province's Governor'. At the same speech, Ranariddh also inflamed his relations with his co-Prime Minister by openly declaring that Hun Sen 'would bring a Communist dictatorship if elected'.[51] Toan Chhay quickly proposed himself as a candidate for the vacant Prime Minister-ship, abandoning Ranariddh. Many others followed such a path.

The decision of the FUNCINPEC party to follow the line they did illustrates well some of the impediments to the type of political transition implied in the export of an alien form of political organisation world-wide. Such notions suggest and anticipate change from single party state systems to those with a multi-party pluralist liberal flavour. However, the Cambodian imperative did not take into consideration, as has been noted earlier, resistance at the elite level to such transitional demands. As long as Ranariddh accepted the terms of the transition as dictated by the CPP's natural domination of Khmer political organisation from elite to mass level, the challenges to the *status quo* could be managed in such a way as not to damage the structures upon which the preservation of elite power rested. As long as such structural impediments to the consequences of this type of imposed transition exist, transition would not proceed in the manner anticipated by the instigators of such change.

A comparison of processes outlined in this chapter and chapter seven initially suggests a contradiction. Earlier, it was argued that Hun Sen would not share power with Ranariddh, but the challenges of Sirivudh and Rainsy created a visible degree of co-operation between Ranariddh and Hun Sen. However, whilst there is a degree of similarity between the two parties' approaches to the 'dissidents', the concern was not a joint one of the nation's well-being or of policy-orientated focus. Rather, the co-operation, or the bilateral agreement over FUNCINPEC's pre-March 1996 approach, was a product of a shared desire to remove obstacles to elite party power and privilege, rather than being more altruistically motivated. Rainsy, and to a lesser degree Sirivudh, independently represented then a check on the strategies and tactics of the CPP and FUNCINPEC with regard to the way in which each leader, and each party, consolidated personal power and access to wealth and privilege. In no sense did the 'joint' approach or policy represent agreement on powersharing; rather, it permitted each leader to reinforce their hold over conditions that permitted their leaders some degree of continued privileges and power.

BLDP

The challenge to political order represented by UNTAC's intervention affected other groups, as well as the main coalition partners. Whilst it is clear that divides or relatively non-confrontational classifications existed prior to political liberalisation, such as those illustrated above in the CPP's case, it is equally clear that the consequences of the re-ordering of political society aggravated already extant political divisions, as well as creating new ones such as in the case of FUNCINPEC. These were managed internally, but were exacerbated over the position party members took on the coalition of CPP and FUNCINPEC.

Thus, in much the same way as Rainsy had represented a threat to the internal, private interests of the coalition, the opposition emanating from the anti-coalition element of the BLDP had to be treated in a similar way.[52] The already extant tension within the BLDP revolved around party President Son Sann's desire to have his son, Son Soubert, in charge after the election.[53] Others rejected such a notion. This split was then manipulated 'to lessen the possibility of dissension within the coalition itself'.[54] In short, the BLDP's capacity to act as a check or balance within the coalition, or even to influence policy, was undermined by the dominant coalition members who then encouraged its reconstruction in a mould favourable to Hun Sen and Ranariddh's interests.

In July 1995, in response to an attempt to have him expelled from the BLDP and his position as Vice President, Ieng Mouly organised his own Congress with the support of Ranariddh and Hun Sen and had himself elected to the leadership of the party. This then marginalised the other element of the BLDP that had been aligned against Ieng Mouly for a number of reasons. In this way, the voices of dissent within the BLDP could be de-legitimised politically by undermining the opposition's position and credibility. The pro-CPP/ Ranariddh element would develop internal support as it was recognised where the source of political patronage would now come from. The process simultaneously reinforced internal disputes; and relocated dissidence to the slothful judicial arena where debate could be decelerated and stymied. Furthermore, the Son Sann element was then persecuted in grenade attacks as it attempted to reform and run its own individual Congress. Lizée observes that the process represented 'a way of discrediting the most vocal opponents of the government' emanating from the BLDP.[55] The coalition's policy on the BLDP split was ordered around opportunism and the desire to continue the relatively stable, but self-serving, political order that had developed through Ranariddh's subservience to Hun Sen.

In the cases of all three major parties, then, a significant characteristic of the period between 1993 and 1997 was the presence of internal divides. In the case of the CPP, resistance revolved around dissatisfaction with the party's position in Khmer politics, as well as with the position of individuals within the party hierarchy. These problems, as the CPP saw them, were coupled to the attendant negation of the capacity to generate personal wealth and private clients to reinforce a power base. In the case of FUNCINPEC, however, the question was more complex and more internally destabilising. Ironically, however, the real issue that pushed FUNCINPEC into a corner of its own making was Ranariddh's desire to preserve coalition stability in order to ensure he personally would not be marginalised by the CPP, or by Hun Sen. This in turn caused resentment and disputes from party representatives with either genuine concerns regarding Cambodia, or with politics that conflicted with Ranariddh's and had therefore to be excluded. For the BLDP, splits which already existed over internal, party issues were exploited by Ranariddh and Hun Sen to both eradicate, as far as was possible, dissent and simultaneously reinforce the stability of the coalition.

Society

The focus in this chapter has been on challenges to the transitional process in the period between the UN elections and the July 1997 fighting. However, there were also forces that in principal buttressed the process of transition embarked upon in 1991. If 1993–1997 can be characterised by a lack of democratic functioning by the political parties in the western sense, it could equally be argued that this period could also be characterised as truly democratic in terms of the social transformation in a participatory context.

Cambodia's transition from a non-participatory, submissive population to one that chose, in secret, to select the Royalists, argues Lizée, saved Cambodia and the UN from a disaster.[56] In the absence of credible societal participation in the UNTAC elections, little of value could have been salvaged from the operation. The eulogies for the polling have been perhaps the only constantly positive attribution in the increasing stream of criticisms of the UNTAC operation.

However, in at least two senses, that moving, dramatic and courageous participation was undermined and its significance qualified. First, the election results were not respected. FUNCINPEC was predominant but was relegated to a joint powersharing position that, in terms of practice, relegated him behind Hun Sun. The peoples' participation generally satisfied conditions for the actual five day process of polling, but in the wider context of accepted results reflecting real conditions, it was less meaningful. It did, of course, satisfy other issues, such as the international community's concern for a 'free and fair' election; this would then permit to be released the massive aid flows so long denied the Khmer population and government. This is used by some to justify the elections in terms of benefits accruing to the population from the process of political transition. However, many NGO representatives and political observers point to the concentration of wealth accumulation in the capital and in fiscal reform and support which rarely seems to extend beyond government, and to the limited benefit accruing to the broader segment of rural Khmer society.

A second critique of participatory significance revolves around the attitude of the elite, who had only begrudgingly participated in the process themselves, to the utility and propriety of universal suffrage. The manner in which it was viewed from within the elite also contributed to the respect in which they held it, which in turn affected their relations with civil society. This applies to all the Khmer leaders, not merely those most regularly demonised as antagonists of western human rights values. Heder, for example, argues that Sihanouk, Sam Rainsy and Ranariddh are characterised by 'deeply illiberal, anti-democratic and antipluralist tendencies'.[57] Vickery and Thayer concur.[58] *The Economist* charged that Prince Norodom Sihanouk is 'a natural autocrat better suited to Paris parties than to presiding over a would-be democracy'.[59] The distinctly undemocratic activities of Cambodia's new 'democrats' are reinforced in the view held of the validity of applying liberal democracy to their country. Some of them are deeply sceptical about the propriety of such an act, and do not respect either their role therein or the commitment made by their population to this western shrine. Sihanouk, for example, claims that

> the majority of the public was not concerned about "liberal democracy" … the reality is that the majority of people judge their government not so much as to how democratic it is, but

how many bridges and hospitals they build and the public services they provide.[60]

He also maintained that

> everything is very special in Cambodia. Nothing is in conformity with liberal democratic principles and even our constitution is one thing and our democracy is another. The Constitution is a paper monument. We can consider it a monument.[61]

His son certainly concurs, taking a semi-Maslowian perspective, in which a pyramidal hierarchy of needs is identified as central to survival. High concepts, such as democracy, would be at the uppermost point of the pyramid, whereas essential concepts, such as rice provision, would constitute the broad base of the triangle, representing the more crucial – at that stage – needs of society. The development specialist and scholar Gilbert Rist cites ancient writings when he interprets and associates Maslow's hierarchy from '*primum vivere, deinde philosophari*: you've got to live before you can philosophise'.[62] Ranariddh, in this tradition surrounded by critics, argues that for the population, despite the unmistakable signal sent through their mass participation in the 1993 and 1998 elections, democracy is something

> to be talked about in idle gossip. When they [the people] have sufficient food, shelter, education, and basic amenities, then democracy can be preached and installed in abundance ... the western brand of democracy and freedom of the press is not applicable to Cambodia.[63]

In a very real sense, elite politics in Cambodia can be interpreted as a charade crafted by politicians who have been forced to embrace democracy under external tutelage and surveillance. That supervision, observation and punishment when the stated line is transcended or ignored is an ongoing process, dominated by governments which firmly believe, for right or for wrong, that Cambodia's transition to western democracy is a necessary precursor to development, globalisation and political and economic integration. They in fact reflect the reverse of Ranariddh's position in their assumptions regarding political and economic liberalisation and globalisation.

The search for the greatest degree of absolute power was both facilitated and limited by the UNTAC operation and the benefits accruing from an 'acceptable' form of democratic transition. Thus, for the exiled opposition, the elections permitted access to the structures of power in Cambodia; but unlike in the Khmer tradition, the system installed in Cambodia came with elite responsibilities towards the electorate. The elite Khmer view of this relationship does not necessarily reflect the western values both explicit and implicit in the 1991 intervention strategy. In Khmer political culture, power can be used in arbitrary fashion to cement the interests not of the population, but of its leaders.

Thus, although high levels of grass-roots participation have accompanied both Cambodian elections, the meaning of this in the broader context of elite political culture is limited. Lao Mong Hay argues that

> even though the significance and value of the [population's] role in a democracy is provided for in the present Constitution ... it is subsumed to personal rivalry in the elite and violent political instability on a number of fronts. Ranariddh and Hun Sen do not like the institutions which may undermine their ability to use power in a self-serving or arbitrary manner.[64]

It seems to confirm that Cambodian political problems 'have to be worked out within the framework of its own cultural, social and other values. Clearly, superimposition of alien values and forms does not resolve this issue'.[65]

The elections of 1993 and 1998 reflect a tension between the need to access political power for the elites, the absence of institutionalised and formal parliamentary opposition, and the lack of political mores and values that make them accountable to the electorate. The role of Cambodia's population is continually subsumed to, and simultaneously is forced to serve, the narrower interests of elites attempting to access or preserve positions of power from which they can create their own fiefdoms of political power and wealth, and from which they reward followers. This system is different more by degree than character from the older Angkorean power structures. Whereas then many were enslaved to serve political and regal authority, the more obvious shackles have disappeared, and have been replaced by a broader model of patronage and clientelism through which more, but certainly not the majority, benefit in comparison with their thirteenth century predecessors. Although now imbued with 'democratic rights' by the Paris Peace Accords, and although such rights are enshrined in the Cambodian Constitution, the effect of broad participation, while appearing to be a transition from an old order to something different, is limited by the barely-transformed elite political culture, and the severity of contest for the fruits of power and the consequences of their denial.

IX

Recreating Elite Stability, July 1997 to July 1998

This period, not unlike others in Cambodia's recent history, is contentious in terms of the fighting which began it and the elections that concluded it. However, both represent further stages in Cambodia's political transition from a single party, vaguely Communist free-market state to a relatively authoritarian ruling coalition via a superficial democracy. Whereas it was the intended outcome of the UNTAC operation and the Paris Accords that Cambodia would 'progress' to a multi-party, democratic parliamentary coalition, this stage of the transition is perhaps better characterised as a shift from an unstable competitive coalition to a stable but non-competitive powersharing body. Even this requires further qualification, insofar as the degree to which power is meaningfully shared is clearly limited by the minority parties' inability to representatively fulfil such an undertaking. Whilst appearing to operate in an open democratic mode, the latter offers 'acceptable' resistance to the formerly ruling elite, giving a superficial impression of powersharing. In fact, at the elite level, no such agreement or function exists beyond the synthetic titles of elite 'opposition' in that coalition.

If the July 1997 fighting was an indigenous solution to Khmer political conflicts, its aftermath appeared to recreate some of the conditions of relative political stability that had preceded Ranariddh's ill-fated attempt to seize more power. A form of stability was restored. Many much-hated road-blocks were removed and there was a reduction in indiscriminate shooting. Some NGO workers became less concerned about the security of some of their Khmer counterpart staff, and there was a recognisable reduction in banditry even in the countryside. A generally more conducive atmosphere descended on

Phnom Penh and the countryside in which the NGO workers and their Khmer colleagues lived and worked.[1] Curtis adds that

> after months of heightened tension, the July coup [sic] permitted a return to normalcy. The post-UNTAC coalition government was restored, the National Assembly was reconvened, and the business of government was conducted with renewed dedication and less overt partyism. Internal security was also improved throughout the country as a result of Hun Sen's eight-point security programme.[2]

At the time of his departure, the then Australian Ambassador Tony Kevin claimed that such improvements

> could not have been achieved under the former coalition government.... Development projects [were] stalled because of disagreement between the parties ... government departments were greatly handicapped by the constant jockeying for position between the two sides.[3]

All was not entirely rosy, however. According to western and some Khmer human rights groups, the number of specifically political killings did not halt with the end to the fighting. Several UN reports attempted to document what were alleged to have been over 60 unlawful killings that they had connected to the CPP. Human rights organisations and the western media generally took the position that Hun Sen originated the fighting and that Ranariddh was a victim of the pre-meditated acts of a 'strongman', as the media referred to him. They argue that these killings represented the clinical eradication of political opposition by the CPP. Peang-Meth claims, along with numerous human rights institutions, that such reports

> presented information collected and verified by the [United Nations Centre for Human Rights – UNCHR] concerning 41, and possibly up to 60, politically-motivated "extra-judicial executions committed by security personnel in their custody".[4]

At times, however, such allegations proved unreliable and embarrassing for the UN and for Mary Robinson, then High Commissioner for Human Rights. After a meeting between Robinson and Hun Sen, the latter 'presented to local and international correspondents four witnesses, including three persons who ... [were] reportedly killed in the 5–6 July incident'.[5] Allegations were also made regarding the whereabouts of Pen Sovan, the country's first Prime Minister after

Pol Pot was ousted. He too came out of hiding to reveal himself alive.[6] Despite a dearth of reportage covering the particular incident, the UNCHR's credibility was seriously undermined, but the incident did not really raise the questions it might have done regarding the reliability of such reports more broadly.

Concerns over reliability are compounded by those who have taken the position that some – not all – of the killings that did occur were settlements of other disputes, for example that between the FUNCINPEC and CPP police chiefs Ho Sok and Hok Lundy.[7] Most claim that the latter murdered the former; however, Khieu Kanharith claimed that this was 'not possible', adding that he 'was with Hok Lundy at Hun Sen's house at the time'.[8] This has not been substantiated from other sources. However, it is quite clear that many of the militia, police and army are not under the tight control of particular leaders within the CPP. This mirrors the manner in which village leaders often act independently of orders from the elite, especially where their personal, political and economic security is at risk. The actions of some of these bodies were clearly divorced from political motives relating directly to the individual leadership of the nation. Vickery contends that although some of the military went on a violent rampage and some civilians were killed as a result, this was more a product of hatred against rich individuals by groups of extremely poor and rarely paid soldiers than it was of a political murder campaign.[9]

Thus, although the summer of 1997 will be most persistently remembered for violence and an inaccurately defined 'coup d'etat', a degree of stability characterised the aftermath as resistance to the freshly forming political elite diminished. A number of issues also became clearer as the year progressed.

'Affected' Democracy and the Elite's Challenge

First, the armed confrontation was part of Cambodia's ongoing transition, but not immediately to democracy. The outbreak of inter-factional war in Phnom Penh represented another stage in the evolution of elite Khmer political culture. This was the recognition that opposition and contest of a political nature were here to stay; but that the relationship between sides was only to be conducted in a specific way favourable to the dominant group or groups. It also emerged from this that the absence of opposition to the ruling elite, in individual party/leader terms or in terms of the governing coalition, produced more stability than when dissent flared.

Recreating Elite Stability, July 1997 to July 1998

Cambodian leaders, effectively under a form of international political and media siege since 1991, took things into their own hands to settle the unresolved conflict transferred from the battlefield to Parliament by the Paris Peace Agreement. The issue was, and had been since the early challenges to Sihanouk after independence from the French protectorate, the question of a challenge to traditional authority from within. This was, by extension, a challenge to the clients of traditional authority; and to the benefits that accrue from such privileged positions within the elite and their supporters. As has been noted earlier, no Khmer leader since independence, whether regal, communist, republican or former peasant, has accepted without resistance a challenge to the absolutism of their authority. As pressures from without have diluted the tradition, the CPP's reluctant acceptance of political challenge has been the most benign in comparison with antecedent. The imposed transition did not take these issues into account when they telescoped over two centuries of western liberal tradition and experience into two years of social experimentation, for a vulnerable and poor country with primary ideals governed less by specific human rights and more by survival through patronage and loyalty.

Another consequence became clear. The framework defining the inter-party relations had originally derived from the CPP's position of power through their active resistance to Ranariddh's destabilising strategies. However, after July 1997, that framework was determined by the CPP's coalition partners who passively declined to escalate opposition to the dominant party, and recognised the degree to which they could express opinion and implement policies with which the CPP disagreed. 'Acceptable' conditions had existed before the consequences of Ranariddh's escalation of rivalry. Then, the Prince had, against the interests of some of his loyalists and political clients, acquiesced to the CPP's domination of political life. After March 1996, however, the framework for relations changed as Ranariddh challenged the terms and conditions by which the CPP had accepted his presence (see chapter eight). It became ever clearer that a key cause of the severity of such treatment of dissent has its origins in the absence of institutionalised political opposition, an issue which this text has addressed at various points. Thus, certain conditions had been more clearly identified to a broader range of observers under which relative political stability could be anticipated. These conditions included, perhaps most importantly, the absence of opposition to the interests of the ruling elite, in individual party/leader terms before

July 1997, or in terms of the more pliable governing coalition thereafter.

The July armed political intercourse established beyond reasonable doubt that there were, to appropriate a term used by Chomsky in a different context, political 'bounds of the expressible'.[10] That is, the terms of reference for relations between the members of the coalition, and equally, between members of parliament opposing the coalition when they existed, were established by the dominant (CPP) party. As long as those terms were adhered to, a limited expression of opposition would be tolerated. When the terms were breached by FUNCINPEC's importation of weapons and agitation with elements of the Khmer Rouge such as Khieu Samphan, it threatened the interests preserved in the *status quo ante*. The debate would then be relocated away from private arbitration and conciliation, to one settled perhaps by guns or tanks. Clearly, of course, opposition was not muted entirely. The media remained relatively active but often cowed somewhat by the death of one of their number.[11] However, after July 1997, some of the main challengers, such as Ranariddh and Rainsy, opposed from overseas. Those who opposed from within were considered exceptionally brave to confront the CPP, or even to refer to the fighting as a 'coup'. However, most opposition within Cambodia knew the boundaries and was relatively muted compared to the dissent expressed between early 1996 and July 1997.

The 'bounds of the expressible' hypothesis is clearly reflected in the question of who was included in the coalition government after the fighting ceased. One of the principal arguments against describing the events of July 1997 as a 'coup' is that the political party of the exiled Prince not only remained in position and relative power; but it appointed, in a democratic vote, a replacement from the remaining ranks of FUNCINPEC.[12] That the vote did not achieve parliamentary quorum was not a product of a lack of a democratic process in the vote. Rather, it was a product of many FUNCINPEC Assembly representatives having fled. A politically powerful FUNCINPEC representative, or one who, like Ranariddh, was a threat to stability as defined by the interests of the powersharing parties, would not be permitted to retake the party helm if the above hypothesis regarding acceptability and boundaries of expression holds true.

Ranariddh's replacement was Ung Huot, formerly Foreign Minister in the FUNCINPEC party structure, and a returnee from Australia. His appointment represented a return to the early days of largely compliant 'opposition' for mutual elite gain. In 1994, it had become apparent to Ranariddh that to achieve the degree of political security he sought, he would have to acquiesce to the dominant position of the CPP elite.

After Ranariddh's departure, Ung Huot's strategy returned FUNCINPEC to the less confrontational pre-March 1996 path to preserve political security, to ride the tide of political power and to be able to enjoy the benefits that this entailed. When he became Education Minister in 1993 after the elections, Ung Huot was acclaimed by elements of the Western media and by many members of UNTAC. He was viewed as having 'appropriate' credentials, in the sense that he had lived in a democratic country (Australia) and had developed democratic values and could be expected to tow the western line.[13] Much later, however, Ung Huot submissively confided that, with reference to his relations with Hun Sen, all was well. 'We very rarely meet', he stated. 'We have little need to. We have stability and co-operation. He is a good leader and I intend to continue this coalition [after the 1998 elections]'.[14] This echoes Hun Sen's comment regarding mutual co-operation with Ranariddh as far back as the first coalition in late 1993 (see chapter seven). Heeger, a political scientist writing in the 1970s on political development, identifies this 'gains' process as one whereby cohesion may be 'simply the result of the ... elites' concern for short-run material gain'. Heeger continues that such associations when institutionalised, for instance, in a coalition, 'serve as allocation centres, generating jobs, loans, economic aid, favourable administration of laws and so forth'.[15] Huot refers to the July fighting as a lose-lose situation, because not only did FUNCINPEC briefly lose a leader and his immediate dependants their privileges, but also the country lost stability and much development aid. Ung Huot declared that

> in the modern days, we talk not about lose-lose, but about win-win. Everyone will be able to share in the government, so everyone wins; there will not be the losers and the price for the losers like there was in the past.[16]

Thus, the association of the remnants of FUNCINPEC with the dominant elite, in Ung Huot's view, facilitated that access to positions of privilege which FUNCINPEC had sought and been denied. The CPP were winners, in Huot's vernacular, as were those FUNCINPEC who chose to accept diminished political power in return for augmented personal economic licence. In this interpretation of 'economic licence', the 1993 post-electoral management of political positions shows precedent. As has been noted (above), certain positions generated more 'opportunities' than others, and were more prized and therefore cost more to buy.[17]

The new political order was defined in terms of denying the past and creating a future which would ensure that many would participate in government by a form of mutual consent dispensed primarily by certain members of the elite and accepted with gratitude by other self-serving interests. When asked about the difference in relations between Ranariddh and Hun Sen, on the one hand, and Ung Huot and Hun Sen, on the other, the newly empowered first Prime Minister declared brusquely:

> that man is Norodom Ranariddh and my name is Ung Huot. To answer your question, different personality, different name. I should not worry too much about Prince Ranariddh. Better to leave this and talk about me. You know Prince Ranariddh; and now you should know me. I was the one who tried to tell him to work together with Hun Sen. But he did not listen to me. I work with Hun Sen and there is peace and stability.[18]

Politicians in Ung Huot's 'new order', claimed the new first Prime Minister,

> will not think of political power in the same way as we have done. And the price will not be so high to pay. Political competition will not be the same, because in a coalition, everyone can win.[19]

In other words, traditional mono-group (the King, or a single political party, or a President) absolutism will be replaced by accommodation of opposition in such a manner as to permit the broadened elite to enjoy the benefits of power, as long as they accept the limitations implicit in the CPP presence to what they might seek to achieve. The issues that raise contention are no longer raised, and the dominant actors reward their opponents by permitting them to retain limited positions of power and patronage which would be a vast improvement over the consequences of unacceptable opposition, the most important of which is exclusion.

The recognition that only certain outcomes were permissible was a function of an externally created tension. On the one hand, there was external pressure for democracy coupled to a certain willingness on the part of the population to vote. On the other hand, there was elite resistance to loss of power and the effects of exclusion which would ensure continued access to some degree of privilege, wealth and the capacity to support clans for the continuity of the elite. Ung Huot's approach to joint, non-confrontational powersharing removed the source of tension by eliminating the impediments to the CPP's consolidation and growth interests whilst simultaneously guaranteeing a limited form of access to the remaining FUNCINPEC elite and its clients as a reward. In so doing, a form of relative domestic stability ensued.

To ensure this stability was preserved required the inclusion of weak, compliant and non-confrontational politicians in the coalition. Equally, however, it required the exclusion of the opposite. This necessarily entailed the maintenance of Ranariddh's exile, which galled some members of the international community, especially meddling band-wagoneers such as US Senator Dana Rohrbacher. Hun Sen's conditions for his return were unacceptable to the Prince, and an effective stalemate came into force with Cambodian and international mediation revolving around a series of efforts to have Ranariddh either reinstalled at best, or, at worst, returned to the country safely. Hun Sen declared that if the King pardoned his son, then the Prince could participate in the election. This would then negate the 'criminality' of his past, which would otherwise be a legal barrier to electoral participation, according to the Constitution. However, the King had to be asked for a Royal Pardon by the 'criminal'; Ranariddh naturally viewed such an act as a tacit admission of guilt. Lao Mong Hay declared that Hun Sen's aim was to 'prevent [Ranariddh] from taking part in the election or else wait so late that there is no time for him to campaign'.[20]

Fragmentation and Reformation: the Opposition

A third post-July pattern was the disintegration and recreation of extra-coalition, parliamentary and quasi-parliamentary opposition. Within the coalition, the remaining opposition to the CPP already exhibited a number of signs of implosion. Whilst the fact that Ung Huot ambled along with the coalition in the guise of FUNCINPEC President is clearly a sign of dissent towards Ranariddh, the former survived mainly because he was little more than an acquiescent compliant who would work with Hun Sen for the status and prestige.[21] This led to dismay within the pro-Ranariddh group of FUNCINPEC, and caused yet further splintering of the party. One member was prompted to declare that 'FUNCINPEC has been chopped into little pieces' as the FUNCINPEC National Assembly Chair, Loy Sim Chheang, announced the formation of his independent *Sangkum Thmei* (New Society) party.[22] Furthermore, in February 1998, Ung Huot, despite leading FUNCINPEC, denounced Ranariddh and formed his own *Reastr Niyum* (Populist) party. The party previously known as FUNCINPEC was divided three ways, and the same competition for party electoral privileges and advantages threatened a number of bitter, if short-lived, legal cases. In total, by the July 1998 elections, FUNCINPEC had splintered into eight bodies. Apart from Sam Rainsy, Ranariddh himself and Loy Sim Chheang, Kong Mony would form, after falling out with the Sam Rainsy Party, the Khmer Angkor Party; Nguon Soeur would canvass with the Khmer Citizen Party; and Khieu Rada would lead the Khmer Unity Party.

Whilst FUNCINPEC came undone, other parties, elements of which were opposed to the CPP's hold on power, were also demonstrating signs of internal collapse. The Buddhist Liberal Democratic Party (BLDP), for example, suffered internal splits that threatened to marginalise its capacity to oppose or check the CPP, while from beyond Parliament, Sam Rainsy's constitutionally contested Khmer Nation Party (KNP), formed in exile, was also sundered by internal strife.

An extension of the processes in the period 1993-1997 is also clearly identifiable in the period between the summers of 1997 and 1998. In the first period, a central and defining characteristic of domestic political discourse was the internal splintering of opposition to the ruling coalition. It may be recalled for example that a split existed within the BLDP. This was between Son Sann and Ieng Mouly, the latter of whom was regarded by many as pro-CPP, the former of whom leaned closer to FUNCINPEC. Similarly, Sam Rainsy was expelled first from FUNCINPEC, and then from the Assembly, and formed the KNP as Ranariddh fell into disrepute within his own party over a number of issues. In the second period, between 1997 and 1998, the final stages of internal fragmentation were over ownership of party names. Two cases in particular illustrate this problem and, more significantly, the erosion of cohesive or ordered opposition to a dominant elite.

Sam Rainsy, formerly FUNCINPEC Minister of Finance, was ejected from that party because he challenged the interests of Hun Sen and Ranariddh; and challenged the popularity of Ranariddh within his party. After forming the KNP, Rainsy continued his tendency towards vociferous and outspoken opposition to the government. He vacillated over support for or opposition to both Ranariddh and Hun Sen at different stages in the evolving pre-1998 electoral environment. One consequence of this was the unilateral declaration of party Presidency by Sam Rainsy's deputy, Kong Mony, in lieu of Rainsy after he became disaffected by Rainsy's unpredictable stance. Kong was known to be pro-CPP and demanded his right to retain the party name and logo. This was important because the KNP was by now associated with Sam Rainsy who would be more popular in elections than the less well known Kong Mony; but the KNP steering committee voted 28-0 to expel the latter.[23] The case went to court.

The behaviour of the Judge appointed to assess his case for legal ownership of the KNP name is illustrative of the problem faced by opposition Parties, and the manner in which the ruling coalition suspended processes which might enhance political transition towards a system which challenged or restrained it. The wrangle over ownership of the name led Rainsy to fall foul of the CPP-dominated Court system in mid-February 1998. Judge Thang Ol failed to turn up at the appointed time, and later claimed that the case was not ready for hearing at trial, despite the hearing having been granted earlier. Some observers in Phnom Penh took the more extreme view that the Courts and Judges were deliberately delaying hearings in order to extend the due date past the final deadline for party registration, thus reducing the number of Parties contesting the election. However, no evidence was presented to prove such allegations. The absence of a timely legal conclusion to the matter forced Sam Rainsy to surrender the fight and re-name his group the Sam Rainsy Party (SRP). However, the issue was not settled in favour of pro-CPP Kong Mony, who had to rename his party the Khmer Angkor Party.[24] This suggests strongly that the Judges involved were probably not as influenced by the CPP as many considered; or that the CPP did not lean on the judiciary to execute its political will. Whilst the legal wrangling and possible inducements from the CPP reflected issues of alleged legal partisanship and patronage respectively, they also reflected the eradication of political opposition through a combination of political immaturity on the part of the opposition and justifiable exploitation of weakness and disorder by the CPP. This would happen in any other country.

A second example of the fracturing and reforming of political opposition was the aggravation of the well-known divide within the

BLDP extant since 1995. The BLDP also had a political history pre-dating the current legislature. Its initial President, Son Sann, was a founder of the Democrat Party in the 1940s. He was a Prime Minister in Sihanouk's government, and fought with the Royalists against the CPP's PRPK forerunners in the 1980s. He represented those interests in the Supreme National Council that attempted to facilitate that stage of Cambodia's political transition from a form of relatively benign authoritarianism to a superficial non-constitutional democracy. Despite this seeming *samakki*, or solidarity, the party split in 1995 over disagreements between Son Sann and Ieng Mouly (see chapter eight and above). One element of the party hierarchy favoured working with Hun Sen's CPP, whereas another favoured FUNCINPEC. The disagreement caused serious rifts in policy formulation, but became a legal issue when, in a similar fashion to the KNP split (above), each side to the dispute claimed the party name and its logo. A Phnom Penh Court of Appeal ruled in favour of Mouly's claim to possession of the party logo; Son Sann's faction of the BLDP became the (Grandfather) Son Sann Party. Eventually, the party split again, as Thach Reng formed the Light of Liberty Party.

These are clear examples of the apparent erosion of resistance to the post-July 1997 ruling FUNCINPEC-CPP coalition. However, both parties successfully reconstituted themselves, recreating political opposition and running reasonably successful election campaigns. Thus, although their 'ownership' was contested, the challenges forced the metamorphosis of those parties into new entities which eventually offered even greater recognition to the original leaders of those parties and therefore probably represented a significant challenge and threat to the ruling coalition's primacy. In other words, although the internal divides had negative consequences in terms of organised opposition to the governing coalition, the manner in which they were eventually remade ensured that those parties represented a potentially more significant threat to the CPP's re-election efforts than they had before.

Democratic Institutions

The necessity for the party name changes was in part a product of a fourth characteristic of the year preceding the 1998 elections. The process of holding elections required constitutionally determined institutions to be created or, where existing, to be used impartially, and for a neutral political environment to be ensured in which a free and fair election could be managed reliably and safely. The new institutions, and their members, were controversial elements both within and without Cambodia. Many argued that, instead of being neutral facilitators of democratic pluralism, organs such as the National Election Committee (NEC) and the Constitutional Council (CC), which would rule on alleged infringements of the conditions guaranteed in the Constitution itself, were state appendages operating to ensure the elections would secure the return of the CPP. They were, it was alleged by some, neither fair, impartial, nor Constitutional. Sam Rainsy, in response to the alleged bias, temporarily withdrew his Khmer Nation Party in February 1998 as a statement of concern through a stage-managed protest.[25] Established institutions, such as the judiciary, were also accused of being vehicles not for democracy, but for the reinforcement of authoritarian hegemony. The party splits noted above were an example of these forces converging and conspiring, it was argued by some, to derail the opposition before the elections and ensure, as far as possible, a relatively uncontested election by creating conditions which would exclude various opposition parties' participation in the polls.

Finally, the elections themselves, perhaps as contentious as their UN-sponsored predecessors, reflected the conditions under which political transition could occur domestically, and the limitations to the character of that transition. As a climax and testing ground for Cambodia's externally initiated and internally affected transition to a 'liberal democracy', they demonstrated clearly how the elite and the organs which serve it have manipulated the enforced conditions of transition into those which are acceptable in the sense that they alter as little as possible the premises of more traditional Khmer elite political organisation.

The progress of democratic institutions since UNTAC's departure has been uneven. Their political evolution has been in part determined by the degree to which the elite is prepared to permit them to develop. In this sense, both the existence and character of such institutions reflect the interests of the ruling coalition, undermining the very essence of neutrality to which they nominally purport. An example of such political partisanship is the manner in which human rights organisations sometimes enjoy popular support; but are often impeded in their investigations by the absence of co-operation on the part of the government. This was most obviously the case with the March 1997 grenade attacks in Phnom Penh aimed at supporters of Sam Rainsy's KNP; and with the alleged execution of over 40 FUNCINPEC members over the July 1997 Phnom Penh fighting.[26]

The Media

One organ that may have had some effect on impartially exposing the limitations on democratic transition, and weaknesses and deficiencies in the modern political system, has fallen foul of a fundamental paradox. The media in Cambodia has flowered since UNTAC's period, and despite periods of government-initiated repression, is viewed by some as one of the most free in Asia. The sheer weight and volume of daily, weekly and fortnightly journals of extremely variable quality encourages such views. However, the Khmer media is far from the impartial check and balance it ostensibly represents in Western European or North American democracies. In fact, the Khmer media is a variant of conventional political opposition insofar as such a concept exists at all.

In other words, rather than acting impartially, it constitutes extra-parliamentary opposition. Much of the 'reporting' is vitriolic and slanderous, with regular references to penis size or impotency of various political or Royal leaders. It therefore generates its own problems as the government refuses to accept such a role for the media in a constitutional democracy; a view regularly trumpeted by both Hun Sen and Ung Huot. In the past, such extra-Parliamentary political confrontation has led to newspaper offices being shut down and proprietors and journalists being murdered or disappeared.[27] It is a further example of the unusual nature opposition takes in Cambodia; and of the strong measures taken against such confrontations by the government.

The National Election Commission (NEC)

Political transition to democracy requires the development and impartial use of other institutions. The late-forming NEC was riddled with accusations of corruption and political and constitutional illegitimacy in the media. Many claimed that the body tasked with the oversight and implementation of polling, from the choice and location of voting sites to the provision of ballot papers, was partisan. There are some signs that the government manipulated, for example, the election of the indigenous NGO representative of that Committee. For example, of those seeking representation, the field was dominated by pro-CPP Chea Chamroeun, who faced pro-democracy activist, and opponent of the CPP, Dr. Lao Mong Hay of the Khmer Institute for Democracy. Senior CPP figures and potential voters attended a 'loyalty lunch' at which Chea Chamreoun handed out hundred dollar bills to seal his bid for the NEC seat. He claimed not to have been alone, arguing that others also offered gifts and money, 'but they paid for only a small banquet'.[28] In other words, they were less wealthy and could therefore afford less largesse. This differs more by degree and less in character from the Western model of vote capture. One key difference is that it is less open in the West and therefore more prone to accusations of corruption. It is still, however, effectively a similar model of vote capturing. It is far from unusual to offer 'incentives' to generate allies, and it is little different from the procedure used to generate accord within the pro-Western Gulf 'allies' in 1990.[29] Lao Mong Hay had no such patronage or finance, and was not elected.

Further underscoring such allegations of impropriety and partiality was the dispute over political party representation on the NEC. Because both BLDP and FUNCINPEC were internally split, they fielded two candidates each for the Committee. But as the factions favoured by the court judgements, even when incomplete, were pro-CPP, the compilation of the NEC became biased towards the CPP, when in fact it should have been a wholly neutral body dedicated to impartial preparation. Many observers feel keenly that this particular institution served the CPP more than any other contender as a result of its politically biased structure. However, structural manipulation of the technical polling and counting process was not visible. The NEC, even if it was deliberately biased, or if the opposition simply was not able to organise and mobilise appropriately, did not affect visibly or significantly the passage of the election.

The 1998 Elections

The second multi-party, universal plebiscite in Cambodia's history took place on 26 July 1998. It was uniquely different from that of 1993; yet it bore remarkable similarities also. It differed in terms of party participation, which almost doubled. Yet the mass participation in 1998 stayed as enthusiastically high as its precedent. In 1998, the entire management and organisation of the polling was Khmer; previously it had been almost exclusively UNTAC in complexion. However, in terms of functioning, it differed little. Almost all areas were covered, and there were again many calls of irregularities. Finally, both elections suffered from a fundamental element of elite political culture and character. The transition from the vanquished to the victors was first challenged, and then led to violence and outright rejection. In both cases, the CPP took the lead position; however, in the first case it manipulated the political environment after the polling. In the second, it won fairly in the polling but enjoyed some institutional advantages in the pre-electoral period. Ultimately, the settling of the trauma and consequences of enforced political transition was more long term in 1998 than it had been in 1993.

Table 2: 1998 elections, confirmed provisional results, 7 September.

	CPP	FUNCINPEC	Sam Rainsy Party	Others
Votes	2,030,802	1,554,374	699,653	617,654
No. of provinces/23	18	4	1	nil
No. of seats/122	64	43	15	nil

The CPP won the elections. As well as producing a different winner from the 1993 polls, the overall results in 1998 were quite different in other ways. Last time, FUNCINPEC won overall in 9 provinces out of 20, taking 58 seats. This time, Hun Sen's CPP won overall in 18 out of 23 Provinces (three have been added since 1993 in the wake of Khmer Rouge defections), giving the CPP 64 seats against FUNCINPEC's 43. This is according to a contested system of seat allocation that allocates remaining votes to parties proportionally. Critics of the applied model claimed the CPP-influenced election institutions and the Constitutional Council (CC) deliberately changed a system which, it was alleged, had been agreed in advance by the main parties. It was alleged that subterfuge had been involved on the part of the NEC and the CC and, by association, the CPP in altering the chosen model without informing the other parties.

This manipulation, it was alleged, gave the CPP a greater majority than they would have had under the system their opposition claims the NEC chose before the elections. The original system, it was claimed, would have reduced the CPP's seats and increased the oppositions' to the point that FUNCINPEC and the Sam Rainsy Party might have been able to form a coalition and eject the CPP from office.[30] Most of the complaints regarding this originated from the losers. However, it was clear that if subterfuge had been involved, the originators could not have known which parties would benefit most. Indeed, all parties would benefit to a degree, but that degree would not be known until the overall results were known. A Cambodian constitution specialist,

Raoul Jennar, argued that 'the formula ... could have benefited any important political party and it benefited indeed, for example, FUNCINPEC in Kompong Cham Province and [the] Sam Rainsy Party in Siem Reap Province'.[31] Therefore 'there was no manipulation' and such claims were nonsense.

The NEC and CC continued to reject both the arguments concerning the choice of seating model, and the various claims and allegations of irregularities, the vast majority of which were unsubstantiated. Although many claims were submitted, 'all those investigated [by September 1998] had proved to be admissible technical irregularities, and not evidence of any calculated pattern of political chicanery'.[32] US Republican Stephen Solarz, never a noted supporter of the CPP, declared that 'the opposition's allegations appear to be characteristic of administrative inefficiencies and minor mistakes that are frequently found even in advanced democracies'.[33] Critics of the NEC and the Constitutional Council demanded that they investigate further, which the two institutions refused to do, to uproar from the media and other vested interest parties. By comparison and in contrast, about two months later, similar allegations of impropriety were made against Britain's version of the NEC. However, in that case, the oversight body's refusal to respond to allegations went virtually unchallenged.[34]

Only one other party came close out of the remaining 36 competing. Sam Rainsy lead the SRP to 15 seats. Ung Huot's *Sangkum Thmei* party embarrassingly failed to win a single seat nation-wide, despite a pre-electoral campaign revolving around shooting criminals after one offence, and building more public toilets (Phnom Penh had but one, near the Royal Palace, inaugurated by Huot; it was flattened after he lost Office). His sense of realism was also revealed when, after getting less than one percent of the vote, he demanded a recount.[35]

Although the contest for power staggered on in Cambodia until the end of September 1998, the dominant CPP won a majority of votes and seats. Many expressed surprise that Hun Sen's former ruling party had turned the tables so convincingly. Because Hun Sen was unpopular with many outside his country, most foreign Cambodia watchers suggested prior to the polls that the only way Hun Sen could win would be by subverting the electoral process. Some even took to disingenuously claiming to have expertise in Khmer politics and electoral procedure, and attempted to discredit the electoral process. For example, an article by Elizabeth Bork originally appeared in the

Washington Post and was reprinted in the *Cambodia Daily*.[36] That author anointed herself with 'electoral expertise' and visited a polling station in which, shortly after lunch, the percentage of voters who had voted was marked in chalk on a board. Bork declared to her readers that this clearly meant the CPP was fabricating attendance figures that would be otherwise impossible to discern. This was nonsense. Any polling station chief could easily extrapolate that figure by subtracting the number of people who had voted (their names were ticked off on a list as they voted) from the voter registration list. From that a percentage could quickly be arrived at in an honest, reliable and not at all sinister fashion.[37]

The majority of representatives from the range of international observer groups, in contrast, agreed that systemic fraud, ballot rigging or counting irregularities were either accidental or, if interpreted as partisan, then on a scale which could not have meaningfully affected the actual outcome.[38] The issue became ever more contested in the months following the polls and through the street fighting in Phnom Penh in mid-September 1998. However, the difference between the first two parties was close to half a million votes. Few believe that irregularities on such a scale would have got past all the observers, national and international. Sven Linder, head of the EU Observation Team, recognised some problems with the NEC, the post-electoral work of which was not 'up to the quality of work displayed before'. However, he argued that

> the NEC and the Constitutional Council could have shown a more open and flexible attitude towards the handling of complaints ... but if those complaints had been handled, [nothing] would have been revealed that would have changed the basic conclusions.... Our observers have seen nothing which [suggests] the will of the voters has been tampered with.[39]

Lakhan Mehrotra, the UN Secretary General's personal representative in Cambodia, concurred, arguing that 'in a short span of time the NEC did what UNTAC did in 1993'.[40] Theo Noel, senior advisor to the NEC and clearly impartial as well as highly experienced, declared the allegations were 'groundless'.[41]

Despite the breadth of acceptance of the election results, from a range of bodies and individuals (other than the losers, of course), a headline *Far Eastern Economic Review* unilaterally and unreasonably declared the elections 'unfree and unfair' following the polling. A clear degree of arrogance, buttressed from a position of authority for which the FEER is normally justifiably credited, may inevitably have led some of its less involved readers to assume wrongdoing on such a scale as to invalidate the election. This was a far cry from the truth. A number of reasonable and reliable explanations for the CPP's victory exist. The following section reviews the 'standard view' of why the CPP won, and then criticises each perspective.

First, it is unreasonable to argue that all the alleged and real misdeeds were the responsibility of a carefully planned strategy emanating from the apex of the CPP to the base. Few individuals in history have ever wielded such power; there have always been competing or parallel interests that dilute such power to one degree or another. It is clear that individuals in any political party do not always follow the leaders exact line. Often they may take their own initiatives after interpreting either their leader's, or their own, ambitions.

Despite such common sense, many had predicted that the polls would be rife with various forms of harassment and intimidation, based on the view that such acts had characterised the pre-electoral strategy of the CPP. Hun Sen stood accused of wrong doings regarding the creation of inappropriate conditions for the elections. However, whilst it is undoubtedly the case that such conditions and events existed to some degree, it is unreasonable and unreliable to blame them all on the elite, or on Hun Sen. As was noted above, the centrality of political power to wider self-preservation and self-aggrandisement applies to most elements and ranks of the governing coalition. Thus, individuals acted independently of the coalition hierarchy to preserve positions lower down the scale they already enjoyed, and which were threatened by local level opposition activism.

For example, a village chief in a small commune on Pochentong Rd, three miles outside Phnom Penh centre, did not admit personally to such misdemeanours. However, he explicitly stated that civilians, police and military were widely known to act in a manner which, while accepted as criminal, was permissible when family or other social groups were threatened by damaging change.[42] Given the unanticipated electoral outcome, and the various questions it and the pre-electoral period raised, the debate in Phnom Penh tended to revolve around the context in which the elections occurred, rather than practice on polling day, with some exceptions.

A second explanation for the CPP's victory has been linked to this and the assumptions that underpin it. This was that the CPP could not win because they were not popular. This position was enhanced when internal CPP surveys reflected the same doubts; those surveys assumed great credibility. According to Frieson, a clear CPP strategy existed involving the use of Grass Roots Strengthening Teams. Their first task was 'to assess the extent of popular support for the CPP through informal public opinion surveys...'.[43] The outcomes raised serious doubts about the CPP's continued political viability. One survey in Kraingyov was particularly disturbing, as it was a pro-CPP area in which Hun Sen had invested in various development projects. On such grounds, and with the guaranteed secrecy of the ballot, Hun Sen, his antagonists argue, should not have been returned the way he was. By extension, this implies for the CPP's antagonists that they must have used suspicious means to win in the manner they did.

Outside Cambodia, these sensations were given credence by associating Hun Sen directly with all manner of human rights and political abuses. Tony Kevin, former Ambassador from Canberra, argued that a limited flow of biased information from Cambodia had created a 'consensus ... among conservatives and liberals alike' in Washington and elsewhere. In this 'consensus', he added, it is believed that 'Hun Sen ... is personally linked to everything bad that happens in Cambodia and that he will ensure an election win by whatever means possible'.[44] However, whilst aspects of this type of rule were apparent, and whilst there was reported intimidation, some of this was not political; some was conducted on a score-settling basis; and some was not ordained from above. Furthermore, intimidation and harassment clearly did not affect everyone.

This said, however, it must be noted that intimidation and harassment take varying forms. What constituted persuasion could be interpreted as coercion. Tony Kevin has made himself unpopular by arguing from such a perspective, but almost anyone who does not maintain the Liberal, anti-Hun Sen position is immediately tarred with partisanship. It is unacceptable to argue, without evidence or without releasing evidence that can be accountably scrutinised independently, that Hun Sen is directly behind every misdemeanour in Cambodia. Nor is it acceptable to maintain the position that all deaths of opposition activists are directly related to organs and institutions of the CPP-led state. The line has to be drawn, however, when one FUNCINPEC activist was found with his eyes missing, his fingers cut off and the flesh on his legs removed from mid-thigh down, as well as other damage. CPP police claimed 'suicide'.[45] Clearly, the messages sent from the elite, designed to ensure increased party membership, loyalty, and a pro-CPP vote, found different translation at grass roots level in differing instances.

The external perception of the CPP and Hun Sen was that they were unpopular. This is clearly at odds with the vote outcome. Focus for an explanation of the results, mainly deriving from outside Cambodia, then turns to the political institutions that managed the elections. If harassment and intimidation cannot be proven to be directly connected to the party elite, then given Hun Sen's 'unpopularity', something else must explain his victory. Attention may then be turned to the political institutions that underpin and manage most elections, in one form or another.

The degree to which the CPP's victory can be definitively or even reasonably explained by manipulation of state institutions is questionable. Few Cambodians were reported as having complained of being unable to either register or vote, in proportion to the number that did not. In some villages, there was nowhere near the degree of fear for CPP representatives suggested in some quarters.[46] Concerns regarding disenfranchisement are undermined by a comparison of the last election's registered voters with that of 1998; and between the registered voters and votes cast in 1998. The figures are similar, reflect demographic changes, and suggest that no such conspiratorial anomaly exists. Furthermore, the Committee for Free and Fair Elections ran a parallel count which differed little from the NEC's verdict and confirmed that party representation in the Assembly was unaffected. In one example, completed recounts on 6 August 1998 in the disputed regions of Takeo Province, revealed the second figures were 'remarkably close to the first tally'.[47] In other words, there were no significant differences to imply that large scale, systemic pre-election fraud deliberately disenfranchised large numbers of Khmer voters.

If the NEC potentially invalidated aspects of the election in the eyes of some, the sceptics found far greater evidence in party political intimidation and harassment. One paper cited a standoff in Pailin, a former Khmer Rouge stronghold, then a private economic fiefdom for Ieng Sary, and now a government municipality. Racist Sam Rainsy Party loyalists were advising residents not to vote for the CPP 'because they're Viêt Namese', to which the CPP representative simply retorted, 'Wait until your leader comes to town'.[48] Another reported incident involved a former Khmer Rouge guerrilla named Sou Kim, who had earlier defected to the government and was now the reserve FUNCINPEC candidate in Pailin. He was allegedly forced to 'flee to Phnom Penh because the Governor of Pailin wanted to arrest him for failing to defect properly' to the CPP.[49] The Sam Rainsy Party won the only seat in Pailin, despite these claims of pre-electoral intimidation and harassment.

Allegations of such harassment were sometimes more widespread than they were substantiated. The UN Human Rights Office cited 143 incidents of alleged intimidation between 27 May and 2 July, according to the *Cambodia Daily* of that date. The UN report claimed that the proportion of those incidents taking place during registration was considerably lower than that occurring after 12 June, 1998. As the official campaign period ran from 25 June to 24 July, observers pointed to a pattern of intimidation centred on the campaigning process. In the middle of this period, for example, amongst several others, a FUNCINPEC activist was killed in the Province of Kompong Thom in an alleged political slaying, according to local reports.[50]

Other concerns abounded. In a widely publicised incident, the CPP in a number of Provinces gave away MSG (mono-sodium glutamate) to people and took thumbprints. The MSG was traded for promises of votes on polling day, claimed many. The CPP stated it was merely giving gifts for political loyalty, and that their acts could not compromise the crucial secrecy of the ballot. This was but one example of more obvious, overt vote securing that all major parties participated in. The CPP ran mock ballots in some provinces, where they carefully 'trained' the electorate which party to 'tick' on the day. The thirty-nine parties each had a number allocated at random, and various CPP representatives reminded voters to pay particular attention to their number, thirty-five. Likewise, FUNCINPEC adopted a similar strategy. However, rather than go to the voters, the voters came to Ranariddh. At an 18 July rally held at the Olympic Stadium in Phnom Penh, Ranariddh exhorted his clan to 'remember to tick number thirty-four', corresponding to FUNCINPEC's place on the ballot paper.[51] Alternatively, at the same rally, Ranariddh asked the crowd which number they would tick, and the reply came back '*samsap buon*' (thirty-four). The Sam Rainsy Party also followed such approaches to vote garnering. None of the parties differed in this respect, and if it was a fault in the eyes of some, it was equally applicable to each group. Thus, to argue that the CPP won because of dubious vote garnering is to miss the point that all the main parties used similar approaches.

Amidst concerns of intimidation, the CPP turned out in huge numbers at regular events in both urban and rural locations to bang the party drum. In the weeks preceding the election, many dawn departures from Phnom Penh inevitably crossed convoys of party agents preparing for a campaign somewhere. The other key parties, as well as some of the less well known groups, also attempted various public campaigning. However, if the intensity of the CPP's rallies does not explain the victory, it is possible that the disunity of the oppositions' does. With FUNCINPEC already split over the response to their leader's ejection after the July 1997 fighting, and with a degree of antipathy between Ranariddh and Rainsy, Hun Sen did not have to adopt 'divide and rule' tactics; the opposition did that itself.[52] Going by election results, had Rainsy and Ranariddh united, they would have achieved a majority of the votes and the outcome would have been quite different.

Other potential reasons abound for the CPP's victory, and what some consider to be a reversal of the hoped-for political transition in Cambodia. 'The CPP', argued the *Cambodia Daily*, 'is the party millions of Cambodians look to for security, and are forever grateful to [them] for freeing them from the nightmare of the Khmer Rouge rule'.[53] Although the *Daily* has a degree of sympathy for the CPP, there is a significant element of truth to this statement. In connection with this notion of security, it is also the CPP which 'builds schools and irrigation systems, and donates rice'.[54] Although clearly the CPP does not do this across the whole country, the phenomenon is well known and clients are mobilised accordingly.

Democratic Intent and Electoral Behaviour in the Opposition

The 'Standard Total View' traditionally, although this is showing some signs of change, has been that the least agreeable of the Khmer leaders is Hun Sen. This perspective is buttressed with the argument that individuals such as Ranariddh and Rainsy have western, democratic credentials and education, and they are more likely to practice democracy. This is nonsense. While Hun Sen has clearly rejected some elements of externally imposed democratic reform, he is far from alone. Whilst Ranariddh and Rainsy were divided more broadly, one area in which they were united was vitriolic, racist propaganda. A common theme seems to unite Khmers in an inflamed hatred of the Viêt Namese. The modern demonisation of the Viêt Namese is a product of quite recent Cambodian and international propaganda. Whilst there is no doubt that a degree of resentment exists because of the annexation in the late nineteenth century of

Kampuchea Krom (southern or lower Cambodia), Thai encroachment from the West is more visible, more frequent, has a longer historical tradition and is more insidious. However, it is rarely a subject of concern or invective. With the exception of the PRPK and CPP, Cambodia's leaders have consistently sought to explain their own problems by blaming the Việt Namese. Furthermore, Pol Pot utilised this nonsense in order to create greater unity in his crumbling Cambodia. His troops raided Việt Namese villages mercilessly, causing Hanoi to respond with force when the last thing they needed was the expense of such an attack and the subsequent international aid they lent to Phnom Penh.

The race issue is an easy tool to use to create unity against the CPP, because of their multi-faceted connection with Việt Nam. Ordinary Khmers have been propagandised into believing that Việt Nam was responsible for Pol Pot's Cambodian genocide.[55] After Hanoi's reluctant and unaffordable incursion and during the course of Việt Nam's presence in the 1980s in Cambodia, propaganda continued to distort history by demonising Hanoi and fabricating myths which suggested a second genocide was underway in Cambodia (see chapter two). Coupling historical enmity to the current dominant party, Ranariddh and Sam Rainsy regularly raised racist invective against the 'Yuon', a term when used contemporarily equating roughly to 'savage', to generate support for their anti-CPP and anti-Việt Namese position. Whilst Rainsy denies such terms are racist, Pol Pot had stated in the Khmer Rouge 'Black Paper', that 'Yuon is the name given by Kampuchea's people to the Việtnamese since the epoch of Angkor and it means "savage"'.[56] The term was also recognised as racist and derogatory by Yasushi Akashi, when the Khmer Rouge during the UNTAC operation used it.[57] Various human rights bodies in Cambodia, indigenous or otherwise, did not address this issue until late, whilst ordinarily pursuing claims against the CPP.

One consequence of Rainsy and Ranariddh's anti-Việt Namese and anti-CPP invective is the western view of Hun Sen's opposition. Rainsy and Ranariddh most recently are generally painted as pro-democracy liberals with western education and values.[58] The possession of such mores fits better with the UN intervention based on pluralism and democracy than Hun Sen's political activities, which change with time in much the same way as any other politician's would. Western preferences, especially during the first half of the 1990s, have revolved around claims to democratic credentials by individuals such as Rainsy and Ranariddh, and around the need to oppose the former 'Communist' who consistently outmanoeuvres, out-wits and out-orates the 'liberals'. Such beliefs are far from reliable or truthful.

Rainsy and Ranariddh's racism and xenophobia, reminiscent of the Pol Pot period, are underpinned further by other anti-pluralist, intolerant tendencies. *The Guardian* described Rainsy as a 'power-hungry spoiler, too convinced of his own righteousness to even consider a compromise with his rivals', which include variously Ranariddh.[59] The Cambodian government and also 'many diplomats' express these views.[60]

Such un-democratic prejudices went unchallenged. When, for example, his party announced their claims of irregularities, Rainsy 'demanded another election', adding that 'we must change the regime'.[61] No irony was noted that Rainsy had effectively demanded Hun Sen's overthrow whether the election results ordered this or not. Furthermore, the papers citing this made no attempt to comment objectively on his statements. In the absence of the criticism that would certainly have been levelled at him had Hun Sen made such statements, Rainsy and Ranariddh simply escalated the crisis and continued to voice their demands. They selfishly brought the system and society to a potential chasm.[62] Yet such behaviour was largely unchallenged. In a letter to US Senators McCain and Kerry, Hun Sen reminded the recipients that Rainsy had, 'in the most vitriolic terms ... called for the overthrow of the government, asked the US to bomb my house, demanded that I step down, and referred to me as a "Yuon" puppet'. Hun Sen concluded that this approach could only put Rainsy 'in the category of a David Duke or a Paula Hanson'.[63]

Ranariddh exhibits similar non-democratic principles. One example of open non-democratic expression was his demand for the Chair of the National Assembly, as a condition for recognising the election. Democratic process enshrined in the Cambodian Constitution stipulates that represented parties submit candidates for election to this post; Ranariddh was not even following the Constitution to which he had pledged allegiance. In a letter to the *Phnom Penh Post*, one reader rhetorically demanded: 'Do Rainsy and Ranariddh say, "give me liberty or give me death"? No, it is more like "give me that lucrative ministerial post, or I create more hell"'.[64] Whilst some Khmer scholars are divided over many issues of their study, in this they do in fact concur closely.[65] Heder maintains, and Vickery accepts to a significant degree, that underlying the calls for democracy and human rights that have been made by Sihanouk, Sam Rainsy, and a few other prominent figures in their criticisms of the Royal government are deeply illiberal, antidemocratic and antipluralist tendencies. If these critics were in power and faced the kind of opposition to which they are subjecting Ranariddh and Hun Sen, they would almost certainly act as intolerantly.[66]

As well as the general weakness, non-democratic values and incoherence of the opposition, their perceived inability to effectively govern and create stability may be another explanation for their electoral unpopularity. Many Cambodians, when randomly surveyed as to their post-electoral desires, stated simply 'stability', or 'peace'. A vote for FUNCINPEC or Sam Rainsy did not necessarily equate to this, whilst ensuring a place for the CPP equates to an absence of political counter-attacks. Not a few long-term NGO representatives also hold such views.[67] The view persists that while Hun Sen may not be popular with many westerners as a political personality, his continued presence in politics offers stability. Furthermore, it is argued anonymously in some quarters, progress would be much more rapid and reliable if he did not have to compete with 'inadequate and vacuous' politicians such as Prince Ranariddh.[68] Although the NGO-popular 'necessity theory' proved to be unpopular with many foreign observers in Cambodia, this approach finds expression amongst many Cambodians tired of political in-fighting punctuating their history and puncturing their economic development.

Cambodia's political transition was no more concluded by the 1998 plebiscite than it was by the 1993 polls. Another stage of transition began in the post-electoral phase, which was dedicated to manoeuvring and bargaining by the defeated groups to gain access to political power denied them by the outcome of the polls. It is worth momentarily comparing events of this period in South America. O'Shaughnessy and Dodson have argued that elections in such circumstances as Nicaragua (1990) and El Salvador (1994) demonstrate a need to bargain after elections, not necessarily with full and complete regard to the outcome of the polling. They refer to this process as 'pact-making to achieve elite consensus on the rules of the game'.[69] The immediate aftermath of both recent Cambodian elections were marked by the absence of such a process. Later on in both cases, pact making characterised the manner in which a solution was arrived at. In 1993, the defeated CPP threatened to resist change and threatened destabilisation. In 1998, the defeated Sam Rainsy Party and, to a less visible degree, Ranariddh's FUNCINPEC party, incited demonstrations in Phnom Penh against the CPP, destabilising the environment. Some viewed the demonstrations as visible evidence of spontaneous democratic responses to an undemocratic and illegal regime; Rainsy was certainly at the forefront of such claims. However, this seems less likely than at first appeared. Individuals seen to be organising the confrontations on behalf of elites paid many 'demonstrators'. The *Phnom Penh Post* questioned whether the demonstrations were 'truly the "people's will" or ... an organised and designed revolution that played on genuine feelings stirred up solely for the gain of political leaders on all sides'.[70] It later observed that

> the massed protests are less "spontaneous" or "driven by the people" as [opposition leaders] may claim, though both phenomena exist.... Diplomats and military analysts agree that the protests are obviously being managed.... Key protesters carry walkie-talkies; perhaps four to five mobile command posts exist to co-ordinate activities.[71]

An earlier edition had claimed that whilst 'Tianenmen Square had a more spontaneous grassroots momentum ... [the Cambodian protests] seems to have Rainsy's hand of public relations slickness caressing it'.[72] A US political observer, anonymously cited in the *Post*, declared that the situation was 'like a remote-controlled demonstration. Some people are in control of these demonstrations'.[73] Several 'protesters' openly admitted to ulterior, opportunistic business motives.[74]

One NGO researcher argued that the manner in which the demonstrations stopped – almost overnight – is further evidence that the protests were manipulated. Indeed, there is clearly documented evidence of Rainsy deceiving Khmers and journalists alike to incite riot and dissent. In one example, an Australian journalist filmed Rainsy talking with factory workers outside Phnom Penh who had been banned from attending the protests. Rainsy translated one worker's narrative as meaning, 'if we go, we will lose our jobs'. The NGO Khmer speaker categorically stated that the interviewee had said he would lose his pay, not his job.[75] The mistranslation, which is hard to do accidentally, was designed to aggravate conditions of repression and to bring credibility to his political campaign and ambitions. This was perhaps the mild element of Rainsy's dangerous incitement and destabilisation programme; racism further fuelled these self-serving policies, designed to create legitimacy by appealing to a common element of anti-Viêt Namese sentiment in Khmer society. It is not without precedent, conceptually. Rainsy's provocation is evident in the formation of the Khmer Nation Party in 1995. Both the logo and the founding date (Jayavarman VII and 9 November, National Day) represented 'a challenge to the very legitimacy of the government' suggesting 'Rainsy was more interested in provocation than meaningful parliamentary opposition'.[76]

As more individuals joined the process, it 'quickly metamorphosed', according to McAuliff, 'into massive anti-government and racist demonstrations having little to do with the elections or democracy'.[77] For example, Jennar notes Rainsy's racial incitement harking back to Pol Pot anti-Viêt Namese racism. Rainsy propagandised and agitated in a dangerous manner in the Khmer-Viêt Nam Friendship Park when he urged Khmers: 'do not form a coalition with one who has a yuon ... head and a Khmer body'.[78] What began as fairly limited protests mushroomed into a far wider confrontation, between pro-SRP loyalists and pro-CPP voters, swollen by government security forces.

Violence escalated as state forces responded to the demonstrations. Simultaneously, FUNCINPEC and the SRP refused to join the government and the Assembly, prompting a potential Constitutional crisis as the mandate of the last government expired imminently. However, the opposition showed a lack of unity. Ranariddh distanced himself by omission from 'Rainsy's destructive strategy', which would inevitably result in clashes with state forces.[79] He may have considered he had less to lose than Ranariddh; he certainly did not consider what was at risk for the people he was using in his attempt to lever himself into a position of authority. Rainsy demonstrated the degree to which he was prepared to go to achieve political power, despite having been conclusively beaten by the CPP.

Although he was clearly not responsible for every act of mass 'democratic' resistance that superseded the elections, in the same way that Hun Sen could not have been responsible for every act of political vandalism in Cambodia before the polls, evidence suggests Rainsy financed poor farmers from the Provinces to take to the streets in his cause.[80] One aid worker with several years' experience in Cambodia went so far as to state that Rainsy was 'putting people's lives at risk and stirring up emotions like [a] warmonger'. She added that 'none of this would be happening if Rainsy hadn't been such a lunatic'.[81] Farmers and poor cyclo drivers were recruited and paid to attend; many others who made up the throng of people were bystanders and curious observers, rather than solely SRP supporters.[82] Tony Kevin maintained that 'Rainsy – a bad loser ... [was] irresponsibly perpetuating the tragedy of Cambodia'.[83] It is clear that some of his concern for the consequences of his actions – the injured and dead – was affected and used cynically to generate support from allies in the international community.

Some described the events as 'popular [anti-government] fury'. Others declared that 'the sentiment was overwhelmingly anti-government'.[84] Such views tended to predominate. However, there was also popular rejection of the SRP protests from those supportive of the election winners. Although a retreat from entrenchment was signalled after a plea from Chea Sim that was accepted by Ranariddh, pro-CPP protesters turned on the Sam Rainsy-ists. What had started as sporadic violence became more intense and indiscriminate, with many innocent individuals being attacked either by SRP supporters or by the state police or CPP supporters. McAuliff observed that

> the images of that weekend [were] haunting. Simple peasants, kromas [scarves] around their necks and clubs in their hands had come to the big city with a message for the opposition's uppity city folk: "We had an election. You lost. Now shut up".[85]

It was also clear that some elements of the CPP anti-protest protesters were also organised; but later, and for less propagandistic reasons more orientated to preservation of the widely accepted *status quo*.[86] Theo Noel, the senior western election advisor to the NEC, told journalists that 'the opposition parties ... should now accept the results of the election gracefully and stop identifying scapegoats to cover up their divisions and their weakness'.[87] Kevin articulated the feelings of many in Phnom Penh when he wrote to the *Phnom Penh Post*:

> In rejecting on unconvincing grounds the mandate given by the Cambodian electorate, Rainsy has shown contempt for his people [sic] and for the international community that observed this election honestly and professionally.[88]

Eventually, the King persuaded Ranariddh and Rainsy to co-operate with Hun Sen. The violence in Phnom Penh ceased, although there was an unclaimed but politically ineffectual rocket attack in Siem Reap on a convoy of vehicles which included Hun Sen. Without the full details of Sihanouk's diplomacy there, it is not possible to draw reliable conclusions as to how the conflict was mediated. Some argue that the driving force was the CPP. Others maintain the King influenced the process significantly. However, if it fits previous patterns and precedent, Ranariddh had it made clear to him that the opposition would not undermine the dominant elite. The monopoly of armed forces enjoyed by the government-elect rendered resistance futile (whether it was just or not). Rainsy was probably warned off, by Ranariddh as well as Sihanouk, because the former was impeding the formation of a government that would empower, in a reduced manner, Ranariddh's FUNCINPEC. He therefore lost allies and legitimacy, as well as exposing himself to a legitimisation of government crackdowns against his protests after Ranariddh formed a government with the CPP. The dominant actor who had won with international legitimacy limited expression; the CPP was quite prepared to accept a degree of powersharing, as long as it fitted within 'the bounds of the expressible'. Rainsy's activities were well outside those boundaries, but Ranariddh's location within them, by virtue of his distance from Rainsy, ensured a degree of facilitation by the CPP. The CPP's Hor Nam Hong warned publicly that in its resistance to the formation of the 1998 government,

> FUNCINPEC should be careful, it should know how far it can go in its manoeuvres.... I know that sometimes one manoeuvres for position, that is fine. But if one does that, we [CPP] have to get serious.[89]

This clearly reflects the 'bounds of the expressible' hypothesis. Hor Nam Hong was defining the terms of the relationship, and identifying the consequences of overstepping the boundaries he laid out on behalf of his party.

The Creation of the Cambodian Senate

Over the following four months, negotiations proceeded with little headway made until an indigenous solution to create a second house for the Executive was floated. The idea was almost an instant success, in Khmer terms. This notion addressed almost at a stroke the superficial and underlying tensions in the Khmer elite. The creation of an un-elected Upper House in Cambodia during the months of October and November 1998 constituted a domestic refinement or extension of the processes set in motion after the 1993 UN-sponsored elections; but perhaps less so in the democratic tradition than at first it appears.[90] In the context of the political and Constitutional impasse that developed after the 1998 election results were made public, the provision of the Senate, confirmed on 13 November 1998, represented two positive achievements in the Cambodian context.[91]

Beyond the national setting, however, it presented significant challenges to democratic transition. First, it allowed the second party, FUNCINPEC, to form part of a coalition on some of its own terms, rather than being a more subordinate partner in a unicameral body dominated by its traditional CPP opposition. This then reduced internal government political confrontation and in doing so may have cleared a path towards some form of broader socio-economic development in Cambodia.

Second, critics claim that the Senate was only established to provide a senior position for Chea Sim, previously leader of the National Assembly but in need of an alternative after Ranariddh was given that post.[92] The *Phnom Penh Post* cited one FUNCINPEC official as saying it was 'nothing but an expensive sinecure for Chea Sim'.[93] Whilst this explanation may suggest a degree of comprehension of the role of the Senate, it misses a wider aspect of its creation. The creation of the Senate also permitted, to a greater degree than would have been possible under a single Lower House (the National Assembly), the continuation of more traditional aspects of Cambodian politics by creating extra positions that perform the task of redistributing wealth through patronage and clientelism. FUNCINPEC members are claimed to have said that 'the Senate was a cash bonanza.... One senator bought his seat for $100,000'.[94] This in turn could be used to preserve political power bases supporting or sustaining either major political party. In effect, it resolved the issue of an increased number of politicians chasing the relatively constant number of beneficial and profitable political posts in the old system.

Sam Rainsy and his supporters have expressed a third criticism of the Senate. He claimed that it was a 'waste of money, only to serve individual interests and will create a lot of confusion within the legislative powers'. He added that on these grounds, he would not vote for it in the procedures necessary to alter the Constitution to permit the Senate's creation.[95] Furthermore, other sources argue that rather than acting in the constitutional liberal sense as a brake and check on abuses of power, the Senate will be used to undermine the democratic functioning of the elected House.[96] This argument is presumably based on the belief that Bills will go to the unelected Senate and can be halted arbitrarily and without recourse to due processes set in motion by the elected representatives of the people. However, the Senate is in no way that powerful; nor is the political process of Cambodian bi-cameralism that primitive. In fact, Bills rejected or amended by the Senate go back to the Lower House where they can be rejected by a second vote in the Assembly.[97] Despite his own protests and arguments, Rainsy accepted seven seats for his party.

The sixty-one-member Senate represented a refinement of the system installed after July 1993, and reflected a desire to manage the crises that developed between 1993 and 1997 over powersharing. As Ung Huot once recognised, the old situation created only losers; a broader distribution of political positions avoids 'lose-lose' to create 'win-win' scenarios.[98] The provision of a National Assembly in 1993 created only a limited number of positions for FUNCINPEC, which were in many instances over-ridden at lower and upper levels. However, the creation of a Senate in 1998 added to available positions and compensated some of the effects of FUNCINPEC's earlier frustrations over grass roots powersharing.

In other words, as the notion of commune level powersharing was largely non-negotiable after March 1996, prompting Ranariddh to increasingly challenge the CPP's privileges, action was taken in the form of the provision of the Senate, to ameliorate the situation by compensating the FUNCINPEC elite which in its own turn may compensate FUNCINPEC's lower level interests. As long as the FUNCINPEC elite is economically empowered through government positions, the people lower down supporting them can be rewarded or compensated. This is not the case with every senior FUNCINPEC politician; however, as a process it constitutes both a tradition and a continuing influence on the transition in Cambodian politics, slowly shifting away from patronage and clientelism and towards an alternative but as yet unclearly-defined model. It is interesting to note that unsubstantiated rumours have suggested that FUNCINPEC party history was repeating itself in 1999. Because Ranariddh had recognised the limits of his power with regard to Hun Sen, and because more elements of his party had been sated by the creation of the senate and the patronage it provided, he had by May 1999 all but ceased to challenge Hun Sen. It was claimed that members of the party were again voicing dissatisfaction at the Prince's record, in the same way they had prior to the March 1996 Congress which precipitated the violence of 1997.[99] Internal party corruption was also an issue, according to the sources involved. A core difference, however, is that Ranariddh has learned the error of his ways and is working to enhance his own advancement as far as possible. Confronting Hun Sen or the

CPP, he has learned, will not provide such an outcome. Since it was still he who controlled much of the military loyal to FUNCINPEC in the integrated government forces, another attempted putsch on Ranariddh's part becomes less likely.

The political transition from a single party state to a competitive multi-party system still requires that the economic needs of the elite be upheld; but it also strains the capacity of a nation's resource base to fulfil such expectations. Increasing the number of government positions, which traditionally come with certain privileges and rewards for loyalty, accommodated the increased demand for such positions commensurate with an expanded polity. It also ameliorated the consequences of political defeat or marginalisation, and the conflict quite frequently attendant upon this. However, resources to finance this will have to be developed from somewhere, and the most obvious route is through corruption, or through patronage and clientelism towards foreign countries and companies.

Despite this, the overall benefits are two-fold in the Cambodian case. First, the provision of the Senate resolved key aspects of multi-party competition for politically powerful positions. Second, in doing so, it generated access to privileges for the increased number of politicians and other government functionaries that accompanied the shift from single party to multi-party system. It thus went some considerable way to removing the block in transition that developed immediately after the 1998 elections. It also suggested a degree of internal political stability as long as these conditions remained unchallenged.

It had limitations, however, in a different context. Whilst it seemed to remove obstacles and create some conditions for political stability, it did little in terms of the expectations of the pro-democracy lobby. The western conceptualisation of government in the service of the people is undermined by the creation of an un-elected Senate. The purpose of this was the political and financial servicing of the elite and its clients, rather than the furthering of open government on meritocratic terms for the benefit of the population as a whole. In a sense, it may be considered a significant step backwards; in England, the debate over the removal of an un-elected Upper House was ironically running simultaneously. However, in the Cambodian context, the provision of the Senate was expedient and appropriate. Without political stability on Cambodian terms, which are constructed more in terms of elite absolutism rather than democratic ideals, stability is a necessary precursor to socio-economic development and the evolution of a political democracy. This is a contentious position which speaks to a wider debate regarding the primacy of democracy and the rule of law before development, or vice versa, depending on one's experience and ideology. However, it is hard to escape the conclusion that Cambodian leadership, whether regal, republican or otherwise, traditionally both resists challenges to its authority and also prioritises itself above its people. As David Chandler has pointed out, Khmer elites do not refer in the language to 'service' in relation to their citizens or subjects, but to 'consumption'.

A second limitation is that it is unlikely in 1999, or in the immediately foreseeable future, that a Senate composed under such conditions and within such a political culture is likely to be broadly politically efficient. Vested interests appear quite likely to subsume accountable or democratically-influenced scrutiny of legislation debated in the National Assembly; in no small part because the Senate was not established with this task as its primary raison d'être.[100] That is, it was not created to address democratic process. Rather, it was created in large part to facilitate the elite power concerns of the defeated FUNCINPEC. It is therefore not necessarily to be expected that democratic functioning will be enhanced by the provision of an apparent check and balance on the legislature. As long as the systems of patronage and clientelism, on the one hand, and the emphasis on political stability before nation-wide socio-economic development, on the other predominate, they will to a significant degree determine political processes in Cambodia.

This development must therefore be evaluated from more than one perspective. Those concerned, for right or for wrong, with stability before democracy, at the expense of western concepts such as separation of political powers and the service of the population, may conclude that the Senate is almost an inspired solution, serving as it does the traditional interests of a Cambodian elite. On the other hand, those concerned for the evolution and spread of democracy as the highest form of political organisation may be less impressed with these recent, and perhaps not unwelcome, developments.[101]

Whilst the details of this transition phase will be as emotionally debated as those of the July 1997 fighting, what seems clearer is that a repeating phenomenon exists in Cambodia's transition away from single party politics, through authoritarian powersharing coalitions, to whatever lies ahead. The absence of opposition institutionalised in parliament or in a collective political consciousness creates circumstances where the contest for power occasions a degree of desperation in defeat. As a result, the results of elections are contested strenuously by the losers and defended vigorously by the victors. The pawns in the middle are the population, used and abused by various leaders to achieve narrow goals which are generally not directly concerned with the wider citizenry.

The acrimonious and destabilising 'debate' over the post-election power transfer is symptomatic of these conditions, and confirms the rejection of opposition which expresses itself or threatens to express itself beyond the bounds of the expressible in Khmer elite political culture. The elections themselves also showed the opposition to the CPP in a nefarious light as they ignored the very human rights issues they themselves claimed to be platformed upon in what they termed as a stark contrast to the CPP. Furthermore, those slips of the democratic veil illustrated well that contrary to popular perception, Ranariddh and Rainsy are as capable of rejecting democracy as Hun Sen is alleged to be. For the time being, western, constitutional liberal democracy is a clear misnomer for a political order based on elite privilege and the protection of clans at the expense of social representation and opposition.

X

Conclusion

The goal of democratisation has been inspired since the 1960s in the developing world as often from without as it has been from within. No democracy is perfect, and most, including those situated in the West, are still on a passage to a more refined variant. In a sense, all democracies are in transition. Cambodia is perhaps at the beginning of the continuum from non-democracy to constitutional pluralism.

Transition itself clearly implies change. For some countries it can be tumultuous, for others it may be smooth. Most, however, demonstrate a tension between continuity of tradition and reform for change. Cambodia's recent political transition reflects a number of tensions that derive from this fundamental confrontation of values, culture and experience. First, it mirrors a gap between on the one hand, democracy as a reliable panacea for civil conflict, and on the other, the subsequent inevitable dilution of absolutist traditional power. Second, it reflects a tension on the one hand between the intentions of international intervention to 'democratise' a state, and on the other, the resistance of entrenched elites such as those in Cambodia to such plans. Third, Cambodia specifically demonstrates a tension between the desire to create valid (for example, neutral) electoral environments in which multi-party competition can meaningfully flourish, on the one hand. However, on the other, it also demonstrates the challenge to this process represented by patronage and clientelism, which reinforces traditional absolutism.

This work has argued that the Cambodian political elite has resisted democratisation in a number of ways. It takes the position that, although a huge infusion of interests and finance sought to push Cambodia down a democratic path, what existed by 1999 was more of

Conclusion

a veneer than a meaningful, substantive democracy. There is no doubt that elements of democracy and democratisation are visibly extant, not least of all in the form of the participatory plebiscite, with some important qualifications. Other institutions indicative of democratic functioning exist, and will continue to exist.

However, many of those that appear democratic are less so when scrutinised more closely. For example, the Senate's core role relates to patronage and clientelism, rather than to an exercise in curbing possible excesses in the National Assembly. Another example is that of political opposition, which is still tenuous, and exists not with freedom to express criticisms of government. Rather, it is aware of the degree to which it can opine on the activities of the core elite, before that elite's reactions become violent. There was by 1999 only a limited sense of a clear separation of powers between the Executive and the judiciary, with the capacity for the former to influence the latter being quite marked in some cases. Thus, some of the core elements of 'democracy' as it is viewed in the West are clearly lacking to one degree or another some eight years after the United Nations arrived to commence the implantation process. No value judgements are attached to this, but explanations for why, in this work's opinion, democracy has been very partially accepted and institutionalised, especially among the elite, are warranted.

In attempting to undertake this, considerable emphasis has been placed, in the preceding chapters, on Khmer political culture and how elites have developed their legitimacy. Those chapters have also noted and argued that patterns of legitimacy and authority permeate different personalities of the elites in Cambodia. Whether they have been labelled Royalist, Republican or Communist, and whether they existed in Monarchical, revolutionary or 'democratic' periods, leaders have demonstrated clear disdain and a lack of respect for democratic principles when their power, position or future has been challenged.

Equally, emphasis has also been placed on the concept of patronage and clientelism, the *khsae*, and the bonds that connect elites to the periphery. These elements of tradition have strong and deep roots in Cambodia. Furthermore, that which might undermine their role has been conspicuous in its absence over the last forty years. As long as no alternative to patronage exists to distribute largesse and wealth, jobs and favours, rewards and gifts, that socio-economic model and the politics that succour it and derive from it are unlikely to be changed significantly. Thus, until broadly accessible wealth extends across Cambodia and undermines poverty and dependency on patrons,

Conclusion

versions of patronage and clientelism will continue to co-exist with narrow elite authority. It has been observed that 'the recipe for dismantling or defusing patron-client relationships [includes] promotion of economic, social and political equality; adequate enforcement of civil and criminal laws; [and] creation of kinship and village solidarity'.[1] It requires only limited scrutiny of events in Cambodia to conclude reasonably that, although there have been some improvements in some of these fields in the last decade, it is not the extent required to 'defuse' the dominant determinant of human organisation. Indeed, the same authors noted that 'the pervasive existence of patron-client relations has almost unanimously been deplored by development planners as an obstacle to accomplish a more democratic direction ... in Cambodia'.[2]

The 'deploring' of this model of organisation clearly implies an emphasis on the inalienable 'rightness' of democracy as the leading political paradigm, in much the same way as authoritarian states dictated the 'purity' or 'ideological correctness' of their chosen path. It must be noted that until the form of *economic* organisation prevalent in Cambodia can be replaced, or its absence compensated for in some way, the application for western ideological reasons of a different *political* form of organisation is more likely than not to lead to new problems of competition for scarce resources amongst many poor people, especially in the rural areas, but not solely restricted to them.

Democracy alone would not provide the essentials of life for many Khmers in either 1993 or 1998. In fact, implanting democracy would undermine economic essentials. Then, broad poverty reinforced patronage and clientelism, and alternative systems of political organisation that did not offer what patronage was proven to provide could not have been sustainable. Whilst the popular plebiscite suggested strongly an internalised belief in democracy as progress, Khmers also voted to ensure a leader would reward them for their loyalty in much the same way as they would under the traditional *khsae* networks. This is clearly not to suggest that no-one voted altruistically, or that people did not refer to personal freedoms associated with democracy, or for a preferred political personality. However, given the levels of socio-economic development outside the key towns and provincial centres, it is unsurprising that individuals would vote for the party or personality that promised them betterment. In a sense, this is little different from elections in the Western democracies. Individuals vote for the party that will improve their lot. So too did Khmers in 1993 and 1998. A core difference is that

Conclusion

Western voters show evidence of making political choices that do not always, immediately or solely affect their desired material well being. A politically accountable and meritocratic system would have been incompatible with economic inequality at that time in Cambodia's political and economic development. Patrons would have been unable to reward clients and clients would have withdrawn support for their leaders. Simultaneously, clients would have become more impoverished relative to the gains they would have accrued under the traditional *khsae* system. Because the majority of Khmers, especially in the rural areas, are relatively poor, voting for openness and accountability – that is, for democracy – would have been counterproductive to their economic and social requirements. Many Khmers were thus not consciously voting for a transformation of political ideology and for democratic change. Many voted because doing so allowed them to make choices about who would best improve their socio-economic lot, regardless of their regal or peasant origins. Such networks of relationships are antithetical to democracy because they are indiscriminate (in the sense that they can be easily altered) and not based on equality of relationships before a set of enforceable laws.

Thus, transition to democracy in Cambodia foundered on two planks of tradition. The absence of an alternative to *khsae* benefits, and the views of absolutism held by the elite, combined to limit the degree to which democracy and its associated institutions have taken root in Cambodia. Cambodia's claimants to legitimate authority, from King Sihanouk to Sam Rainsy, have demonstrated values and beliefs almost diametrically opposed to those underpinning Western 'democracy'. None have demonstrated great levels of tolerance, of the acceptance of difference, or of the notion of a legitimate Opposition. Absolutism, derived from traditions pre-dating Angkorean domestic organisation, is a core element of authority and legitimacy in Cambodia. In fact, the minimal influences to the contrary present in Cambodia during the 1980s have reinforced for all parties the legitimacy of absolutism. Many influences associated with political 'advancement' in other parts of the world did not find expression in the internationally isolated Phnom Penh of that period. Soviet and Viêt Namese influence was of a similar authoritarian nature, reflecting to a degree the regime type of the two states at that time. Earlier, Pol Pot and Lon Nol's largely unfettered authoritarian ways served to reinforce absolutism, and Sihanouk's leadership after independence was not noted for its tolerance.

Conclusion

These planks of traditional social, economic and political organisation came face to face with a potential nemesis when the UN attempted to superimpose 'modernising' democracy on Cambodia's traditional institutions. In a very real sense, the most convincing of explanations for democracy's experiment with Cambodia lie in this conjuncture. Democracy, from the perspective of the entrenched elite, manifested itself in political competition which would inevitably undermine the support it relied on to retain power. The moment Opposition was introduced, the fight to preserve power for the entrenched group commenced. Similarly, the moment the Opposition arrived with the intention of taking some or all power from the incumbents, confrontation was inevitable. This also characterises politics in Western states. However, two key elements absent from the contemporary Western model are continuing views of absolutism, and the inclination to resort to violence to resolve political conflict. The latter reflects the absence of a tradition in Khmer society of mechanisms, processes and institutions that exist to mediate and settle arguments.[3]

Another cultural rock on which democracy foundered was the absence of Opposition legitimacy. Clearly, opposition forces arose and have existed before in Khmer political history. However, their presence historically has not been viewed as legitimate by the absolutists who have dominated Cambodia. There has not been the experience of opposition as a part of a government or party's own legitimacy as there has been to a degree in Western European parliamentary democracies. This remained, to a significant degree, the case in 1991, and was the case, but to a lesser degree, in 1999. There is another important ramification for Khmer democracy contained within this shortfall. Opposition has limited access to political power and to the state, as the CPP demonstrated in 1993. It is not funded by the state, as it is in other countries. Taxes generated by the state finance not merely the government or a coalition of forces, but also the 'loyal Opposition', whose task it is to act as a check on government excesses or improprieties and corruption. In Cambodia, this has not been the case. If the ruling elite does not view Opposition as legitimate, there is no good reason to finance it from tax. This, amongst other things, has ensured that no institutions have arisen to accommodate opposition. This in turn ensures that economic marginalisation is a consequence of political exclusion. As has been observed earlier, this can have very serious and sometimes violent consequences in a country with diverse levels of poverty such as Cambodia.

Conclusion

Applying these generalisations to the cases of transition that have formed the core of this work might test the degree to which they are valid in the Cambodian experience. From the outset, the single party State of Cambodia (SoC) and its forebears the PRPK were resistant to the changes implicit and explicit in the Paris Agreements of 1991. The introduction of Opposition to a dominant single party model exaggerated the notion of marginalisation. Hence, the need to manage the fallout from this was exacerbated, as resources could not be made to go as far as would be required by the presence of many new patrons competing for clients and political support in elections. However, this was clearly not the only reason for the SoC's resistance to the developing PPA. Members of the party, including Hun Sen, regarded the peace proposals with some degree of mistrust, and with good reason. They did not expect a UN force to act impartially; after all, the UN had excluded a legitimate and *de facto* government in favour of a group of Khmers proven by a UN Truth Commission to have committed genocide. Many other issues attached to the UN and in particular aspects of its make up caused the party grave concern.

Simultaneously, the notion of empowerment and inclusion, as opposed to disempowerment and potential exclusion, explains the Khmer Rouge support for transition. An important qualification is that the Khmer Rouge was not committing to democracy. Rather, they were committing to a process that would permit them access to power denied by the Phnom Penh government over the previous decade by the expedient of war. The evidence clearly showed an imperative to participation; but not for the lofty ideal of liberal democracy. Testing its reverse helps corroborate this proposition. That is, when the Khmer Rouge viewed the process to which they committed in 1991 as threatening to marginalise them, they ceased to participate in it in June 1992.

When the CPP demanded equal power with FUNCINPEC, after the May 1993 elections in which they came second, their concern was exclusion and marginalisation. Many Khmers recognise openly that government positions are a means to economic improvement.[4] This may be for themselves directly, for their families, or for the political clans that make up the *khsae*. The reduced number of positions in the new Constituent Assembly after May 1993 affected, most obviously, the 32 resignees who had to make way for competent and often younger technocrats, and others deemed important for governance. However, the importance of equal powersharing across Ministries far exceeded the significance of the resignees' act. Those positions of power were not always or necessarily related to places on the Assembly. That is, party members could occupy positions within the Ministries without having portfolio in the Assembly. Real power in Cambodia lay less in the legislative Assembly and more in the Executive. If fifty-fifty powersharing to accommodate its coalition partners implied a proportional loss of positions for the CPP, either more positions would have to be created, or significant numbers of the CPP would be marginalised. In the event, despite meddling from the US Mission, the fifty-fifty solution permitted some form of positive gain for the CPP, without which the likelihood of a peaceful post-election transition would have been markedly reduced.

Resistance to democratisation continued after the initial experiment in 1993. The period of struggle that followed the formation of the four-party coalition was marked by several interwoven themes. A struggle to enhance the degree to which FUNCINPEC and the CPP could develop or maintain clients began almost immediately after the Constituent Assembly legislated its successor, the National Assembly. The nature of this conflict was not one of political legitimacy in the eyes of the electorate, as one might imagine after a usurping of a poll outcome by one party or another. Rather, it can be viewed as a balance of power struggle. The most important third party actor became the Khmer Rouge, disenfranchised in part by itself and in part by the UN's failure to neutralise the political environment in which the election took place. The struggle in this sense was more simple and perhaps more cynical than ones involving complicated relations of kin and patronage. The Khmer Rouge were exiled and outlawed, and therefore beyond the key source of power distribution in Phnom Penh. FUNCINPEC had access to this, but only to a limited degree and without sufficient status to be able to reward its *khsae*. The CPP blocked both of these groups from their ambitions. It is perhaps unsurprising with hindsight that the balance of power evolved the way it did. The consequence was the July 1997 fighting, a war by proxy between the CPP and the Khmer Rouge, as well as a more direct clash between elements of FUNCINPEC and the CPP.

These patterns of behaviour clearly demonstrate themes of resistance to democratisation and power sharing. They continued to dominate the process of electoral selection preceding and superseding the 1998 polls. In a very real sense, those elections had parallels with the struggle of 1993, except the roles and positions of the key actors were reversed. In 1993, the CPP lost and contested the election on the grounds of procedural irregularities, of which there were inevitably

Conclusion

many, some more suspicious than others. In 1998, the Opposition SRP and FUNCINPEC lost, and contested the election on the grounds of systemic fraudulence. This time, however, the winners dominated the military forces and the defeated were left with primarily verbal resistance. Linking the three elements, of 1993, 1998, and the period in between was the contest for distribution and ownership of power amongst anti-democratic absolutists. A core difference after the 1998 elections, however, was the solution to the impasse that broke out between the CPP and the SRP, with FUNCINPEC vacillating in the middle. The creation in 1993 of the Assembly did not provide the positions and benefits to the increased number of political protagonists created by the UN intervention. The Senate, on the other hand, redistributed power amongst Chea Sim and Ranariddh, and simultaneously acted as job creation at lower levels for both main parties, as well as for the SRP. As long as this continues to satisfy FUNCINPEC and the SRP, the CPP remains unthreatened and able to carry out what it perceives as its responsibilities. As long as no voices of dissent on serious, 'high' issues such as elite powersharing are raised, then peace will likely follow, if the pattern of events prior to this is a reliable informant of process. However, such forms of and approaches to social, political and economic organisation do not reflect the kind of democracy that had been planned for Cambodia.

This is not necessarily to criticise overly the Cambodian role in the process of democratisation. In a very real sense, significant progress has been made in terms of a beginning. However, the route to Liberal democracy, if it must be followed, is a long one. It is hardly surprising that the institutional changes upon which democracy depends have been marginal in the last nine years. Both regal absolutism and liberal democracy have taken thousands of years to evolve and produce the generally refined institutions extant at the turn of the third Millennium. Cambodia's democratisation, over a period of less than a decade, cannot be expected to eliminate or marginalise the great forces that have determined its political evolution over the last thousand years.

There has been, then, a clash. Absolutism and patronage confronted equality and plurality. In the attempt to duplicate the European model, many issues have been overlooked or ignored. Perhaps most important amongst them are that the European model was largely internally evolving whereas Cambodia's experience was thrust from without. Furthermore, rather than European democratisation being grafted onto an already existing and resistant set of institutions, the preceding models, those of the *ancienne regime*, were first vanquished. Lizée notes that

> the fact that this [European] model emerged from particular historical, sociological and political circumstances and that, precisely for this reason, it might not readily be transferable to certain countries escaped most of those who were thinking along these lines.[5]

In order to sustain democracy, various institutions must be *in situ* to support the new pretender, and the old pillars of society which stand in contrast to such impositions have to be dismantled. In Cambodia, the attempt was made by external parties to superimpose democracy onto a system still supported by those older pillars. This is hardly the fault of Cambodians, few of whom other than Ranariddh and the Khmer Rouge had any choice in the matter. Cambodians were not consulted *en masse*, and Hun Sen was against the implementation techniques of the plan. It is thus unsurprising that there has been resistance from many quarters. Cambodia's political transition to democracy, if endure one it must, depends on many years of socio-economic reorganisation, from the traditional institutions to models of capitalism which do not exclude large numbers of poor people (many will argue that such a model cannot exist because it is a contradiction in terms).

As other forms of wealth distribution replace patronage and clientelism, the power that elites have derived traditionally from clients will be undermined, and absolutism will probably give way gradually to greater acceptance of the legitimacy of power sharing and opposition. Simultaneously, the consequences of political defeat will not find as much expression in socio-economic marginalisation. It is a process that reflects much literature reviewing experiences in Africa and Latin America. It is not perfect, and it is not to say Cambodia's political transition will be flawless if these conditions are met. However, it is to say that externally imposed democratisation and its consequences are core causes of much of Cambodia's political instability and violence since 1991.

It is important at this closing point to illustrate the manner in which such analysis is denied by those seeking to excuse the shortcoming of major institutions entrusted with pursuing and institutionalising the assumptions which define the end of the Cold War and post-Soviet evolution. Failure to comply with the evolving 'norms', of the consolidation of democracy as the highest and final form of political

Conclusion

organisation, and of the assumptions regarding its applicability and propriety to non-Western states, results in blame being apportioned. Thus, if a peacekeeping and democratisation programme is not seen to work in the manner in which it was intended, responsibility is placed with the 'patient' rather than with the institutions administering the medicine. There is much evidence of such mischief regarding Cambodia. This is not to say only one side to this contest is responsible. However, analysis and opinion that inform future policy needs to be considered much more carefully if Jarat Chopra's 'institutional memory' problem is to be challenged. In other words, if key figures and institutions persist in blaming Khmers for problems which have other origins, as this work has tried to show, political transitions elsewhere are destined to have overlooked key aspects which are central to the phenomenon.

The propensity to blame Khmers has a long tradition. For example, in early 1996, the US General Accounting Office (GAO) published a document assessing the state of Cambodia three years after UNTAC completed its mandate. It noted that

> since UNTAC ended its mandate in late 1993, Cambodia has made limited progress.. towards ... holding constitutionally required national elections by 1998 ... [and] meeting international human and political rights standards.[6]

It then went on to argue that these conditions should be evaluated with reference to post-UNTAC developments. In other words, the peacekeeping operation and its consequences – indicating failed political transition to the democratic model – should be absolved of responsibility for the travails then facing Cambodia. It was the implicit argument of the GAO that the well-documented US secret bombings and invasion of Cambodia prior to 1970, the civil war between 1970 and 1975, the genocide between 1975 and 1979, and the long civil war up to 1991 should

> not be used as a benchmark for measuring the current government's progress.... [T]he standards of behaviour set out in the.... Paris Peace Accords implemented by UNTAC ... are the appropriate standards for assessing the current government's progress....[7]

In other words, failure to continue within a democratic framework explains the problems facing the government in Phnom Penh in the wake of UNTAC's departure. It denies the role of powerful forces

Conclusion

such as absolutism and patronage, of pre-UNTAC conditions, and of the many experiences that shaped Cambodia's current political evolution. It also rejects the notion that the UN intervention and the overt and plainly stated Liberal agenda upon which such assumptions of propriety rest may be held in part responsible for the current situation. This process shifts responsibility for the outcome of the intervention from the UN, the Perm-5 and the west more generally, onto Cambodians, which deflects enquiry away from the issue of intervention and political transition.

The 'blame anyone but us' culture has poignant precedent regarding Cambodia. The London *Times* reported in 1998 that Henry Kissinger who, with Richard Nixon, sanctioned the murderous and illegal bombing of much of Cambodia in the late 1960s and early 1970s, had little sympathy for external explanations for the Pol Pot period. He asked, 'why should we [the West] flagellate ourselves for what Cambodians did to each other?'.[8] Kissinger's self-serving Aesopian revisionism and flagrant denial of truths imply that the West bears no responsibility for the rise to power of Pol Pot and of the international impoverishment of the 1980s. Such claims reflect a tradition of blaming Khmers for acts which, while exhibiting levels of Khmer complicity, irrefutably also reveal western responsibility.

US institutions are not alone in blaming Khmers and denying a historical angle to contemporary instability. UN secretary-general Kofi Annan claimed, shortly after the July 1997 fighting, that 'the UN operation was successful in helping to establish national institutions which could lead to stability and economic development'.[9] He continued to claim that the UN could not be held accountable for what happens after it departs a country. This also reflects the GAOs perspective (above), which was to separate the UN from events superseding its departure. It is both wrong and simply not enough to blame everything on Cambodia and Cambodians, and it is dangerous to express and reinforce analyses which suggest that western institutions and assumptions cannot be held to book for the problems of political transition Cambodia has experienced.

Underlying this habit of locating blame on the 'patient', and the concomitant refusal to accept the challenge traditionalism represents to the 'modernising' forces of democratisation, is a branch of what SM Mohammed Idris refers to as 'Vasco da Gama Syndrome'. The characteristics of this syndrome are, he writes,

Conclusion

a profoundly arrogant assessment of ... [Western] civilizational abilities and achievements ... invariably accompanied by an almost pathological drive to interfere, intervene and dominate peoples, cultures and situations that it considers inferior.[10]

In a very real sense, the failure of democratic transition in Cambodia is a product of the continuity of such thinking and assumptions as underpin and articulate the 'Liberal Project' and the flawed conclusions upon which that agenda rests.

Notes

Preface

1 See A Schlesinger, Jr, *Has Democracy a Future?* Foreign Affairs, September–October 1997, p. 2; and F Zakaria, *The Rise of Illiberal Democracy*, Foreign Affairs, November–December 1997, p. 23.
2 MRJ Vatikiotis, *Political Change in Southeast Asia: Trimming the Banyan Tree*, Routledge, 1996, p. 82.
3 B Schwarz, *The Diversity Myth: America's Leading Export*, Atlantic Monthly, May 1995, p. 60.
4 See SP Riley, *Africa's 'New Wind of Change'*, The World Today, vol. 48, no. 7, July 1992.
5 T Young, *'A Project to be Realised': Global Liberalism and Contemporary Africa*, Millennium: Journal of International Studies, vol. 24, no. 3, p. 1, 1995.
6 R Burbach, O Nunez and B Kagarlitsky, *Globalisation and its Discontents: The Rise of Postmodern Socialisms*, Pluto, 1997, p. 35. Readers unfamiliar with this text should note that the authors are highly critical of this phenomenon, rather than supportive of it.
7 S Lawson, *Democracy and the Problem of Cultural Relativism: Normative Issues for International Politics*, Global Society: Journal of Interdisciplinary International Relations, vol. 12, no. 2, May 1998, p. 264. Lawson also cites C Ake, *The Unique Case of African Democracy*, International Affairs, vol. 69, no. 2, 1993, and M Alagappa, *Democratic Transition in Asia: The Role of the International Community*, Honolulu, East-West Center Special Reports, no. 3, October 1994.
8 This statement does not imply that policy consensus existed in the capital cities of the USA, the Soviet Union or China. The terms are used for clarity of expression.
9 See amongst others, *Fresh Paths to Peace: New Dimensions of UN Peacekeeping Operations*, Work in Progress, vol. 14, no. 3, June 1995, p. 1 (United Nations University).

Notes

10 This concept finds expression in, for example, F Fukuyama, *The End of History and the Last Man*, Hamish Hamilton, 1992.
11 For a survey and discussion of this phenomenon in Africa, see TD Sisk and A Reynolds (eds.), *Elections and Conflict Management in Africa*, United States Institute of Peace, 1998.
12 Of course, pressure appeared from below in several cases, such as South Africa; however, the facilitation of change lay in the hands of the international intervenors to a significant degree.
13 Shaw reminds that the conflict spread to Kompong Som, for example, where 'the CPP military were searching through hotels looking for FUNCINPEC supporters and military ... [and] FUNCINPEC governors were told to flee or die ... in Stung Treng'. E-mail correspondence from Battambang with Graham Shaw, 11 November, 1998.
14 Zakaria (1997), p. 27.
15 J Chopra, *United Nations Authority in Cambodia*, Thomas J Watson Jr. Institute for International Studies, Occasional Paper no. 15, 1994, p. 49.
16 JM Sanderson, 'UNTAC: Successes and Failures', in H Smith (ed.), *International Peacekeeping: Building on the Cambodian Experience*, Australian Defence Studies Centre, 1994, p. 31.

I

1 This term is used by some to identify the period after the 'détente' of the 1960s and 1970s which followed the climb-down from potential nuclear hostilities over the Cuban Missile Crisis of 1962. It differs temporally from the 'first' Cold War which, it is often suggested, began shortly after the end of the Second World War. The second Cold War marks for many an escalation of tensions previously 'simmering' during 'détente'. Not long after the Viêt Namese invasion of Cambodia in December 1978, an anti-western Ayatollah took over from the Shah of Persia in Iran, and the Soviet Army invaded Afghanistan. Not long before the Viêt Namese invasion, Hanoi had signed a 25-year Treaty of Friendship with Moscow, reinforcing the Sino-Soviet split and strengthening US-Chinese relations. Many other events signalled increased international hostility and tension.
2 M Vickery, *Cambodia 1975-1982*, Southend, 1984, p. 247.
3 Chang Pao-min, *Beijing Versus Hanoi: The Diplomacy Over Kampuchea*, Asian Survey, vol. 23, no. 5, 1988, p. 599.
4 M Haas, *Cambodia, Pol Pot and the United States: A Faustian Pact*, Praeger, 1989, p. 445; J Pilger, *Heroes*, Pan 1989, pp. 31–2.
5 WS Turley, *The Khmer War: Cambodia after Paris*, Survival, vol. 32, no. 5, 1990.
6 WJ Duiker, *The Communist Road to Power in Vietnam*, Westview, 1996, p. 368.
7 David Munro and John Pilger, *Year Zero: the Silent Death of Cambodia*, ATV-TV (London), 1980.
8 Vickery (1984), p. 247.
9 The KNUFNS changed its name to the Kampuchean National United Front for National Construction, after the 'Salvation' had been achieved.

Notes

10 It will be noted that Bou Thang's name appears again later, in an alleged anti-Hun Sen 'coup' seventeen years later in 1994. For a detailed discussion of the origins of the Salvation Front, see Vickery (1984), pp. 190–3.
11 SJ Hood, *Dragons Entangled: Indochina and the China-Viêt Nam War*, ME Sharpe, 1992; Duiker (1996), p. 368.
12 See D Chandler, *The Tragedy of Cambodian History: Politics, War and Revolution since 1945*, Yale University Press, 1991, chp. 8; Duiker (1996), chp. 13; Hood (1991), chp. 7.
13 Vickery (1984), p. 190.
14 Ibid.
15 Ibid., p. 191.
16 For detailed accounts of the camps and the politicisation of the occupants, see L Mason and R Brown, *Rice, Rivalry and Politics: Managing Cambodian Relief*, Notre Dame, 1986; and J Reynell, *Political Pawns: Refugees on the Thai-Kampuchea Border*, Oxford, 1989.
17 JE Heininger, *Peacekeeping in Transition: The United Nations in Cambodia*, Twentieth Century Fund Press, 1994, p. 10. Between 1979 and 1982, the Party of Democratic Kampuchea, or Khmer Rouge, took sole possession of Cambodia's seat at the United Nations. See also FZ Brown, 'Soviet-American Conflict and Co-operation in Indochina', in GW Breslauer et al (eds.), *Beyond the Cold War: Conflict and Co-operation in the Third World*, Institute of International Studies, *University of California at Berkeley*, 1991. For a discussion of the status, origins and meaning of the CGDK, see C Etcheson, *Civil War and the Coalition Government of Democratic Kampuchea*, Third World Quarterly, vol. 9, no. 1, January 1987.
18 DP Chandler, *A History of Cambodia*, Westview, 1993, p. 234.
19 In the early stages of the war in Viêt Nam, Hanoi had adeptly maintained sound relations with both Moscow and Beijing. However, as China's relations with the USSR soured, and as Viêt Nam's strengthened with the Soviet Union, China increasingly resented, ands became hostile to, Viêt Nam's policies. The situation was aggravated after Viêt Nam and the USSR signed their 25-year Friendship Treaty (in 1978), and as Viêt Nam attacked China's Khmer Rouge client.
20 Alagappa uses a similar, but less qualified, expression in *The Cambodian Conflict: Changing Interests*, Pacific Review, vol. 3, no. 3, 1990.
21 There is no attempt here to maintain that there was a deliberately co-ordinated, jointly organised policy operating between Beijing and Washington. However, mutual interests directed similar policies. For an introduction to the diplomacy of the period, see E Mysliwiecz, *Punishing the Poor: the International Isolation of Kampuchea*, Oxfam, 1989. See also Mason and Brown (1986); Reynell (1989); and Haas (1989).
22 Pilger, *Heroes*, Pan, 1989, p. 423. See also Haas (1989).
23 Heininger (1994), p. 10.
24 J Pilger, *Organised Forgetting*, New Statesman and Society, 1 November, 1991, p. 10. This view is shared by authors such as Brown and Mason (1986); Mysliwiecz (1989); and Haas (1989).
25 C Peschoux, *The 'New' Khmer Rouge: Reconstruction of the Movement and Reconquest of the Villages 1979–1990 – A Preliminary Assessment*, English language draft, unpublished (published in French).

Notes

26 Heininger (1994), p. 10.
27 *The United Nations in Cambodia, 1991–1995, UN Blue Book Series*, vol. 2, 1995, p. 5.
28 *Report of the International Conference on Kampuchea*, New York (13–17 July 1981), A/CONF.109/5, p. 11.
29 *Yearbook of the United Nations, 1981*, pp. 240–1. See also T Findlay, *Cambodia: The Legacy and Lessons of UNTAC, SIPRI Research Report no. 9*, Open University Press, 1995, p. 4.
30 Heininger (1994), p. 11. Beijing viewed 'the Cambodian conflict as the main drain on Vietnam's resources' (A. Lakshmana Chetty, *Cambodia: Waiting for Whom?*, Sri Venkateswara University, India, (unpublished, undated paper, p. 17). Chetty further maintains that 'China … rebuffed years of Viêtnamese contacts on normalisation', as does K Mahbubani, in *The Kampuchean Problem: A Southeast Asian Perspective, Foreign Affairs*, vol. 62, no. 2, Winter 1983/1984, p. 418. However, this is refuted from several sources. See, for example, Hood (1992), ch. 3.
31 B Kiernan, *Genocide and Democracy in Cambodia: The Khmer Rouge, the United Nations and the International Community, Yale University Monograph*, 1994, p. 200.
32 S Heder, *Kampuchea 1980: Anatomy of a Crisis, Southeast Asia Chronicle*, vol. 77, February 1981, p. 10. Much of the rest of the article attempts to describe Viêt Namese domination and inefficiency and corruption in aid distribution, from the perspectives of interviewees living in Thailand who had fled from the Viêt Namese. There was no attempt to offer a balanced perspective from within Cambodia from the aid workers or journalists who had already gone there.
33 Pilger (1 November, 1991), p. 10. This view is shared by authors such as Brown and Mason (1986); Mysliwiecz (1989); and Haas (1989).
34 L Beuls, *Determinants of Peacekeeping Policy in Cambodia: Keeping Up With Interests?*, Paper at Second Pan-European International Relations Conference, ECPR, 13–16 September, 1995, p. 8.
35 Kiernan (1993), note 58, p. 253. See also M Vickery, *Cambodia (Kampuchea): History, Tragedy and Uncertain Future, Bulletin of Concerned Asian Scholars*, vol. 21, Nos. 2–4, April–December 1989, p. 54.
36 Kiernan (1993), p. 253. See also Vickery (1989), p. 54.
37 Kiernan (1993), p. 202. The nature of this event was disguised elsewhere. Nayan Chanda claimed that ASEAN 'had difficulty persuading [Schultz] to support' the regional attempt at reconciliation (*Civil War in Cambodia?, Foreign Policy* no. 76, Fall 1989, p. 38). For corroboration of the US role, see Vickery (1989), p. 54.
38 Haas (1989); esp. part two; and Pilger (1989).
39 J Pilger, *The West's War in Cambodia, New Statesman and Society*, 28 May, 1993, p. 14. See also M Vickery, *Cambodia: A Political Survey, Regime Change and Regime Maintenance in Asia and the Pacific*, no. 14, Australian National University, 1994; and Pilger (1989).
40 Chang Pao-min (1988), p. 429. This speech is discussed in Carlyle Thayer, *Prospects for Peace in Kampuchea: Soviet Initiatives and Indochinese Responses, Indonesia Quarterly*, vol. 17, Part two, 1989.

Notes

41 J Tessifore and S. Woolfson (eds.), *A Global Agenda: Issues before the 47th General Assembly*, University Press of America, 1992, p. 84. See also *The Economist*, 8 April, 1989.
42 Pao-min (1988), p. 430. See also Hood (1992), p. 75. When Gorbachev came to power, he initiated a joint Chinese-Soviet Commission for a series of exchange missions, to enhance diplomacy between Moscow and Beijing.
43 Hood (1992), p. 75. Rapprochement worked both ways; Beijing made several concessions to the USSR to underscore the diplomacy of the period. For a discussion of these issues, see S Long, *China and Kampuchea: Political Football on the Killing Fields*, Pacific Review, vol. 2, no. 2, 1989, pp. 151–2.
44 See for example Kiernan (1993).
45 Pao-min (1988), p. 430.
46 Ibid., p. 431. This view was supported by Hun Sen in an interview in Phnom Penh with the author, 1 January, 1994.
47 DR SarDesai, *Viêtnam: the Struggle for National Identity*, Westview, 1992, ch. seven; and Chang Pao-min, *Kampuchean Conflict: The Diplomatic Breakthrough*, Pacific Review, vol. 1, no. 4, 1988. See also *The Economist*, 8 April, 1989. The new foreign policy thrust from Moscow has also been described as 'the crucial catalyst for a new eagerness to expedite a resolution of the Kampuchea conflict...' (see Pao-min (1988), p. 429).
48 Kiernan (1993), p. 198. The phrase most often used is 'from a battlefield to a market place'. However, Bangkok was also keen to solve the border refugee issue.
49 Private correspondence from Professor M Leifer, London School of Economics, 24 March, 1993. See also M Osbourne, *Sihanouk: Prince of Light, Prince of Darkness*, Allen and Unwin, 1994, p. 254.
50 *The Economist* 30 September, 1989. See also Sesser (1992), p. 63; and Kiernan (1993), p. 205. Ieng's comments came during an interview, 24 December, 1997, Pailin, Cambodia.
51 Kiernan (1993), p. 202. See also *Far Eastern Economic Review*, 2 March, 1989.
52 J Pilger, *New Statesman and Society*, 21 July, 1995, p. 14. See also Kiernan (1993), p. 205.
53 Kiernan (1993), p. 208.
54 Ibid., p. 95.
55 Interview with Hun Sen, Phnom Penh, 1 January, 1994.
56 Interview with Khieu Kanharith, Phnom Penh, 10 April, 1996. Kanharith was referring to Hun Sen's pragmatism, tempered by resistance to core issues they believed at the time to be biased against them.
57 Hun Sen agreed to this on the condition that the central 'clique' of the Khmer Rouge, including among others Pol Pot, would not be party to the negotiations.
58 Heininger (1994), p. 10.
59 Interview with Hun Sen, Phnom Penh, 1 January, 1994. Khieu Kanharith also noted the tension between these two positions in an interview, 10 April, 1996.

Notes

60 Vickery (1984), p. 14.
61 *The Economist*, 6 May, 1989. See also *The Economist*, 5 August, 1989, p. 44; and Kiernan (1993), p. 197. The 'right terms' included constitutional changes which would make the Prince more than a mere figurehead: the difference, perhaps, between Presidential powers in the French Fourth and Fifth Republics.
62 *The Economist*, 30 September, 1989. See also Sesser (1992), p. 63.
63 Sesser (1992), p. 63. See also Kiernan (1993), p. 205.
64 J Pilger, *New Statesman and Society*, 21 July, 1995, p. 14. See also Kiernan (1993), p. 198 and 205; and Beuls (1995), p. 8.
65 Lizée (1993), p. 36. See also *The Economist*, 25 February, 1989, p. 63.
66 *The Economist*, 30 September, 1989.
67 *The Economist*, 29 July, 1989, p. 61.
68 Interview with Hun Sen, 1 January 1994, Phnom Penh.
69 Summary of World Broadcasts, 10 August 1989, Phnom Penh home service, 13:00 GMT, 5 August 1989
70 Chetty (unpublished, undated paper), p. 5. See also SWB 13 November, 1989, Xinhua 18:34 GMT, 11 November, 1989. Vickery contends that he was inclined to do this because it provided an opportunity to develop greater political power than would be afforded him as a 'figurehead' in a Hun Sen-dominated Cambodia. See Vickery (1989), p. 57.
71 *The Economist*, 30 September, 1989, p. 71.
72 Interview with Hun Sen, 1 January, 1994, Phnom Penh.
73 *The Economist*, 28 October, 1989, p. 80. See also A James, *Peacekeeping in International Politics*, Macmillan, 1990, pp. 270–1.
74 Chetty (unpublished, undated paper), p. 6. See also T Koh, *The Paris Negotiation on Cambodia: A Multilateral Negotiation that 'Failed'*, *Negotiation Journal*, vol. 6, no. 2, 1990, pp. 85–7.
75 This was the *'Framework for A Comprehensive Political Settlement of the Cambodia Conflict'*, signed in August 1990. The draft text was an amended version of a US Congressman's plan, taken up by the Australians, keen for a role in East Asia ('Framework Document').
76 M Leifer, *Powersharing and Peacemaking in Cambodia? School of Advanced International Studies Review: A Journal of International Affairs*, vol. 12, no. 1, 1992, p. 145; and G Evans and B Grant, *Australia's Foreign Relations In the World of the 1990s*, Melbourne University Press, 1992, ch. 13.
77 *'Framework Document'*, Article 7, section one.
78 Berdal and Leifer in J Mayall, (ed.), *The New Interventionism 1991–1994: United Nations experience in Cambodia, former Yugoslavia and Somalia*, Cambridge University Press, 1996, p. 34.
79 Interview with Hun Sen, 1 January, 1994, Phnom Penh.
80 Ibid.
81 Vickery, (1994), pp. 3–4.
82 Chetty (unpublished, undated paper), p. 20.
83 Interview with Hun Sen, Phnom Penh, 1 January, 1994. This pragmatism is thematic in CPP thinking. For continuity, see interview with Khieu Kanharith, 10 April, 1996.
84 Leifer (1992), p. 146.

Notes

85 Ratner (1995), p. xvii.
86 Heininger (1994,) p. 133.
87 MC Ott, *Cambodia: Between Hope and Despair, Current History: A Journal of Contemporary World Affairs*, December 1997, p. 433.
88 David Ashley in *Phnom Penh Post*, 2–15 June, 1995, vol. 4, no. 11, p. 6.
89 JA Jeldres, *The UN and the Cambodian Transition, Journal of Democracy*, vol. 4, no. 4, October 1993, p. 107.
90 *The Independent*, 24 October, 1991.
91 J Pilger, *Distant Voices*, Vintage, 1992, p. 178.
92 Ratner (1995), p. 158.

II

1 Interview with Ieng Sary, 24 December, 1997, Pailin, Cambodia. See also D Roberts, *More Honoured in the Breech: Consent and Impartiality in the Cambodian Peacekeeping Operation, 1993, International Peacekeeping*, vol. 4, no. 1, April 1997; JE Heininger, *Peacekeeping in Transition: The United Nations in Cambodia, Twentieth Century Fund Press*, 1994, p. 133; SR Ratner, *The New UN Peacekeeping: Building Peace in Lands of Conflict after the Cold War, St. Martin's*, 1995.p. xvii and p. 158; JA Jeldres, *The UN and the Cambodian Transition, Journal of Democracy*, vol. 4, no. 4, October 1993, p. 107; *The Independent*, 24 October, 1991; JA Schear, 'Riding the Tiger: The United Nations and Cambodia's Struggle for Peace', in WJ Durch (ed.), *United Nations Peacekeeping, American Policy, and the Uncivil Wars of the 1990s*, Macmillan, 1997; and M Leifer, *Powersharing and Peacemaking in Cambodia? School of Advanced International Studies Review*, vol. 12, no. 1, 1992.
2 *Newsweek*, 24 September, 1990, p. 45.
3 RH Taylor (ed.), *The Politics of Elections in Southeast Asia, Cambridge University Press*, 1996, p. 10.
4 *Phnom Penh Post*, vol. 4, no. 25, 15–28 December, 1995.
5 *Phnom Penh Post*, vol. 3, no. 17, 26 August–8 September, 1994, p. 8.
6 K Frieson, 'The Cambodian Elections of 1993: A Case of Power to the People?' in RH Taylor (ed.), *The Politics of Elections in Southeast Asia, Cambridge University Press*, 1996, p. 224.
7 KB Hadjor, *Dictionary of Third World Terms*, Penguin, 1993, p. 66.
8 See DW Ashley, 'The Failure of Conflict Resolution in Cambodia: Causes and Lessons', in FZ Brown and DG Timberman (eds.), *Cambodia and the International Community: The Quest for Peace, Development and Democracy, Institute of Southeast Asian Studies* (Singapore), 1998.
9 See M Vickery, *Cambodia 1975–1982*, Southend, 1984, p. 13.
10 Frieson in Taylor (ed.), (1996), p. 225.
11 Vickery (1984), p. 13.
12 M Ward, 'Constraints on Re-Building Cambodia's Economy', *Conference on Cambodia's Economy*, University of Washington, Seattle, 1994, p. 3; cited in G Curtis, *Cambodia Reborn? The Transition to Democracy and Development, United Nations Research Institute for Social Development* (UNRISD), 1998, pp. 206, note 9.

Notes

13 *Phnom Penh Post*, vol. 3, no. 17, 26 August–8 September, 1994, p. 15. See also RE Elson, *The End of the Peasantry in Southeast Asia: A Social and Economic History of Peasant Livelihood, 1800—1990s*, Macmillan, 1997, p. 25.
14 See, for a detailed review of the military positioning, B. Kiernan, (ed.), *Genocide and Democracy in Cambodia: The Khmers Rouges, the United Nations and the International Community*, Yale University Press, 1993, p. 209.
15 Interview with Hun Sen, 1 January, 1994, Phnom Penh.
16 Ibid.
17 J Chopra, *United Nations Authority in Cambodia*, Thomas J Watson Jr. Institute for International Studies, Occasional Paper no. 15, 1994, p. 30.
18 *The Economist*, 1 June, 1991, p. 54.
19 B Schwarz, *The Diversity Myth: America's Leading Export*, Atlantic Monthly, May 1995, p. 60.
20 Ibid.
21 Ibid.
22 See, amongst many others, M Haas, *Cambodia, Pol Pot and the United States: The Faustian Pact*, Praeger, 1989; and E Mysliwiecz, *Punishing the Poor: the International Isolation of Kampuchea*, Oxfam, 1989. For detailed accounts of the international geopolitics of the period, see L Mason and R Brown, *Rice, Rivalry and Politics: Managing Cambodian Relief*, Notre Dame, 1986; J Reynell, *Political Pawns: Refugees on the Thai-Kampuchean Border*, Oxford, 1989; M Vickery, *Cambodia (Kampuchea): History, Tragedy and Uncertain Future*, Bulletin of Concerned Asian Scholars, vol. 21, nos 2–4, April–December 1989; B Kiernan, *The Cambodian Crisis, 1990–1992: The UN Plan, the Khmer Rouge, and the state of Cambodia*, Bulletin of Concerned Asian Scholars, vol. 24, no. 4, 1992; and Kiernan (1993).
23 Paul Davies, *Cambodia: Interference is not Aid*, unpublished paper, 26 May, 1992, p. 4.
24 See, for example, JM Sanderson, 'UNTAC: Successes and Failures', in H Smith (ed.), *International Peacekeeping: Building on the Cambodian Experience*, Australian Defence Studies Centre, 1994, p. 17. Others were generally optimistic. See also K Farris, *UN Peacekeeping in Cambodia: On Balance, a Success*, Parameters, vol. 24, no. 1, 1994; and MW Doyle & N Suntharalingum, *The UN in Cambodia: Lessons for Complex Peacekeeping*, International Peacekeeping, vol. 1, no. 2, 1994.
25 M Hong, *The Paris Agreement on Cambodia: In Retrospect*, International Peacekeeping, vol. 2, no. 1, Spring 1995, p. 94.
26 Anonymous telephone interview, senior UN representative, Battambang, 10 September, 1993. This view was supported by some NGO representatives with longer experience of politics in Cambodia.
27 Schear in Durch (ed.)1997, p. 139.
28 Interview with Hun Sen, 1 January, 1994, Phnom Penh.
29 Schear in Durch (ed.)1997, p. 139.
30 See, for example, T Thomas, *Into the Unknown: Can the United Nations Bring Peace to Cambodia? Journal of International Affairs* vol. 44, no. 2, 1991.

Notes

31 FZ Brown, *Cambodia in Crisis: The 1993 Elections and the United Nations*, Asian Update, *The Asia Society*, 1993, p. 5. This is also strongly inferred in Hong (1995), p. 94.
32 Anonymous telephone interview, senior UN representative, Battambang, 10 September, 1993.
33 See Pol Pot, *Clarification of Certain Principled Views to Act as the Basis of Our Views and Stance*, 6 February, 1992, p. 4; and S Heder and J Ledgerwood, *Propaganda, Politics and Violence in Cambodia: Democratic Transition under United Nations Peacekeeping*, ME Sharpe, 1996. p. 74. Heder cites the following internal Khmer Rouge documents: *What Will Cambodia's situation Be Like in the Upcoming Decades* (1987); *Viewpoints on How Always to Organise and to Establish the Conditions for Ensuring Well the Livelihood of Our Ranks and Our People and Ensuring Well the Preservation, Defence, Consolidation and Expansion of the Forces in Our Ranks and Our People* (11 April 1988); and Pol Pot, *What is the Current Situation in Kampuchea? What Will It Be Like in the Future?* (December 1988).
34 Interview with Hun Sen, 1 January, 1994, Phnom Penh. See also
35 *International Report, Radio Australia*, 16:00hrs UTC, 14 June, 1993.
36 D Roberts, *Meddling while Phnom Penh Burned: the US Role in the Cambodian Secession, June 1993, Bulletin of Concerned Asian Scholars*, vol. 30, no. 3, July–September 1998.
37 Interviews with Hun Sen, 1 January, 1994, Phnom Penh; and Ieng Sary, 24 December, 1997, Pailin, Cambodia.
38 Kiernan (1992), p. 15. See also J Pilger, *Distant Voices*, Vintage, 1992, p. 198; and Leifer (1992), p. 148. Figures at 17 August 1992 for numbers of soldiers in cantonment stood at: CPP: 9817; KPNLF: 5876; FUNCINPEC: 3445; NADK: zero. See also RM Jennar, *Dialogue of the Deaf in a Volatile Context, Cambodian Chronicles* V, EFERC, 7 September, 1992, p. 4.
39 W Durch, *The Evolution of UN Peacekeeping: Case Studies and Comparative Analysis*, Macmillan, 1994, p. 467.
40 Kiernan (1992), p. 17.
41 Interview with UN District Electoral Supervisor, Kompong Speu Province, in Norwich, 23 November, 1995. Ramon Miranda-Ramos, an IPSO during the elections, concurred with this view, sampled during the mobile polling phase in Takeo Province.
42 V Simone & AT Feraru, *The Asian Pacific: Political and Economic Development in a Global Context*, Longman 1995, p. 222. See also M Alagappa, *Political Legitimacy in Southeast Asia: The Quest for Moral Authority*, Stanford, 1995.
43 Simone & Feraru (1995), p. 222.
44 F Zakaria, *The Rise of Illiberal Democracy, Foreign Affairs*, November–December 1997, p. 27. Frieson makes a similar comment in Taylor (ed.), (1996), p. 227.
45 There *have* been elections in Cambodia since independence. They were not universal suffrage selecting from a multi-party candidature and were restricted mostly to the assembly. The results were also decided in advance; and one party maintained dominance throughout that period.

Notes

See M Vickery, *Kampuchea: Politics, Economics and Society*, Pinter, 1986; and DP Chandler, *The Tragedy of Cambodian History: Politics, War and Revolution since 1945*, Yale University Press, 1991, chs 3, 4 and 5. Pre-independence elections, whilst generally free and fair, exhibited limited political freedom due to intolerance of a communist party; or acceptance of the role of the French Union in Cambodian political sovereignty. See M Vickery, *Phnom Penh Post*, vol. 1, no. 6, 25 September, 1992, p. 2.

46 R Jennar, *UNTAC: 'International Triumph' in Cambodia?*, Security Dialogue, vol. 25, no. 2, 1994, p. 147. William Shawcross notes that 'Cambodians have always lived under authoritarian regimes. Intimidation by these rulers has been part of everyday life'. (*Killing Field Election*, BBC2 Assignment, May 1993). See also Chandler (1991); Vickery (1986); Chopra (1994), pp. 47–8; Kiernan (1993), p. 291; DGE Hall, *A History of Southeast Asia*, Macmillan, 1981, part IV; Chandler (1993), ch. 11; and E Becker, *When the War Was Over: Cambodia's Revolution and The Voice of its People*, Touchstone, 1986. The lineage can be traced back yet further to the Angkorean period. See Chandler (1994).

47 Some of the policies invoked out of pragmatism by younger cadre, especially Hun Sen after 1985, were not of a Leninist ilk. Market reforms and property laws that were in direct contravention to Leninist ideology were applied to overcome the most obvious threats to economic development. For examinations of the theoretical debate surrounding ideology, see Vickery (1984), p. 250.

48 See B Kiernan, *How Pol Pot Came to Power*, Verso, 1985; and Chandler, (1991).

49 See Vickery (1986); and Chandler (1991), ch. 6.

50 Although Hun Sen's name is always associated with the PRK, he did not become PM until 1985. In the months immediately after the establishment of the Kampuchean Peoples Revolutionary Council (KPRC), the leadership consisted of Pen Sovan, Heng Samrin, Chea Sim, Keo Chenda, Chan Ven, Dr. Nou Beng and Mok Sokun, as well as Hun Sen in charge of Foreign Affairs.

51 The country's name has been a key to identifying the politics of each period. Under Sihanouk after independence, it was the Kingdom of Cambodia; under Lon Nol it was the Khmer Republic; under Pol Pot it was Democratic Kampuchea (a misnomer); under Heng Samrin-Hun Sen, it was the People's Republic of Kampuchea; and finally, with the ascendancy of Sihanouk, it has now reverted to a Kingdom.

52 Impressions gained from interviews and conversations conducted in Cambodia between 1991 and 1993.

53 S Heder, *Cambodia's Democratic Transition to Neoauthoritarianism*, Current History: A Journal of Contemporary World Affairs, December 1995, p. 426.

54 Curtis (1998), p. 17

55 Ibid., p. 17

56 Interview with Hun Sen, 1 January, 1994; interview with Major-General Bunno Nuon, Pailin, Cambodia, 24 December, 1997.

57 ES Muskie, *Exploring Cambodia: Issues and Reality in a Time of Transition*, Centre for National Policy, Washington DC, October 1990, p. 23.

Notes

58 *Camnews*, Reuter (Phnom Penh), 27 April, 1996.
59 Leifer (1992), p. 140.
60 Schear in Durch (1997), p. 139.
61 See M Vickery, *Cambodia: A Political Survey, Regime Change and Regime Maintenance in Asia and the Pacific*, no. 14, Australian National University, 1994, p. 1.
62 See Chandler (1994).
63 Jennar (November 1992), p. 3.
64 Schear in Durch (1997), p. 139.

III

1 J Pilger, *Heroes*, Pan, 1989.
2 Impressions gained from informal, often impromptu, discussions with rural Khmers over the last nine years in Cambodia. Although black propaganda and intellectual dishonesty has created a myth concerning the brutality and nature of the Viêt Namese so-called 'occupation force', the majority of Khmers take a far more positive view of the 1980s. For accurate, first hand scholarly commentary, see S Thion, *Watching Cambodia, White Lotus* (Bangkok), 1993. For other scholarly perspectives on this issue, see M Vickery, *Kampuchea: Politics, Economic and Society*, 1986; M Vickery, *Cambodia 1975–1982*, Southend, 1984; DP Chandler, *The Tragedy of Cambodian History: Politics, War and Revolution since 1945*, Yale University Press, 1991.
3 Vickery (1984), p. 231.
4 For a clear discussion of the consequences of intervention, and the effects on Cambodia of aid denied, see E Mysliwiecz, *Punishing the Poor: the International Isolation of Kampuchea*, Oxfam, 1989.
5 See Mysliwiecz (1989).
6 RM Jennar, *Cambodia Chooses, Cambodian Chronicles IX*, 14 May, 1993, p. 1. See also S Prasso, *Cambodia: A Heritage of Violence*, World Policy Journal, vol. 11, no. 3, 1994.
7 *Far Eastern Economic Review*, 27 April, 1995, p. 31.
8 For a brief discussion of the changing nature of the Cambodian political leadership, see *Far Eastern Economic Review*, 31 October, 1991, p. 12.
9 *Oxfam News*, Winter 1993, p. 8. See also Prasso (1994).
10 M Vickery, *Cambodia 1975–1982*, Southend, 1984, p. 7. See pp. 2-7 for an interesting discussion of this with some illuminating anecdotes and examples.
11 Ibid., p. 17.
12 Ovesen, I-B Trankell and J Ojendal, *When Every Household is an Island: Social Organization and Power Structures in Rural Cambodia*, Uppsala, 1996, p. 42.
13 *The Independent on Sunday*, 21 October 1990, p. 5.
14 Correspondence from PA Donnelly to author, 1 June 1999.
15 See, amongst many others, SJ Hood, *Dragons Entangled: Indochina and the China-Viêt Nam War*, ME Sharpe, 1992, p. 73.
16 Interview with under-secretary of state Suy Mong Leang, Council of Ministers, Phnom Penh, 8 January, 1998.

Notes

17 *Far Eastern Economic Review*, 9 January 1992, p. 11; *New York Times*, 2 May, 1991. These views were corroborated by Suy Mong Leang – Interview with under-secretary of state Suy Mong Leang, Council of Ministers, Phnom Penh, 8 January, 1998.
18 RM. Jennar, *The Lost Gamble, Cambodian Chronicles VI*, EFERC, 11 November, 1992, p. 13.
19 J Chopra, *United Nations Authority in Cambodia, Thomas J Watson Jr. Institute for International Studies*, Occasional Paper no. 15, 1994, p. 31.
20 Frieson in Taylor (ed.), (1996), p. 227. See also D Chandler, *Brother Number One: A Political Biography of Pol Pot*, Westview Press, 1992, p. 51.
21 *The Economist*, 23 November, 1991, p. 85.
22 For a discussion of the nature of the post-1979 political regimes in Cambodia, see M Vickery, *The Cambodian People's Party: Where did it come from, where is it going?*, *Southeast Asian Affairs*, 1994; and M Vickery, *Kampuchea: Politics, Economics and Society*, Pinter, 1986 (ch. 5).
23 M Leifer, *Tigers, Tigers, Spurning Rights, Times Higher Education Supplement*, 21 April, 1995, p. 16. See also FC Deyo, *The Political Economy of the New Asian Industrialism*, Cornell, 1987; and R Wade, *Governing the Market: Economic Theory and the Role of government in East Asia*, Princeton, 1990.
24 Vickery (1986), p. 55
25 Ibid., p. 250.
26 Ibid., p. 57.
27 See Vickery (1984), chp. 2.
28 Ibid., p. 211.
29 Interviews conducted during a five-month research exercise in Cambodia, June to October, 1991.
30 DG Porter, *The Myth of the Bloodbath: North Vietnam's Land Reform Reconsidered, Bulletin of Concerned Asian Scholars*, Vol. 5, No. 2, 1973.
31 See *The Economist*, 1 February, 1992, p. 63; D Roberts, *Cambodia: Problems of a UN-brokered Peace, The World Today*, vol. 48, no. 7, July 1992, p. 130; *The Economist*, 25 January, 1992, p. 59; and *The Independent*, 29 January, 1992.
32 For a discussion of political theory and the economic framework of the mid-1980s, see Vickery (1984), p. 250.
33 Ibid., p. 239.
34 *The Independent on Sunday,* 17 November, 1991. The Prince's memories do not generally include the brutality with which he dominated the political and court scene in this period; nor do they generally make references to the poverty and corruption of life in that decade. His views are certainly through rose-tinted spectacles.
35 Sihanouk quoted in *The Economist*, 23 November, 1991, p. 85. Taxi-dancers are often prostitutes.
36 Frieson, in Heder and Ledgerwood (eds.), (1996), p. 185.
37 Observations made in a five month research exercise to Cambodia, June to October, 1991.
38 See Pilger (1989).
39 Son Sen was the military commander of the NADK before he was murdered on Pol Pot's orders in July 1997.

Notes

40 *NGO Resource Project - Daily Report*, 15 May, 1993, Phnom Penh. This 'protection' line was a consistent theme of the CPP's political platform throughout campaigning and the election: Hun Sen's 'stump speeches point out that CPP is the only party in the race which has built anything [and which] promises protection from the Khmer Rouge'.

41 J Pilger, *Distant Voices*, Vintage, 1992, p. 233. See also *The Guardian*, 28 November, 1992; *The Independent*, 28 November, 1992; and *The Times*, 28 November 1992.

42 *Far Eastern Economic Review*, 12 December, 1991, p. 10.

43 See *Far Eastern Economic Review*, 9 January, 1992, p. 11; *The Independent*, 21 December, 1991; *The Guardian*, 24 December, 1991; *The Economist*, 25 January, 1992, p. 59; and *The Economist*, 1 February, 1992, p. 63.

44 K Farris, *UN Peacekeeping in Cambodia: On Balance, a Success*, Parameters, vol. 24, no. 1, 1994, p. 49.

45 MW Doyle & N Suntharalingum, *The UN In Cambodia: Lessons for Complex Peacekeeping*, International Peacekeeping, vol. 1, no. 2, 1994, p. 131. See also RM Jennar, *UNTAC: 'International Triumph' in Cambodia?*, Security Dialogue, vol. 25, no. 2, 1994, p. 152; and JA Schear, 'Riding the Tiger: The United Nations and Cambodia's Struggle for Peace', in WJ Durch (ed.), *United Nations Peacekeeping, American Policy, and the Uncivil Wars of the 1990s*, Macmillan, 1997.

46 Doyle & Suntharalingum (1994), p. 131. See also Jennar (1994), p. 152.

47 Ibid., p. 153.

48 *Far Eastern Economic Review*, 27 February, 1992.

49 Jennar, (1994), p. 153.

50 *Index on Censorship*, 1 May, 1993, p. 5.

51 Interview with Pho Bun Naraddh, Pailin Hotel, Phnom Penh, July 1993.

52 *The Guardian*, 14 January, 1992.

53 Jennar (1994), p. 152. See also *The Daily Telegraph*, 6 April and 24 May, 1993.

54 A Acharya, *Cambodia, the United Nations and the Problems of Peace*, Pacific Review, vol. 7, no. 3, 1994. p. 303. See also *The Daily Telegraph*, 6 April and 24 May, 1993.

55 Farris (1994), p. 43.

56 These estimates were first presented in *Report of the secretary-general on Cambodia containing his proposed implementation plan for UNTAC, including administrative and financial aspects*, S/23613, 19 February, 1992. Cited in *The United Nations in Cambodia, 1991–1995*, UN Blue Book Series, vol. 2, 1995, p. 12.

57 In conversation with Dr. Peter Carey, (Cambodia Trust NGO), 23 April, 1993, Phnom Penh; and in discussion with Dr. John Mackinlay, King's College, London, 17 May, 1998. See also *Far Eastern Economic Review*, 30 July, 1992, p. 18.

58 *Far Eastern Economic Review*, 30 July, 1992, p. 18.

59 Interviews with Ieng Sary, 24 December, 1997, Pailin, Cambodia; and with S Heder, *School of Oriental and African Studies*, London, 1997, 14 November, 1997.

60 For a review of personnel contributors to the UNTAC operation, see *The United Nations in Cambodia, 1991–1995*, UN Blue Book Series, vol. 2, 1995, p. 23.

Notes

61 Ibid., p. 17.
62 See D Roberts, *Sympathy with the Devil? The Khmer Rouge and the Politics of Consent*, Contemporary Security Policy, vol. 19, no. 2, August 1998.
63 See D Roberts, *More Honoured in the Breech: Consent and Impartiality in the Cambodia Peacekeeping Operation*, International Peacekeeping, April 1998; and S Heder and J Ledgerwood, *Propaganda, Politics and Violence in Cambodia: Democratic Transition under United Nations Peacekeeping*, ME Sharpe, 1996.
64 *Far Eastern Economic Review*, 25 June, 1992, p. 12; *Far Eastern Economic Review*, 2 July, 1992.
65 G Will, *The Elections in Cambodia: Taking Stock of a UN Mission*, Aussenpolitik, no. IV, 1993, p. 398. Some take the position that there were never real threats from the NADK. Heder notes that internal documents demonstrated the provision of 'plans to have the capability to attack polling stations if there was an order to do so'; and that there was 'a contingency plan to make sure that [the NADK had] the capability to launch such attacks'. Heder and Ledgerwood (1996), p. 100.
66 *Phnom Penh Post*, vol. 2, no. 8, 9-22 April, 1993, p. 1. This warning came directly on the heels of the anti-Viêt Namese pogroms in Phnom Penh and the Northwest. For a detailed account of NADK plans for anti-polling retribution, see Heder and Ledgerwood (1996), chp. 3.
67 T Findlay, *Cambodia: Legacy And Lessons of UNTAC, SIPRI*, 1995, p. 35.
68 Interview with Ieng Sary, 24th December, 1997, Pailin, Cambodia. See also *Phnom Penh Post*, vol. 2, no. 2, 15-28 January, 1993, p. 2; and SM Hill and SP Malik, *Peacekeeping and the United Nations*, Issues in International Security, Dartmouth, 1996.
69 *Far Eastern Economic Review*, 25 June, 1992, p. 21.
70 *Far Eastern Economic Review*, 28 January, 1993, p. 5.
71 *Far Eastern Economic Review*, 30 July, 1992, p. 18, cited in Acharya (1994), p. 301.
72 See, for example, *Far Eastern Economic Review*, 23 July, 1992, p. 8.
73 *Phnom Penh Post*, vol. 1, no. 10, 20 November – 3 December, 1992, p. 6; *Far Eastern Economic Review*, 23 July, 1992, pp. 8–9.
74 Interview with Stephen Heder, *School of Oriental and African Studies*, 14 November, 1997.
75 Ibid.
76 Email correspondence with General JM Sanderson, 16 March, 1998.
77 Ibid.
78 Ibid.
79 Correspondence with Lt. General Michel Loridon, dated 23 April, 1999.
80 Email correspondence with General JM Sanderson, 16 March, 1998.
81 Correspondence with Lt. General Michel Loridon, dated 23 April, 1999.
82 *Far Eastern Economic Review*, 30 July, 1992, p. 19. This is a reference to the defeat of the French garrison in Viêt Nam in 1954 by Ho Chi Minh and General Vo Nguyen Giap's Viêt Minh troops.

Notes

83 This term was adopted by Akashi to describe his diplomacy.
84 S/RES/792, 30 November, 1992. The sanctions were transmitted through reference to Article VII of Annex 2 of the PPA, and were designed to 'prevent the supply of petroleum products to the areas occupied by any Cambodian party not complying with the military provisions' of the PPA.
85 *Far Eastern Economic Review*, 30 July, 1992, p. 18.
86 JM Sanderson, *The Dilemma of Force: Don't Dabble in War, Work in Progress – The United Nations University*, vol. 14, no. 3, June 1995, p. 9. This view reflects concerns such as using the relevant Chapter of the UN Charter; the problem of maintaining international consensus; logistics of conflict when most of the force was not deployed; the uneven quality of some troop contributors, such as the Bulgarians (see Farris, 1994); and the tactical disadvantages which prompted warnings of a Dien Bien Phu-esque defeat.
87 Correspondence from Lt. General Michel Loridon, dated 8 April, 1999.
88 Field notes, Phnom Penh, June 1993.
89 Vickery (1984), p. 2.
90 BA Brown, *Cambodia's Shaky Step, Freedom Review*, vol. 24, no. 4, July–August 1993.
91 *Phnom Penh Post*, June 2–15, 1995, vol. 4, no. 11, p. 8; see also *Phnom Penh Post*, vol. 3, no. 17, 26 August – 8 September, 1994, p. 8.
92 *Cambodia: Agenda for Rehabilitation and Reconstruction, The World Bank*, East Asia and Pacific Region, Country department I, June 1992, New York, pp. 156–157. Even though the date of the report is June 1992, most of it was conducted prior to UNTAC deployment, which was principally from March 1992. See also Vickery (1986).
93 R Pinkney, *Democracy in the Third World, Open University Press*, 1993, p. 120.
94 Schear (1997), p. 158.
95 Ibid., p. 158.
96 *The United Nations in Cambodia, 1991–1995, UN Blue Book Series*, vol. 2, 1995, p. 38.
97 MC Williams, *Keeping the Peace In Cambodia, Survival: IISS Quarterly*, vol. 38, no. 3, 1996, p. 148 (review essays).
98 Cambodian term for the voters booth.
99 DP Chandler, *The Tragedy of Cambodian History Revisited, School of Advanced International Studies Review*, vol. 14, no. 2, 1994.
100 *The United Nations in Cambodia, 1991–1995, UN Blue Book Series*, vol. 2, 1995, p. 44.
101 Field Notes from UNTAC HQ. See also *UN Blue Book Series*, p. 5; Heininger (1994); D Roberts (1994); and Jennar (1994).
102 Chandler (1994), p. 89.
103 Ibid., p. 89.
104 *Phnom Penh Post*, vol. 2, no. 9, April 23–May 6, 1993, p. 1.
105 Frieson, in Heder and Ledgerwood (eds.), (1996), pp. 185–96.
106 *Secretariat News*, UNHQ, New York (Phnom Penh), May–June, 1993, p. 1.
107 Chopra (1994), p. 49.

Notes

108 *Freeness and Fairness of the Cambodian Elections: Statement by Mr. Akashi*, 10 June, 1993, Phnom Penh.
109 Field Notes from UNTAC HQ's announcement of election results, 30 May–10 June, 1993, Phnom Penh. See also Heininger (1994); D Roberts (1994); Jennar (1994).

IV

1 JM Sanderson, 'UNTAC: Successes and Failures', in H Smith (ed.), *International Peacekeeping: Building on the Cambodian Experience*, Australian Defence Studies Centre, 1994, p. 25.
2 RM Jennar, UNTAC: International Triumph' in Cambodia?, *Security Dialogue*, vol. 25, no. 2, 1994, p. 153. See also Sanderson in Smith (ed.) (1994), p. 25.
3 JM Sanderson, 'The Humanitarian Response in Cambodia: The Imperative for a Strategic Alliance', in J Whitman and D Pocock (eds.), *After Rwanda: The Co-ordination of UN Humanitarian Assistance*, Macmillan, 1996, pp. 186–7.
4 J Chopra, *United Nations Authority in Cambodia*, Thomas J Watson Jr. Institute for International Studies, Occasional Paper no. 15, 1994, p. 29.
5 J Mackinlay L Minear and J Chopra, *A Draft Concept of Second Generation Multinational Operations 1993*, Thomas J Watson Institute for International Studies, Brown University, 1993, p. 17.
6 Sanderson in Smith (1994), p. 18.
7 Ibid., p. 18.
8 T Findlay, *Cambodia: The Legacy and Lessons of UNTAC*, SIPRI 1995; JE Heininger, *Peacekeeping in Transition: The United Nations in Cambodia*, Twentieth Century Fund Press, 1994, p. 69; Chopra (1994), pp. 27–30.
9 JA Schear, 'Riding the Tiger: The United Nations and Cambodia's Struggle for Peace', in WJ Durch (ed.), *United Nations Peacekeeping, American Policy, and the Uncivil Wars of the 1990s*, Macmillan, 1997, pp. 153–4.
10 Schear in Durch (ed.) 1997, pp. 153–4.
11 Interview with J Mackinlay, King's College London, 26 June, 1998; J Chopra et al, *Report on the Cambodian Peace Process*, Norwegian Institute of International Affairs, no. 165, February 1993, p. 20.
12 Chopra et al (1993), p. 20.
13 E-mail correspondence with General John Sanderson, 20 September, 1998.
14 Chopra et al (1993), p. 19.
15 Findlay (1995); Chopra et al (1993); Heininger (1994).
16 Chopra (1994), p. 28.
17 Sanderson in Smith (1994), p. 17.
18 Findlay (1995), p. 23.
19 E-mail correspondence with General John Sanderson, 20 September, 1998.
20 Schear in Durch (ed.), 1997, p. 154.
21 Ibid.

Notes

22 A Acharya, *Cambodia, the United Nations and the Problems of Peace*, *Pacific Review*, vol. 7, no. 3, 1994, p. 300.
23 Three categories of control were identified in the PPA. The first group, consisting of five Ministries, were under direct control, and were most likely to be able to affect the electoral outcome. The second grouping, consisting of at least four ministries, were under supervision or control. There was a third group, but that was only under investigation upon specific requests. These ministries were those deemed to have the least potential effect on the vote.
24 *The Economist*, 15 August, 1992. This claim is also suggested in R Amer, *The United Nations Peacekeeping Operation in Cambodia: Overview and Assessment*, *Contemporary Southeast Asia*, vol. 15, no. 2, 1993, p. 215.
25 *Return to Year Zero, Viewpoint '93*, CTV, May 1993.
26 Doyle (1995), p. 38.
27 S Heder and J Ledgerwood (eds.), *Propaganda, Politics, and Violence in Cambodia: Democratic Transition under United Nations Peacekeeping*, ME Sharpe, 1996, p. 187.
28 Chopra (1994), p. 32.
29 *NATO Review*, August 1994, p. 26.
30 Interview with Ty Sopath, Slar Kram Village, Siem Reap, 22 May, 1993. See also *The Review of the Cambodian Human Rights Task Force*, Issue no. 4, 1 May 1993, Phnom Penh, p. 6.
31 The US General Accounting Office supports this argument. See *National Security and International Affairs Division*, Report no. B-270716, p. 10.
32 Interview with Marcella Gange, UNV, 23 November, 1995 (Norwich, England). See also L McLean, 'Civil Administration in Transition: Public Information and the Neutral Political/Electoral Environment', in Smith (ed.), (1994), p. 52.
33 McLean in Smith (1994), p. 48.
34 C Arnson and D Holiday, 'Cambodia', in *The Lost Agenda: Human Rights and UN Field Operations, Human Rights Watch*, 1993, p. 37. The Force Commander offered a number of thoughts about quality of staff in Whitman and Pocock (1996), p. 186.
35 Schear in Durch (1997), p. 155.
36 MW Doyle & N Suntharalingum, *The UN In Cambodia: Lessons for Complex Peacekeeping*, *International Peacekeeping*, vol. 1, no. 2, 1994, p. 25. See also Jennar, (1994), p. 125.
37 W Shawcross, *Cambodia's New Deal*, Contemporary Issues Paper no. 1, *Carnegie Endowment for International Peace*, 1994, p. 13; and *The Spectator*, 22 May, 1993, p. 10.
38 US General Accounting Office, *National Security and International Affairs Division*, Report no. B-270716, p. 11.
39 Anonymous interview, UNTAC Civilian Administrator, Phnom Penh, 25 June, 1993.
40 J Hippler, *Pax Americana? Hegemony or Decline*, Pluto, 1994, p. 84. See Shawcross (1994), p. 13. Shawcross agrees that UNTAC was 'unable to take control of the five key areas' stipulated in the PPA.
41 *The Economist*, 6 May, 1989, p. 68; and *The Economist*, 25 February, 1989, p. 63.

Notes

42 *Fourth Progress Report of the secretary-general on the United Nations Transitional Authority in Cambodia*, S/25719, 3 May, 1993, p. 15. See also Heininger (1994), chp. 6.
43 *Fourth Progress Report ...*, p. 14. See also Schear in Durch (1997), p. 155.

V

1 For a variety of easily digestible discussions on the causes of the Khmer Rouge's withdrawal, see *NATO Review*, August 1994, p. 26; *The Daily Telegraph*, 13 June, 1992; *The Economist*, 20 June, 1992, p. 8; *The Guardian*, 6 January, 1993; *Far Eastern Economic Review*, 30 July, 1992, p. 18; *The Guardian*, 3 September, 1990; *The Daily Telegraph*, 13 June, 1992; *Phnom Penh Post*, vol. 2, no. 11, 21 May–3 June, 1993, p. 1; *Phnom Penh Post*, vol. 1, no. 4, 27 August, 1992, p. 1; *Far Eastern Economic Review*, 12 November, 1992; J Branegan, *Time*, 29 June, 1992, no. 26, p. 48; *Oxford Analytica Daily Brief*, 29 January, 1993; and T Findlay, *Cambodia: The Legacy and Lessons of UNTAC, SIPRI* 1995.
2 S Heder, *Cambodia's Democratic Transition to Neoauthoritarianism, Current History: A Journal of Contemporary World Affairs*, December 1995, p. 427.
3 *Far Eastern Economic Review*, 30 July, 1992, p. 15.
4 Although the four parties that had been fighting each other since 1979 dominated the elections, another 16 parties, many of which had been nurtured and developed overseas at varying stages, joined the fray.
5 Interview with Stephen Heder, *School of Oriental and African Studies*, 14 November, 1997.
6 See for examples, *Phnom Penh Post*, vol. 7, no. 18, 21 August–3 September 1998, p. 12.
7 Ibid.
8 S Heder and J Ledgerwood (eds.), *Propaganda, Politics, and Violence in Cambodia: Democratic Transition under United Nations Peacekeeping*, ME Sharpe, 1996, ch. 3.
9 Pol Pot, *Clarification of Certain Principled Views to Act as the Basis of Our Views and Stance*, 6 February, 1992, p. 4.
10 See Heder and Ledgerwood (eds.), (1996), p. 74. Heder cites the following internal Khmer Rouge documents: *What Will Cambodia's situation Be Like in the Upcoming Decades* (1987); *Viewpoints on How Always to Organise and to Establish the Conditions for Ensuring Well the Livelihood of Our Ranks and Our People and Ensuring Well the Preservation, Defence, Consolidation and Expansion of the Forces in Our Ranks and Our People* (11th April 1988); and Pol Pot, *What is the Current Situation in Kampuchea? What Will It Be Like in the Future?* (December 1988).
11 *Far Eastern Economic Review*, 10 February, 1994, p. 26.
12 Pol Pot (1992), p. 11.
13 Interview with anonymous UN representative, Phnom Penh, 15 December, 1997.
14 Interview with Ieng Sary, 24 December, 1997, Pailin; corroborated in Pol Pot (1992), p. 11. The notion of a significant advantage is constantly reiterated throughout this document.

Notes

15 Pol Pot (1992), p. 11.
16 Interview with Stephen Heder, *School of Oriental and African Studies*, 14 November, 1997.
17 Ibid.
18 Interview with Ieng Sary, 1997.
19 Heder and Ledgerwood (eds.), (1996), p. 104.
20 Interview with NADK Colonel Saing Rin, Pailin, 23 December, 1997.
21 Interview with Major-General Nuon Bunno, Pailin, 23 December, 1997. Nuon was a senior advisor in the Mixed Military Working Group of the Supreme National Council during the UNTAC period. He was privy to the Khmer Rouge elite and its decision-making process, and closely advised Khieu Samphan and Pol Pot.
22 Heder and Ledgerwood (eds.), (1996), p. 104.
23 Ibid., pp. 76–7. Christophe Peschoux, a UN Human Rights Cambodia specialist, supported this evidence, and corroborated the building of barracks and cantonment areas. Interview with Christophe Peschoux, United Nations Centre for Human Rights, Phnom Penh, 8 January, 1998.
24 Interview with Ieng Sary, Pailin, 24 December, 1997.
25 R Normand, *The Teachings of Chairman Pot*, *The Nation*, 3 September, 1990.
26 Interview with Christophe Peschoux, United Nations Centre for Human Rights, Phnom Penh, 8 January, 1998.
27 Interview with Stephen Heder, 1997. See also *Far Eastern Economic Review*, 22 August, 1996, p. 15.
28 Interview with Ieng Sary, 1997.
29 Heder and Ledgerwood (eds.), (1996), p. 77.
30 Field notes in Phnom Penh, April–May 1993
31 Interview with Stephen Heder, 1997.
32 Heder and Ledgerwood (eds.), (1996), p. 77.
33 Interview with Ieng Sary, 1997. This was corroborated as a general theme in Pol Pot (1992).
34 Interview with Major-General Nuon Bunno, Pailin, 23 December, 1997.
35 Pol Pot (1992), p. 4.
36 Ibid., p. 12 and 21.
37 Ibid.
38 Interviews with Ieng Sary and Stephen Heder (1997).
39 Ibid.
40 Interview with Ieng Sary, 24 December, 1997, Pailin, Cambodia.
41 Ibid.
42 Ibid., corroborated in Pol Pot (1992), and further supported in interview with Major-General Bunno Nuon.
43 Pol Pot (1992), p. 13.
44 Heder and Ledgerwood (eds.), (1996), p. 94.
45 Ibid., p. 94.
46 For a discussion of the attempts, and the reasons they failed, see D Roberts, *Sympathy with the Devil? The Khmer Rouge and the Politics of Consent*, Contemporary Security Policy, vol. 19, no. 2, August 1998. See also D Roberts, *A Dangerous Game: Managing Consent in the Cambodian Peacekeeping Operation*, Studies in Conflict and Terrorism, vol. 21, no. 1, Jan. 1998; T Findlay, *Cambodia: The Legacy and Lessons of UNTAC*,

Notes

SIPRI Research Report no. 9, 1995, p. 44; *Report of the secretary-general on the Implementation of Security Council Resolution 783* (1992), 15 November, 1992, *S/24800*, p. 2; and SM Hill and SP Malik, *Peacekeeping and the United Nations*, Dartmouth, 1996, p. 95.

VI

1 *Phnom Penh Post*, vol. 2, no. 12, 6–12 June, 1993. See also RM Jennar, *Cambodian Chronicles VI: Samdech Preah Upayuvaraj Norodom Sihanouk EFERC*, 29 June, 1993, p. 7; *NGO Resource Project – Daily Reports*, 10 & 11 June, 1993; *Phnom Penh Post*, vol. 2, no. 12, 3–6 June, 1993, p. 3; and Letter from Yasushi Akashi to Chea Sim, (CPP President), 9 June, 1993, p. 2.
2 For a detailed analysis, see D Roberts, *Meddling while Phnom Penh Burned: the US Role in the Cambodian Secession, June 1993, Bulletin of Concerned Asian Scholars*, vol. 30, no. 3, July–September 1998.
3 Letter CPP/C/UN/93, no. 41, Phnom Penh, 4 June, 1993. See also letter CPP/C/UN/93, no. 25, 16 May, 1993.
4 *Bangkok Post*, 13 June, 1993; *The Independent*, 14 June, 1993. For a fuller review, see *The Economist*, 5 June, 1993, pp. 71–2.
5 BBC World Service, 13:00hrs UTC, 10 June, 1993.
6 *NGO Resource Project – Cambodia – Daily Report*, 1 June, 1993, p. 1.
7 See letters 32 CPP/C/UN/93 (27 May, 1993); 11 & 14 CPP/C/UN/93 (April and May 1993); and 28 CPP/C/UN/93 (24 May, 1993). Such impressions were noted by Hun Sen. See interview with Hun Sen, 1 January, 1994, Phnom Penh (private residence). See also Phnom Penh National Radio of Cambodia Network, 13:00 GMT, 3 May, 1996: FBIS-EAS-96-087, 3 May, 1996. Observations from Site 106, Siem Reap, Cambodia, in the first two days of the polling, corroborate claims of irregularities and dubious procedure, as well as suspicious happenings.
8 BBC World Service, 13:00hrs UTC, 10 June, 1993.
9 Interview with Marcella Gange, UNV, 23 November, 1995 (Norwich).
10 Jennar (29 June, 1993), p. 7.
11 Interview with United Nations Human Rights representative, 26 May, 1993, Takeo Province.
12 Interview with Khieu Kanharith, CPP Minister for Information, 12 April, 1996, Phnom Penh.
13 The *Cambodia Times*, 7–13 June, 1993, p. 1. See also *The Economist*, 5 June 1993, p. 72; and *Phnom Penh Post*, vol. 2, no. 13, 18 June–1 July, 1993, p. 15. Jennar records the date of this meeting as 1 June, 1993.
14 *Phnom Penh Post*, June 6–12, 1993, p. 2.
15 See, for example, *Bangkok Post*, 3 June, 1993; and *The Economist*, 5 June, 1993, p. 71.
16 *NGO Resource Project – Cambodia – Daily Report*, 4 June, 1993, Phnom Penh; and *Phnom Penh Post*, vol. 2, no. 12, 6–12 June, 1993, p. 1.
17 Ibid., p. 1. The *Cambodia Times* suggested the arrangement was to stop 'squabbles' between the parties (7–13 June, 1993, p. 2). See also Jennar (29 June, 1993), p. 16.

Notes

18 *Rapport de Norodom Sihanouk*, 3 June, 1993, Phnom Penh (FUNCINPEC Offices, Phnom Penh).
19 *Phnom Penh National Radio of Cambodia Network*, 1300 GMT 3 May 1996: FBIS-EAS-96-087, 3 May, 1996.
20 Ibid.
21 M Vickery, *Cambodia: A Political Survey, Regime Change and Regime Maintenance in Asia and the Pacific*, no. 14, Australian National University, 1994, p. 22.
22 Ibid.
23 TG Weiss (ed.), *The United Nations and Civil Wars*, Lynne Rienner, 1995, p. 145.
24 *Message de Samdech Preah Norodom Sihanouk du Cambodge à ses respectés et bien-aimés Compatriotes*, Phnom Penh, 4 June 1993 (FUNCINPEC Offices, Phnom Penh).
25 *Bangkok Post*, 5 June, 1993. See also *The Cambodia Times*, 14–20 June, 1993, p. 2.
26 *Bangkok Post*, 6 June, 1993. See also *The Cambodia Times*, 14–20 June, 1993, p. 2, and Jennar (29 June, 1993), p. 15.
27 *Phnom Penh Post*, June 6–12, 1993, p. 1.
28 *Bangkok Post*, 6 June, 1993.
29 *NGO Resource Project – Cambodia – Daily Report*, 4 June, 1993, Phnom Penh. See also *Bangkok Post*, 16 June, 1993. See also *NGO Resource Project – Cambodia – Daily Report*, 16 June, 1993, Phnom Penh, p. 2; Jennar (29 June, 1993,) p. 17; and *The Cambodia Times*, 14–20 June, 1993, p. 2.
30 *NGO Resource Project – Cambodia, Daily Report*, 11 June, 1993, Phnom Penh.
31 *Phnom Penh Post*, June 6–12, 1993, p. 2. Shawcross trivialized this event by describing the convoy as 'a brace of generals'; see Shawcross (1994), p. 24.
32 JA Jeldres, *The UN and the Cambodian Transition, Journal of Democracy*, vol. 4, no. 4, October 1993, p. 112.
33 *Bangkok Post*, 7 June, 1993. Interestingly, the following day Kanharith rejected any connection between the two issues, denying such reports attributed to Sok An (CPP spokesman) and arguing that the two were 'separate questions'. See *NGO Resource Project – Cambodia – Daily Report*, 8 June, 1993, Phnom Penh.
34 Jennar (29 June, 1993), p. 18.
35 See *Cambodia Times*, 21–27 June, 1993, p. 3.
36 Ibid.
37 S Heder, *CPP Secessionism, Resignations from the Assembly and Intimidation of UNTAC: Background and Theories*, Information/Education division, UNTAC 12, Phnom Penh, 13 June, 1993.
38 Ibid., p. 6.
39 Ibid.
40 Ibid.
41 Ibid.
42 Ibid., p. 2.
43 Roberts (1998), p. 20.

Notes

44 Jennar (29 June, 1993), p. 16.
45 Correspondence with Michael Vickery, 15 March, 1999.
46 Ibid.
47 See M Vickery, 'Resignation of CPP candidates and Their Replacements: A counter analysis to "CPP Secessionism, Resignations from the Assembly and Intimidation of UNTAC: Background and Theories', by Stephen Heder"', Phnom Penh, 24 June 1993, pp. 5–7.
48 Heder (13 June, 1993).
49 Vickery (24 June 1993).
50 Ibid., p. 2.
51 *Bangkok Post*, 16 June, 1993. See also *NGO Resource Project – Cambodia, Daily Report*, 15 June, 1993, p. 1.
52 *Phnom Penh Post*, vol. 2, no. 13, 18 June–1 July, 1993, p. 2.
53 Interview with Khieu Kanharith, Phnom Penh, 10 April, 1996 (private residence).
54 Communiqué of the Cambodian People's Party, 20 June, 1993, Phnom Penh.
55 Ibid.
56 The *Cambodia Times*, 21–27 June, 1993, p. 1. See also Jeldres (1993), p. 113.
57 Jennar (29 June, 1993), p. 18.
58 Ibid, p. 17
59 US Mission 'non-paper', 3 June, 1993. This item was issued almost as soon as Sihanouk's initiative had been made public, suggesting a particularly strong stand.
60 *NGO Resource Project – Cambodia – Daily Report*, 9 June, 1993, Phnom Penh.
61 Ibid.
62 SJ Randall, *Peacekeeping in the Post-Cold War Era: the United Nations and the Cambodian Elections of 1993, Contemporary Security Policy*, vol. 16, no. 2, 1995, p. 187.
63 J Pilger, *Return to Year Zero, The New Internationalist*, no. 242, April 1993, p. 7.
64 Letter from M Vickery to 'Z' Magazine, Massachusetts, 9 May, 1994.
65 B. Kiernan, (ed.), *Genocide and Democracy in Cambodia: The Khmers Rouges, the United Nations and the International Community*, Yale University Press, 1993.
66 *US General Accounting Office, Review of US Assistance to Cambodia*, June 1993: Job Code 711012.
67 Interview between Helen Long and Khieu Kanharith, Provisional National Government of Cambodia, Phnom Penh, 3 September, 1993 (notes passed to author).
68 These include, for example, Stephen Heder and Dr. Lao Mong Hay.
69 *Time Asia*, 22 March, 1999, full interview transcript, p. 4.
70 Impression gleaned from attending speeches, rallies and meetings during the 1993 and 1998 campaign periods.
71 Simone & Feraru (1995), p. 222.
72 ES Muskie, *Exploring Cambodia: Issues and reality in a Time of Transition*, Centre for National Policy, Washington DC, October 1990, p. 23.

Notes

73 This term draws on the romanticisation in Khmer society of the merit and heroism of struggle to achieve various objectives. It finds expression through perspectives of Buddhism, and is not unique to Cambodia

74 D Ashley, 'The Failure of Conflict Resolution in Cambodia', in FZ Brown and DG Timberman, *Cambodia and the International Community: The Quest for Peace, Development and Democracy*, Asia Society, 1998, p. 57.

75 In discussion with M Vickery, 26 July 1998; in interview with Stephen Heder, School of Oriental and African Studies, 14 November 1997.

76 See, for example, R Pinkney, *Democracy in the Third World*, Open University Press, 1993, p. 114; and E Wolf, 'Kinship, Friendship, and Patron-Client Relations', in M Banton, (ed.), *The Social Anthropology of Complex Societies*, Tavistock, 1966.

77 Ashley in Brown and Timberman (1998), p. 69.

78 Interview between J Brown and Reginald Austin, August 1993 (notes passed to author).

79 JM Sanderson, 'UNTAC: Successes and Failures', in H Smith (ed.), *International Peacekeeping: Building on the Cambodian Experience*, Australian Defence Studies Centre, 1994, p. 27.

80 *The Agreement*...

81 Sihanouk's status in Khmer society implies a degree of moral authority from which to take the lead. Political authority, however, was only vested upon the Prince when he was made Head of state in the first promulgation of the Constituent Assembly after the introduction of the interim coalition.

82 Correspondence with M Vickery, 12 November, 1997.

83 For corroboration of this argument, see P Lizée, *Cambodia in 1995: From Hope to Despair*, Asian Survey vol. XXXVI, no. 1, January 1996, p. 84.

84 Ashley in Brown and Timberman (1998), p. 53.

VII

1 J McAuliff, *Welcome to Cambodia, Where Nothing is Ever as it Seems*, Indochina Interchange, September 1997, p. 3. See also G Curtis, *Cambodia Reborn? The Transition to Democracy and Development*, United Nations Research Institute for Social Development (UNRISD), 1998, p. 23.

2 Curtis (1998), p. 23.

3 G Curtis, *Cambodia Reborn? The Transition to Democracy and Development*, United Nations Research Institute for Social Development (UNRISD), 1998, p. 16.

4 FZ Brown, *Drawing the lines of 'acceptable democracy'*, Phnom Penh Post, vol. 4, no. 22, November 3–16, 1995, p. 9. See also *Phnom Penh Post*, vol. 5, no. 7, March 1996, p. 10.

5 *Phnom Penh Post*, vol. 2, no. 24, 19 November—2 December, 1993, p. 1.

6 Ibid., p. 2.

7 *Phnom Penh Post*, vol. 4, no. 5, 10–23 March, 1995, p. 7.

8 Ibid.

9 *NGO Resource Project-Cambodia*, 4 June, 1993, p. 2.

10 Ibid.

Notes

11 *Phnom Penh Post*, vol. 2, no. 24, 19 November–2 December, 1993, p. 2.
12 Ibid.
13 See letter from Michael Vickery to *Z Magazine*, May 9, 1994; and *Camnews*, 16 September, 1997.
14 Attempted interview, US Embassy, June 1993, Phnom Penh
15 In discussion with Ann Bradley, Phnom Penh, IRI presentation, 1993.
16 *The Times*, 6 June, 1995. See also *Phnom Penh Post*, vol. 4, no. 17, 25 August–7 September, 1995, p. 1, p. 8.
17 *Cambodia Daily*, 19 September, 1998, p. 6.
18 Ibid., p. 7.
19 Ibid., p. 7.
20 The significance of this issue is raised in R Pinkney, *Democracy in the Third World*, Open University Press, 1993, p. 101.
21 M Vickery, *Cambodia 1975–1982*, Southend, 1984, p. 22.
22 *The Nation*, 12 February 1994. See also D Ashley, 'The Failure of Conflict Resolution in Cambodia', in FZ Brown and DG Timberman, *Cambodia and the International Community: The Quest for Peace, Development and Democracy*, Asia Society, 1998, p. 54.
23 Statement of Chea Sim, originally broadcast over Phnom Penh Radio, 10 November, 1998 (BBC Summary of World Broadcasts, 12 November, 1998).
24 Interview with Lao Mong Hay, 6 January, 1998, Phnom Penh.
25 Frieson in Taylor (ed.), (1996), p. 231.
26 Curtis (1998), p. 25.
27 Ashley, in Brown and Timberman (1998), p. 54.
28 RM Jennar, *The Cambodian Dilemma, Cambodian Chronicles* XII, EFERC 17, 7 April, 1994, p. 14. See also Ashley, in Brown and Timberman (1998), p. 54.
29 H Watkin, *Cambodia Democracy Fails to Blossom in Feudal Society*, *Camnews*, 2 March, 1998.
30 Ashley, in Brown and Timberman (1998), p. 55.
31 W Shawcross, *Cambodia's New Deal: A Report by William Shawcross*, Carnegie Endowment for International Peace, 1994, p. 44.
32 *The Daily Telegraph*, 27 September, 1993.
33 *Cambodia Daily*, 27 September, 1993, p. 5.
34 *Phnom Penh Post*, vol. 3, no. 6, 25 March–7 April, 1994, p. 6.
35 *Phnom Penh Post*, vol. 4, no. 6, 8–21 April 1994, p. 9; *Phnom Penh Post*, vol. 3, no. 9, 6–19 May, 1994, p. 20.
36 *Far Eastern Economic Review*, 30 September, 1993, p. 10. See also *The Nation*, 29 January, 1994.
37 *The Nation*, 12 February, 1994. See also Shawcross (1994), p. 40.
38 *The Nation*, 12 February, 1994.
39 Ashley, in Brown and Timberman (1998), p. 53.
40 Interview with Hun Sen, 1 January, 1994, Phnom Penh. See also *The Nation*, 29 January, 1994.
41 Interview with Hun Sen, 1 January 1994, Phnom Penh.
42 *Bangkok Post*, 16 September, 1993.
43 JA Jeldres, *The UN and the Cambodian Transition, Journal of Democracy*, vol. 4, no. 4, October 1993, p. 115.

Notes

44 *The Nation*, 12 February, 1994; *NGO Resource Project – Cambodia, Weekly Report* 24–29 September, 1993, p. 2.
45 Shawcross (1994), p. 41.
46 *Phnom Penh Post*, vol. 3, no. 6, 25 March–7 April, 1994, p. 7.
47 *Phnom Penh Post*, vol. 4, no. 4, 24 February–9 March, 1995, p. 1.
48 Ibid.
49 *Phnom Penh Post*, vol. 3, no. 17, 26 August–8 September, 1994, p. 8
50 Shawcross (1994), p. 41; *Cambodia Daily*, 25 March, 1996, p. 8.
51 Jennar (7 April, 1994), pp. 8–9.
52 *Cambodia Daily*, 25 March, 1996, p. 8.
53 *Phnom Penh Post*, vol. 4, no. 21, 20 October–2 November, 1995, p. 1; *Cambodia Daily*, 25 March, 1996, p. 8.
54 *Phnom Penh Post*, vol. 4, no. 21, 20 October–2 November, 1995, p. 1.
55 Interview with anonymous FUNCINPEC official, Phnom Penh, 13 August, 1998.
56 *Phnom Penh Post*, vol. 4, no. 21, 20 October–2 November, 1995, p. 1.
57 Ibid., p. 3.
58 Ibid., p. 3.
59 Shawcross (1994), p. 44.
60 *Cambodia Daily*, 25 March, 1996, p. 1.
61 *South China Morning Post*, 20 March 1999.
62 Ashley, in Brown and Timberman (1998), p. 62. This description and commentary takes no account of Ranariddh's inability to implement such an undertaking.
63 *Background on the July 1997 Crisis: Prince Ranariddh's Strategy of Provocation, Ministry of Foreign Affairs and International Cooperation*, Phnom Penh, 9 July 1997, p. 4.
64 *Cambodia Daily*, 25 March, 1996, p. 1
65 Ashley, in Brown and Timberman (1998), p. 63. See also ch. 9.
66 *Cambodia Daily*, 18–20 July, 1997, p. 14.
67 *Cambodia Daily*, 25 March, 1996, p. 8.
68 Ashley, in Brown and Timberman (1998), p. 54.
69 Ibid.
70 *Summary of World Broadcasts* (SWB) FE/2603, 4 May 1996, B/2.
71 *The Economist*, 15 August, 1996, p. 16. See also the *Far Eastern Economic Review*, 14 November, 1996, p. 22.
72 MW Doyle, 'Peacebuilding in Cambodia: The Continuing Quest for Power and Legitimacy', in Brown and Timberman (1998), p. 82.
73 *Summary of World Broadcasts* (SWB) FE/2603, 4 May 1996, B/2.
74 Ibid.
75 *Background on the July 1997 Crisis: Prince Ranariddh's Strategy of Provocation, Ministry of Foreign Affairs and International Cooperation*, Phnom Penh, 9 July 1997, p. 6 (*White Paper*).
76 This was corroborated in interview with under-secretary of state Suy Mong Leang, Council of Ministers, Phnom Penh, 8 January, 1998.
77 *Cambodia Daily*, 19 November 1996, p. 8; *The Economist*, 16 November, 1996, p. 93; *The Guardian*, 20 November, 1996.
78 *The Guardian*, 20 November, 1996. See also Ashley's 'KR papers', *Phnom Penh Post*, vol. 7, no. 13, 3–16 July, 1998, p. 9.

Notes

79 Ibid.
80 *Far Eastern Economic Review*, 21 August, 1997, p. 17. See also *The Economist*, 16 November, 1996, p. 93.
81 *The Independent*, 13 August, 1996; *The Telegraph*, 10 September, 1996; *The Guardian*, 10 September, 1996.
82 Interview with Ieng Sary, 24 December, 1997, Pailin.
83 Ibid. Stephen Heder corroborates the split. (Interview with S Heder, *School of Oriental and African Studies*, London, 14 November, 1997). See also *Far Eastern Economic Review*, 22 August, 1996, pp. 14–16.
84 Ashley, in Brown and Timberman (1998), p. 67. For a discussion of the internally-originating splits, see, amongst others, *Far Eastern Economic Review*, 22 August, 1996, pp. 14–16.
85 See Ashley, in Brown and Timberman (1998), p. 69.
86 *White Paper*, p. 12.
87 G Curtis, *Cambodia Reborn? The Transition to Democracy and Development*, United Nations Research Institute for Social Development (UNRISD), 1998, pp. 193, note 57.
88 *The Guardian*, 18 June 1997; see also *The Independent*, 18 June 1997.
89 *White Paper*, p. 12.
90 Ibid., p. 12.
91 *The Times*, 17 June, 1997; *Reuter Insurance Briefing*, 20 June, 1997.
92 *Reuter Insurance Briefing*, 18 June, 1997. He has 'dared' Ranariddh to leave government before when Ranariddh objected to his policies, and warned that such an action would be met with a military response.
93 J McAuliff, *Welcome to Cambodia, Where Nothing is Ever as it Seems*, Indochina Interchange, September 1997, p. 4.
94 Curtis (1998), p. 51.
95 *White Paper*, p. 8. This incident was widely reported in the Khmer and international press.
96 Ibid., p. 8.
97 It must be noted that Pol Pot's adoption of 'Liberalism' and environmentalism prior to UNTAC's arrival bears comparison with his 'rejection' of communism in 1982 when the CGDK was formed. Western support for a 'communist' body would have been harder to justify; in fact, the evidence gathered to date suggests Pol Pot had not changed ideological direction, but was sufficiently aware to manipulate the concerns of the wider actors in order to further his own goals. For a discussion of this, see Vickery (1984), p. 251.
98 *Far Eastern Economic Review*, 17 July, 1997, p. 15.
99 *The Guardian*, 18 June, 1997.
100 Curtis (1998), pp. 192-3, note 55.
101 *Far Eastern Economic Review*, 17 July, 1997, p. 15.
102 For different views of the immediate and personality origins of the 'coup', see *Far Eastern Economic Review*, 17 July, 1997, 21 August, 1997 and 28 August, 1997; and M Vickery, *A Non-standard View of the 'Coup'*, Phnom Penh Post, vol. 6, no. 17, 29 August–11 September, 1997, p. 11; McAuliff (September 1997); and Tony Kevin in *Phnom Penh Post*, vol. 7, no. 15, 24–30 July, 1998, p. 4 and in *Phnom Penh Post*, vol. 7, no. 18, 21 August–3 September 1998, p. 12.

Notes

103 See, amongst others, Var Huoth, *Cambodia's Elections were Fair, Washington Post* (letters), 1 September, 1997; *The Guardian*, 11 July, 1997; and *International Herald Tribune*, 14 July, 1997.
104 Chea Sim, cited in Curtis (1998), p. 53.
105 See also Y Imagawa, *The Recent Situation in East Asia and Cambodia, Asia-Pacific Review*, vol. 5, no. 1, 1998, p. 134.
106 *White Paper*, p. 12.
107 Curtis (1998), p. 192 (note 55).
108 D Ashley's interpretation of the 'KR papers', *Phnom Penh Post*, vol. 7, no. 13, 3–16 July, 1998, p. 9.
109 Ibid.
110 Curtis (1998), p. 193, note 58.
111 This is a reference to Hun Sen's artificial eye.
112 Lizée (1995), p. 83.
113 H Watkin, *Cambodia Democracy Fails to Blossom in Feudal Society, Camnews*, 2 March, 1998.

VIII

1 J McAuliff, *Welcome to Cambodia, Where Nothing is Ever as it Seems, Indochina Interchange*, September 1997, p. 3.
2 Ibid.
3 M Vickery, *The Cambodian People's Party: Where Has It Come From, Where Is It Going? Southeast Asian Affairs*, 1994, p. 102. This was corroborated in an interview with Hun Sen, 1 January, 1994, Phnom Penh.
4 *Cambodia Daily*, 13 September, 1993, p. 1. See also interview with Khieu Kanharith, 10 April 1996; and interview with Hun Sen, 1 January, 1994 (both Phnom Penh).
5 *Cambodia Daily*, 13 September, 1993, p. 1.
6 See M Vickery, *Cambodia: A Political Survey, Regime Change and Regime Maintenance in Asia and the Pacific*, no. 14, Australian National University, 1994.
7 *Cambodia Daily*, 16 September, 1993, p. 6; 21 September, 1994, p. 6.
8 *Cambodia Daily*, 13 September, 1993, pp. 1–2.
9 See Vickery (1994), for a discussion of political biographies and the relative weight of such elements within the CPP.
10 See, for examples, J-F Bayart, *The State in Africa: The Politics of the Belly*, Longman, 1993, especially ch. 3; BC Smith, *Understanding Third World Politics: Theories of Political Change and Development*, Macmillan, 1996; V Randall and R Theobald, *Political Change and Underdevelopment: A Critical Introduction to Third World Politics*, Macmillan 1985; MRJ Vatikiotis, *Political Change in Southeast Asia: Trimming the Banyan Tree*, Routledge, 1996; and M Alagappa (ed.), *Political Legitimacy in Southeast Asia: The Quest for Moral Authority*, Stanford University Press, 1995.
11 *Phnom Penh Post*, vol. 3, no. 14, 15–28 July, 1994, p. 8.
12 Interview with Khieu Kanharith, 10 April 1996, Phnom Penh; and again on 11 December 1997.
13 *Phnom Penh Post*, vol. 3, no. 14, July 15–28, 1994, p. 3; p. 8.

Notes

14 Ibid., p. 1.
15 *Phnom Penh Post*, vol. 4, no. 25, 30 December 1994–12 January, 1995, p. 20.
16 *Phnom Penh Post*, vol. 3, no. 14, July 15–28, 1994, p. 3; p. 7.
17 W Shawcross, *Cambodia's New Deal: A Report by William Shawcross*, Carnegie Endowment for International Peace, 1994, p. 42.
18 Vickery (1984), p. 14.
19 Ibid.
20 *Phnom Penh Post*, vol. 3, no. 14, 15–28 July, 1994, p. 1.
21 *Bangkok Post*, 6 September, 1994.
22 Vickery (1994), p. 115.
23 Shawcross (1994), p. 44.
24 Details of Rainsy's sacking appeared in *Financial Times*, 21 October, 1994. Regarding Rainsy's lack of democratic principles and his anti-Viêt Namese racism, see, for example, *Cambodia Daily*, 30 July, 1998, p. 1; *Cambodia Daily*, 13 July, 1998, p. 1.
25 *Phnom Penh Post*, vol. 3, no. 21, 21 October–3 November, 1994, p. 1. See also *Phnom Penh Post*, vol. 4, no. 9, 5–18 May, 1995, p. 1.
26 *The Guardian*, 23 June, 1995.
27 S Heder, *Cambodia's Democratic Transition to Neoauthoritarianism*, Current History, vol. 94, no. 447, 1995, p. 426.
28 Ibid., p. 428.
29 D Ashley, 'The Failure of Conflict Resolution in Cambodia', in FZ Brown and DG Timberman, *Cambodia and the International Community: The Quest for Peace, Development and Democracy*, Asia Society, 1998, p. 61; *Phnom Penh Post*, vol. 4, no. 11, June 2–15, 1995, p. 3. See also Heder (1995).
30 Heder (1995), p. 425.
31 Vickery (1994), p. 115.
32 Ibid. See also McAuliff (September 1997), p. 3.
33 Interviews with Hun Sen, Khao Samriddh and Khieu Kanharith.
34 Interview with Lao Mong Hay, 6 January, 1998, Phnom Penh.
35 Ibid.
36 Interview with under-secretary of state Suy Mong Leang, Council of Ministers, Phnom Penh, 8 January, 1998.
37 Ashley, in Brown and Timberman (1998), p. 61. See also *Camnews*, 2 February, 1998.
38 For an internal FUNCINPEC admission of this, see statement of Veng Sereyvudh, *The Nation*, 12 February 1994.
39 Shawcross (1994), p. 44. Shawcross, an ardent critic of the CPP, often levels such criticisms at that Party. However, unlike in the cited instance, he does not attempt to excuse or apologise the CPP.
40 BBC2, *Correspondent*, 1997
41 P Lizée, *Cambodia in 1995: From Hope to Despair*, Asian Survey, vol. XXXVI, no. 1, 1995, pp. 84–85. See also Camnews, *Prince Arrested, jailed for alleged assassination plot*, 21 November, 1995.
42 *Background on the July 1997 Crisis: Prince Ranariddh's Strategy of Provocation*, Ministry of Foreign Affairs and International Cooperation, Phnom Penh, 9 July 1997, p. 3 (*White Paper*).
43 Lizée (1995), p. 85.

Notes

44 Interview with under-secretary of state Suy Mong Leang, Council of Ministers, Phnom Penh, 8th January, 1998.
45 Interview with Khieu Kanharith, Phnom Penh, 11 December, 1997.
46 Ashley, in Brown and Timberman (1998), p. 62. This was corroborated in interview with Lao Mong Hay, 6 January, 1998, Phnom Penh.
47 McAuliff (September 1997), p. 3.
48 For corroboration of this, see Ashley, in Brown and Timberman (1998), p. 63. See also McAuliff (September 1997), p. 3. For an announcement of the creation of the KNP, see *Phnom Penh Post*, vol. 4, no. 19, 22 September–5 October, 1995, p. 1.
49 *The Guardian*, 12 July, 1997.
50 The further wooing of Toan Chhay involved negotiations with a senior CPP military adviser. See *Cambodia Daily*, 18–20 July, 1997, p. 14.
51 *Phnom Penh Post*, vol. 6, no. 10, 16–29 May, 1997, p. 3.
52 See, for a brief discussion, Heder (1995), p. 428.
53 NGO Forum Meeting with Ieng Mouly, Phnom Penh, 12 September, 1995 (statement, p. 4).
54 Lizée (1995), p. 85.
55 Ibid., p. 85. See also Heder (1995), p. 428.
56 J Chopra, *United Nations Authority in Cambodia*, Thomas J Watson Jr. Institute for International Studies, Occasional Paper no. 15, 1994, p. 49.
57 Heder (1995), p. 429.
58 In discussion with both authors, Phnom Penh, July 1998.
59 *The Economist*, 28 August 1993, p. 15.
60 *Cambodia Daily*, 8–10 March, 1996, p. 1.
61 Ibid.
62 G Rist, *The History of Development: From Western Origins to Global Faith*, Zed, 1997, p. 166. See also R Carmen, *Autonomous Development: Humanizing the Landscape – an Excursion into Radical Thinking and Practice*, Zed, 1996.
63 *The Times*, 6 June, 1995. See also *Phnom Penh Post*, vol. 4, no. 17, 25 August–7 September, 1995, p. 1, p. 8.
64 Interview with Dr. Lao Mong Hay, 6 January, 1998, Phnom Penh.
65 *The Bangkok Post*, 1 August, 1994.

IX

1 Statements and comments made in numerous formal and informal discussions with representatives of a range of foreign NGOs, December 1997–January 1998, Cambodia; and July–September 1998, Cambodia. See also *Phnom Penh Post*, vol. 7, no. 18, 21 August–3 September, 1998, p. 2.
2 Curtis (1998), pp. 54—55.
3 *Phnom Penh Post*, vol. 6, no. 19, 26 September–9 October, 1997, p. 9.
4 A Peang-Meth, *Understanding Cambodia's Political Developments*, Contemporary Southeast Asia, vol. 19, no. 3, December 1997, p. 298.
5 *National Voice of Cambodia*, Phnom Penh, 13.00 GMT, 23 January, 1998: SWB Online, p. 1. The individuals cited were Major Vhau Keang, Major Chin Vannak, and Major Sot Laisak.

Notes

6 Huw Watkin, *Hun Sen berates rights workers for telling 'lies'*, Camnews, 27 August, 1997.
7 Discussions with Michael Vickery, Cambodia, July–August, 1998. David Hawk, of the UN Human Rights Centre in Phnom Penh, agreed that this was possible. Discussion with D Hawk, UN Human Right Office, Phnom Penh, 15 December, 1997. Khieu Kanharith, CPP Minister of Information, also took a similar position. Interview with K Kanharith, Phnom Penh, 11 December, 1997.
8 Interview with Khieu Kanharith, Phnom Penh, 11 December, 1997.
9 In discussion with Michael Vickery, 30 July, 1998, Phnom Penh.
10 N Chomsky, *Necessary Illusions: Thought Control in Democratic Societies*, Pluto, 1989
11 See, for example, D Ashley, 'The Failure of Conflict Resolution in Cambodia', in FZ Brown and DG Timberman, *Cambodia and the International Community: The Quest for Peace, Development and Democracy*, Asia Society, 1998.
12 See, amongst others, Var Huoth, *Cambodia's Elections were Fair*, Washington Post (letters), 1 September, 1997; *The Guardian*, 11 July, 1997; *International Herald Tribune*, 14 July, 1997; *The Nation*, 7 August, 1997; and *The Sunday Nation*, 10 August, 1997.
13 Correspondence with M Vickery, 2 May, 1999. As far as Australia's 'democratic' traditions go, some question and refute this strongly, often citing racial harassment and abuse of ethnic minorities. See, for example, J Pilger, *A Secret Country*, London Cape, 1989.
14 Interview with Ung Huot, 8 January, 1998, Council of Ministers, Phnom Penh.
15 GA Heeger, *The Politics of Underdevelopment*, St. Martin's, 1974, p. 52.
16 Interview with Ung Huot, 8 January, 1998, Council of Ministers, Phnom Penh.
17 *The Nation*, 12 February 1994. See also Statement of Chea Sim, originally broadcast over Phnom Penh Radio, 10 November, 1998 (BBC Summary of World Broadcasts, 12 November, 1998); Interview with Lao Mong Hay, 6 January, 1998, Phnom Penh; D Ashley, 'The Failure of Conflict Resolution in Cambodia', in FZ Brown and DG Timberman, *Cambodia and the International Community: The Quest for Peace, Development and Democracy*, Asia Society, 1998, p. 54.
18 Interview with Ung Huot, 8 January, 1998, Council of Ministers, Phnom Penh.
19 Ibid.
20 Interview with Lao Mong Hay, 6 January, 1998, Phnom Penh. See also *Complications over Pardon threaten deposed Prince's Return*, Camnews, 20 February, 1998.
21 *Support for Deposed Cambodian co-Premier dives as Royalists split Again*, Camnews, 1 February, 1998.
22 D Roberts, *Hun Sen Confounds and Consolidates*, Jane's Intelligence Review, October 1998.
23 Camnews, *Sam Rainsy will go to Court Tomorrow*, 8 February, 1998.
24 *Cambodia Daily – Weekend*, 27 June, 1998, p. 34.

Notes

25 *Leading Cambodian Dissident withdraws Party from electoral Process*, Camnews, 1 February, 1998.
26 See *Cambodia Daily*, 31 March, 1997, p. 1.
27 There are many examples. One is the temporary closure of *Prayuth* (Fighter), in September 1998.
28 *Phnom Penh Post*, vol. 6, no. 26, January 2–15, 1998, p. 1. Chea won 84 out of 156 votes from the NGO community.
29 R Clark, *The Fire This Time: US War Crimes in the Gulf*, Thunder's Mouth Press, 1994, p. 155; D Kellner, *The Persian Gulf TV War*, Westview, 1997, pp. 37–50; and DM and MK Rivage-Seul, *A Kinder and Gentler Tyranny: Illusions of a New World Order*, Praeger, 1995, p. 47.
30 For a discussion of the variables and outcomes, see *Phnom Penh Post*, vol. 7, no. 17, 7–20 August, 1998, p. 2.
31 RM Jennar, *Cambodia Once Again Victim of Disinformation*, Cambodia Research Centre, October 1998, p. 1.
32 *Phnom Penh Post*, vol. 7, no. 18, 21 August–3 September 1998, p. 12.
33 Letter from Hun Sen to US Senators John McCain and John Kerry, Phnom Penh, 3 October, 1998.
34 *The Guardian*, 1 October, 1998, p. 10.
35 *Phnom Penh Post*, vol. 7, no. 17, 7–20 August, 1998, p. 5.
36 See Elizabeth Bork, *Miracle on the Mekong or Sullied Show?*, Washington Post, reproduced in *Cambodia Daily*, 10 August, 1998, p. 17.
37 Ibid.
38 Summary of views expressed in official and unofficial statements of foreign and national observers, in Phnom Penh, August 1998. See also *Phnom Penh Post*, vol. 7, no. 18, 21 August–3 September 1998, p. 9.
39 R Birsel,. *Cambodia Votes Complaints said Mishandled*, Camnews, 30 September, 1998.
40 *Phnom Penh Post*, vol. 7, no. 18, 21 August–3 September 1998, p. 9.
41 Ibid., p. 17.
42 Interview with village chief, Pochentong Road, Phnom Penh, 10 July 1998.
43 K Frieson, 'The Politics of Getting the Vote', in Heder and Ledgerwood (eds.) (1996), p. 188.
44 *Phnom Penh Post*, vol. 7, no. 15, July 24–30, 1998, p. 4.
45 Ibid, p. 3.
46 Notes from villages and communes visited in July and August, 1998, in Battambang, Phnom Penh, Takeo and Kandal.
47 *Phnom Penh Post*, vol. 7, no. 17, 7–20 August, 1998, p. 3.
48 *Cambodia Daily*, 13 July, 1998, p. 2.
49 Ibid., p. 2.
50 *Cambodia Daily*, 8 July, 1998, p. 9.
51 Ranariddh speech at pre-election campaign rally, Olympic Stadium, Phnom Penh, 18 July, 1998.
52 For a discussion of early 1998 splits manifesting themselves publicly, see *Royalist Divisions Erode Challenge to Strongman*, Camnews, 2 February, 1998.
53 *Cambodia Daily* (Weekend), 27 June 1998, p. 12.
54 Ibid.

Notes

55 The first reference I have to this came from an educated Cambodian living in England. It has been repeated too many times since to have accurately and precisely documented every event.
56 See Thion (1993), p. 230.
57 For an interesting discussion of the longer origins of the term, dating to Alexander the Great's arrival in the Indus around 326 BC, see ibid., pp. 230–4.
58 *The Guardian*, 8 September, 1998.
59 Ibid.
60 Ibid.
61 *Cambodia Daily*, 30 July, 1998, p. 1.
62 See, for similar observations, J McAuliff, *Cambodia News Digest*, 22 September, 1998, pp. 1–2.
63 Letter from Hun Sen to US Senators John McCain and John Kerry, Phnom Penh, 3 October, 1998. See for corroboration *South China Morning Post*, 26 August, 1998.
64 *Phnom Penh Post*, vol. 7, no. 19, 4–17 September, 1998, p. 12.
65 For Stephen Heder's analysis, see S Heder, *Cambodia's Democratic Transition to Neoauthoritarianism, Current History*, vol. 94, no. 447, 1995, p. 431. This position was endorsed in discussion with Michael Vickery, Battambang, Cambodia, 25 July, 1998. It was also supported in discussion with Michael Fowler, a journalist and lawyer in Phnom Penh, and in discussion with Craig Etcheson, Phnom Penh, August 3, 1998.
66 S Heder, *Cambodia's Democratic Transition to Neoauthoritarianism, Current History: A Journal of Contemporary World Affairs*, December 1995, p. 429.
67 Informal survey of opinions taken at various points between July and August 1998; and during December 1998 and January 1999.
68 In regular discussions with experienced NGO workers, this impression was given frequently over a period of time.
69 LN O'Shaughnessy and M Dodson, *Political Bargaining and Democratic Transitions: A Comparison of Nicaragua and El Salvador, Journal of Latin American Studies*, vol. 31, no. 1999, p. 114.
70 *Phnom Penh Post*, vol. 7, no. 21, 18 September–1 October, 1998, p. 5.
71 Letter from Hun Sen to US Senators John McCain and John Kerry, Phnom Penh, 3 October 1998. See for full text *Phnom Penh Post*, vol. 7, no. 20, 12–17 September, p. 1.
72 *Phnom Penh Post*, vol. 7, no. 19, 4–17 September, 1998, p. 1.
73 *Phnom Penh Post*, vol. 7, no. 21, 18 September–1 October, 1998, p. 5.
74 *Phnom Penh Post*, vol. 7, no. 19, 4–17 September, 1998, p. 5.
75 Interview with Brittis Edman, Phnom Penh, 22 December, 1998.
76 M Vickery and R Amer, *Democracy and Human Rights in Cambodia*, Final Draft Report, *SIDA*, 1995, p. 8.
77 J McAuliff, *Cambodia News Digest*, 22 September, 1998, p. 2.
78 RM Jennar, *AFP/Phnom Penh: One of the Less Trustworthy Sources of Information on Cambodia, Cambodia Research Centre*, October 1998, p. 10. In 1978, Jennar writes, the Khmer Rouge told Khmers to 'kill people with a Yuon mind and a Khmer body'.
79 One western NGO worker, for example, declared that some of the people she spoke with had openly told her this of themselves.

Notes

80 In discussion with two NGO workers, one of whom spoke Khmer and lived close to the Khmer-Viêt Namese Friendship Monument, dubbed 'Democracy Square' by Rainsy and some of the farmers he bribed to riot.
81 E-mail correspondence with Brittis Edman, Red Barna, 11 September, 1998.
82 See RM Jennar (October 1998), p. 4.
83 *Phnom Penh Post*, vol. 7, no. 18, 21 August–3 September 1998, p. 12.
84 *The Guardian*, 10 September, 1998.
85 McAuliff (September 1998), p. 7.
86 *Phnom Penh Post*, vol. 7, no. 21, 18 September–1 October, 1998, p. 2.
87 *Phnom Penh Post*, vol. 7, no. 18, 21 August–3 September 1998, p. 17.
88 Ibid., p. 12.
89 *Phnom Penh Post*, vol. 7, no. 23, 16–29 October, 1998, p. 6.
90 *Cambodia Daily*, 14 Nov p. 3; *Cambodia Daily*, 19 November, 1998 pp. 1–2.
91 Ibid.
92 See, for examples, FOCUS, 25 March, 1999, *Camnews*, 25 March 1999.
93 *Phnom Penh Post*, vol. 8, no. 4, 19 February–4 March, 1999, p. 2.
94 *Phnom Penh Post*, vol. 8, no. 9, 30 April–13 May, 1999, p. 3.
95 *Phnom Penh Post*, vol. 8, no. 4, 19 February–4 March, 1999, p. 2.
96 *Kyodo News Service*, 2 March, 1999; FOCUS, 25 March, 1999, *Camnews*, 25 March 1999.
97 *Camnews*, 25 March, 1999.
98 Interview with Ung Huot, 8 January, 1998, Council of Ministers, Phnom Penh.
99 *Phnom Penh Post*, vol. 8, no. 9, 30 April—13 May, 1999, p. 2.
100 See *Reuter* statement (Camnews), 19 November, 1998, Phnom Penh.
101 See *Cambodia Daily*, 14 November 1998, p. 3; and *Cambodia Daily*, 19 November 1998, pp. 1–2.

X

1 See J Ovesen, I-B Trankell and J Ojendal, *When Every Household is an Island: Social Organization and Power Structures in Rural Cambodia*, Uppsala, 1996, p. 42.
2 Ibid, p. 84.
3 Ibid., p. 71.
4 M Vickery. *Cambodia 1975-1982*, Southend, 1984, p. 15.
5 P Lizée, *The Challenge of Conflict Resolution in Cambodia, Canadian Defence Quarterly*, September 1993, p. 40.
6 *General Accounting Office Report 'Cambodia'*, National Security and International Affairs Division, B-270716, 29 February, 1996, p. 4
7 Ibid., p. 4.
8 *The Times*, 17 April, 1998.
9 *Far Eastern Economic Review*, 17 July, 1997, p. 17. In point of fact, the bombers ranged freely over far more of Cambodia than is usually understood. In August 1998, for example, unexploded munitions, which

could only have come from heavy bombers, were found in the geographical centre of the country, as opposed to 'merely' along the Cambodian-Viêt Namese border.

10 SM Mohammed Idris, *The Message from Calicut – 500 Years after Vasco da Gama, Third World Resurgence*, no. 96, September 1998, p. 22.

Bibliography

Acharya, A, *Cambodia, the United Nations and the Problems of Peace*, Pacific Review, vol. 7, no. 3, 1994.

Akashi, Y, *Freeness and Fairness of the Cambodian Elections: Statement by Mr. Akashi*, 10 June, 1993, Phnom Penh.

Alagappa, M, *Political Legitimacy in Southeast Asia: The Quest for Moral Authority*, Stanford, 1995.

—— *The Cambodian Conflict: Changing Interests*, Pacific Review, vol. 3, no. 3, 1990.

Amer, R, *The United Nations Peacekeeping Operation in Cambodia: Overview and Assessment*, Contemporary Southeast Asia, vol. 15, no. 2, 1993.

Arnson and Holiday, 'Cambodia', in *The Lost Agenda: Human Rights and UN Field Operations*, Human Rights Watch, 1993.

Background on the July 1997 Crisis: Prince Ranariddh's Strategy of Provocation, Ministry of Foreign Affairs and International Cooperation, Phnom Penh, 9 July 1997.

Bangkok Post.

Banton, M, (ed.), *The Social Anthropology of Complex Societies*, Tavistock, 1966.

Bayart, J-F, *The State in Africa: The Politics of the Belly*, Longman, 1993.

BBC World Service.

Becker, E, *When the War Was Over: Cambodia's Revolution and The Voice of its People*, Touchstone, 1986.

Beuls, L, *Determinants of Peacekeeping Policy in Cambodia: Keeping Up With Interests?*, Paper at Second Pan-European International Relations Conference, ECPR, 13–16 September, 1995.

Breslauer et al (eds.), *Beyond the Cold War: Conflict and Co-operation in the Third World*, Institute of International Studies, University of California at Berkeley, 1991.

Brown and Timberman (eds.), *Cambodia and the International Community: The Quest for Peace, Development and Democracy*, Institute of Southeast Asian Studies (Singapore), 1998.

Bibliography

Brown, BA, *Cambodia's Shaky Step*, Freedom Review, vol. 24, no. 4, July–August 1993.

Brown, FZ, *Cambodia in Crisis: The 1993 Elections and the United Nations*, Asian Update, The Asia Society, 1993.

Burbach, Nunez and Kagarlitsky, *Globalisation and its Discontents: The Rise of Postmodern Socialisms*, Pluto, 1997.

Cambodia News Digest.

Cambodia: Agenda for Rehabilitation and Reconstruction, The World Bank, East Asia and Pacific Region, Country department I, June 1992, New York.

Carmen, R, *Autonomous Development: Humanizing the Landscape – an Excursion into Radical Thinking and Practice*, Zed, 1996.

Chanda, N, *Civil War in Cambodia?*, Foreign Policy no. 76, Fall 1989.

Chandler, D, *The Tragedy of Cambodian History: Politics, War and Revolution since 1945*, Yale University Press, 1991.

—— *Brother Number One: A Political Biography of Pol Pot*, Westview Press, 1992.

—— *A History of Cambodia*, Westview, 1993.

Chang Pao-min, *Beijing Versus Hanoi: The Diplomacy Over Kampuchea*, Asian Survey, vol. 23, no. 5, 1988.

Chomsky, N, *Necessary Illusions: Thought Control in Democratic Societies*, Pluto, 1989.

Chopra et al, *Report on the Cambodian Peace Process*, Norwegian Institute of International Affairs, no. 165, February 1993.

—— *United Nations Authority in Cambodia*, Thomas J Watson Jr. Institute for International Studies, Occasional Paper no. 15, 1994.

Clark, R, *The Fire This Time: US War Crimes in the Gulf*, Thunder's Mouth Press, 1994.

Communiqué of the Cambodian People's Party, 20 June, 1993, Phnom Penh.

Curtis, G, *Cambodia Reborn? The Transition to Democracy and Development*, United Nations Research Institute for Social Development (UNRISD), 1998.

Daily Telegraph.

Davies, P, *Cambodia: Interference is not Aid*, unpublished paper, 26 May, 1992.

Deyo, FC, *The Political Economy of the New Asian Industrialism*, Cornell, 1987.

Doyle and Suntharalingum, *The UN in Cambodia: Lessons for Complex Peacekeeping*, International Peacekeeping, vol. 1, no. 2, 1994.

Duiker, W, *The Communist Road to Power in Vietnam*, Westview, 1996.

Durch, WJ, (ed.), *United Nations Peacekeeping, American Policy, and the Uncivil Wars of the 1990s*, Macmillan, 1997.

Elson, RE, *The End of the Peasantry in Southeast Asia: A Social and Economic History of Peasant Livelihood, 1800–1990s*, Macmillan, 1997.

Etcheson, C, *Civil War and the Coalition Government of Democratic Kampuchea*, Third World Quarterly, vol. 9, no. 1, January 1987.

Far Eastern Economic Review.

Farris, K, *UN Peacekeeping in Cambodia: On Balance, a Success*, Parameters, vol. 24, no. 1, 1994.

Bibliography

Findlay, T, *Cambodia: The Legacy and Lessons of UNTAC, SIPRI Research Report no. 9*, Open University Press, 1995.
Framework for A Comprehensive Political Settlement of the Cambodia Conflict..
Fukuyama, F, *The End of History and the Last Man*, Hamish Hamilton, 1992.
Haas, M, *Cambodia, Pol Pot and the United States: A Faustian Pact*, Praeger, 1989.
Hall, DGE, *A History of Southeast Asia*, Macmillan, 1981.
Heder, S, *Kampuchea 1980: Anatomy of a Crisis, Southeast Asia Chronicle*, vol. 77, February 1981.
—— *CPP Secessionism, Resignations from the Assembly and Intimidation of UNTAC: Background and Theories*, Information/Education division, UNTAC 12, Phnom Penh, 13 June, 1993.
—— *Cambodia's Democratic Transition to Neoauthoritarianism, Current History: A Journal of Contemporary World Affairs*, December 1995.
Heder and Ledgerwood (eds.), *Propaganda, Politics and Violence in Cambodia: Democratic Transition under United Nations Peacekeeping*, ME Sharpe, 1996.
Heeger, GA, *The Politics of Underdevelopment*, St. Martin's, 1974.
Heininger, JE, *Peacekeeping in Transition: The United Nations in Cambodia*, Twentieth Century Fund Press, 1994.
Hill and Malik, *Peacekeeping and the United Nations*, Issues in International Security, Dartmouth, 1996.
Hippler, J, *Pax Americana? Hegemony or Decline*, Pluto, 1994.
Hong, M, *The Paris Agreement on Cambodia: In Retrospect, International Peacekeeping*, vol. 2, no. 1, Spring 1995.
Hood, SJ, *Dragons Entangled: Indochina and the China-Viêt Nam War*, ME Sharpe, 1992.
Imagawa, Y, *The Recent Situation in East Asia and Cambodia, Asia-Pacific Review*, vol. 5, no. 1, 1998.
Index on Censorship.
International Herald Tribune.
June to October, 1991.
James, A, *Peacekeeping in International Politics*, Macmillan, 1990.
Jeldres, JA, *The UN and the Cambodian Transition, Journal of Democracy*, vol. 4, no. 4, October 1993.
Jennar, RM, *Dialogue of the Deaf in a Volatile Context, Cambodian Chronicles* V, EFERC, 7 September, 1992.
—— *The Lost Gamble, Cambodian Chronicles VI*, EFERC, 11 November, 1992.
—— *Cambodian Chronicles VI: Samdech Preah Upayuvaraj Norodom Sihanouk EFERC*, 29 June, 1993.
—— *The Cambodian Dilemma, Cambodian Chronicles* XII, EFERC 17, 7 April, 1994.
—— *UNTAC: 'International Triumph' in Cambodia?, Security Dialogue*, vol. 25, no. 2, 1994.
—— *Cambodia Once Again Victim of Disinformation, Cambodia Research Centre*, October 1998.
—— *AFP/Phnom Penh: One of the Less Trustworthy Sources of Information on Cambodia, Cambodia Research Centre*, October 1998.

Bibliography

Kellner, D, *The Persian Gulf TV War*, Westview, 1997.

Kiernan, B, *How Pol Pot Came to Power*, Verso, 1985.

—— *The Cambodian Crisis, 1990–1992: The UN Plan, the Khmer Rouge, and the state of Cambodia*, Bulletin of Concerned Asian Scholars, vol. 24, no. 4, 1992.

—— *Genocide and Democracy in Cambodia: The Khmer Rouge, the United Nations and the International Community*, Yale University Monograph, 1993.

Killing Field Election, BBC2 Assignment, May 1993).

Koh, T, *The Paris Negotiation on Cambodia: A Multilateral Negotiation that 'Failed'*, Negotiation Journal, vol. 6, no. 2, 1990.

Kyodo News Service.

Lakshmana Chetty, A, *Cambodia: Waiting for Whom?*, Sri Venkateswara University, India, (unpublished, undated paper).

Lawson, S, *Democracy and the Problem of Cultural Relativism: Normative Issues for International Politics, Global Society: Journal of Interdisciplinary International Relations*, vol. 12, no. 2, May 1998.

Leifer, M, *Powersharing and Peacemaking in Cambodia? School of Advanced International Studies Review: A Journal of International Affairs*, vol. 12, no. 1, 1992, Evans and Grant, *Australia's Foreign Relations In the World of the 1990s*, Melbourne University Press, 1992.

Leifer, M, *Tigers, Tigers, Spurning Rights*, Times Higher Education Supplement, 21 April, 1995.

Letter 28 CPP/C/UN/93, no. 28, Phnom Penh, 24 May, 1993.

Letter CPP/C/UN/93, no. 25, 16 May, 1993.

Letter CPP/C/UN/93, no. 32, Phnom Penh, 27 May, 1993.

Letter CPP/C/UN/93, no. 41, Phnom Penh, 4 June, 1993.

Letter from M Vickery to 'Z' Magazine, Massachusetts, 9 May, 1994.

Letter from Yasushi Akashi to Chea Sim, 9 June, 1993.

Letters CPP/C/UN/93, 11 and 14, Phnom Penh, April and May 1993; and Lizée, P, *The Challenge of Conflict Resolution in Cambodia*, Canadian Defence Quarterly, September 1993.

—— *Cambodia in 1995: From Hope to Despair*, Asian Survey vol. XXXVI, no. 1, January 1996.

Long, S, *China and Kampuchea: Political Football on the Killing Fields*, Pacific Review, vol. 2, no. 2, 1989.

Mackinlay, Minear and Chopra, *A Draft Concept of Second Generation Multinational Operations 1993*, Thomas J Watson Institute for International Studies, Brown University, 1993.

Mahbubani, K, *The Kampuchean Problem: A Southeast Asian Perspective*, Foreign Affairs, vol. 62, no. 2, Winter 1983/1984.

Mason and Brown, R, *Rice, Rivalry and Politics: Managing Cambodian Relief*, Notre Dame, 1986.

Mayall, J, (ed.), *The New Interventionism 1991–1994: United Nations experience in Cambodia, former Yugoslavia and Somalia*, Cambridge University Press, 1996.

McAuliff, J, *Welcome to Cambodia, Where Nothing is Ever as it Seems*, Indochina Interchange, September 1997.

Message de Samdech Preah Norodom Sihanouk du Cambodge à ses respectés et bien-aimés Compatriotes, Phnom Penh, 4 June 1993 (FUNCINPEC Offices, Phnom Penh).

Bibliography

Mohammed Idris, SM, *The Message from Calicut – 500 Years after Vasco da Gama, Third World Resurgence*, no. 96, September 1998.
Munro and Pilger, *Return to Year Zero, Viewpoint '93*, CTV, May 1993.
—— *Year Zero: the Silent Death of Cambodia*, ATV-TV (London), 1980.
Muskie, ES, *Exploring Cambodia: Issues and Reality in a Time of Transition*, Centre for National Policy, Washington DC, October 1990.
Mysliwiecz, E, *Punishing the Poor: the International Isolation of Kampuchea*, Oxfam, 1989.
National Security and International Affairs Division, Report no. B-270716.
National Voice of Cambodia, Phnom Penh.
NATO Review.
New York Times.
NGO Forum Meeting with Ieng Mouly, Phnom Penh, 12 September, 1995 statement.
NGO Resource Project - Daily Report, Phnom Penh.
Normand, R, *The Teachings of Chairman Pot, The Nation*, 3 September, 1990.
O'Shaughnessy and Dodson, *Political Bargaining and Democratic Transitions: A Comparison of Nicaragua and El Salvador, Journal of Latin American Studies*, vol. 31, no. 1999.
Osbourne, M, *Sihanouk: Prince of Light, Prince of Darkness*, Allen and Unwin, 1994.
Ott, MC, *Cambodia: Between Hope and Despair, Current History: A Journal of Contemporary World Affairs*, December 1997.
Oxfam News.
Oxford Analytica Daily Brief.
Ovesen, Trankell and Ojendal, *When Every Household is an Island: Social Organization and Power Structures in Rural Cambodia*, Uppsala, 1996.
Peang-Meth, A, *Understanding Cambodia's Political Developments, Contemporary Southeast Asia*, vol. 19, no. 3, December 1997.
Peschoux, C, *The 'New' Khmer Rouge: Reconstruction of the Movement and Reconquest of the Villages 1979–1990 – A Preliminary Assessment*, English language draft, unpublished (published in French).
Phnom Penh National Radio of Cambodia Network.
Phnom Penh Post.
Pilger, J, *Organised Forgetting, New Statesman and Society*, 1 November, 1991.
—— *Heroes*, Pan, 1989.
—— *A Secret Country*, London Cape, 1989.
—— *Distant Voices*, Vintage, 1992.
—— *The West's War in Cambodia, New Statesman and Society*, 28 May, 1993.
Pinkney, R, *Democracy in the Third World*, Open University Press, 1993.
Pol Pot, *Clarification of Certain Principled Views to Act as the Basis of Our Views and Stance*, 6 February, 1992.
Porter, DG, *The Myth of the Bloodbath: North Vietnam's Land Reform Reconsidered, Bulletin of Concerned Asian Scholars*, Vol. 5, No. 2, 1973.
Prasso, S, *Cambodia: A Heritage of Violence, World Policy Journal*, vol. 11, no. 3, 1994.
Radio Australia.

Bibliography

Randall and Theobald, *Political Change and Underdevelopment: A Critical Introduction to Third World Politics*, Macmillan 1985.

Randall, SJ, *Peacekeeping in the Post-Cold War Era: the United Nations and the Cambodian Elections of 1993*, Contemporary Security Policy, vol. 16, no. 2, 1995,.

Rapport de Norodom Sihanouk, 3 June, 1993, (FUNCINPEC Offices, Phnom Penh).

Ratner, SR, *The New UN Peacekeeping: Building Peace in Lands of Conflict after the Cold War*, St. Martin's, 1995.

Report of the International Conference on Kampuchea, New York (13–17 July 1981), A/CONF.109/5.

Report of the secretary-general on Cambodia containing his proposed implementation plan for UNTAC, including administrative and financial aspects, S/23613, 19 February, 1992.

Reuter Insurance Briefing.

Review of the Cambodian Human Rights Task Force, Issue no. 4, 1 May 1993, Phnom Penh.

Reynell, J, *Political Pawns: Refugees on the Thai-Kampuchea Border*, Oxford, 1989.

Riley, SP, *Africa's 'New Wind of Change'*, The World Today, vol. 48, no. 7, July 1992.

Rist, G, *The History of Development: From Western Origins to Global Faith*, Zed, 1997.

Rivage-Seul, DM and MK, *A Kinder and Gentler Tyranny: Illusions of a New World Order*, Praeger, 1995.

Roberts, D, *Cambodia: Problems of a UN-brokered Peace*, The World Today, vol. 48, no. 7, July 1992.

—— *A Dangerous Game: Managing Consent in the Cambodian Peacekeeping Operation*, Studies in Conflict and Terrorism, vol. 21, no. 1, Jan. 1998.

—— *More Honoured in the Breech: Consent and Impartiality in the Cambodia Peacekeeping Operation*, International Peacekeeping, April 1998.

—— *Meddling while Phnom Penh Burned: the US Role in the Cambodian Secession, June 1993*, Bulletin of Concerned Asian Scholars, vol. 30, no. 3, July–September 1998.

—— *Sympathy with the Devil? The Khmer Rouge and the Politics of Consent*, Contemporary Security Policy, vol. 19, no. 2, August 1998.

—— *Hun Sen Confounds and Consolidates*, Jane's Intelligence Review, October 1998.

S/RES/792, 30 November, 1992.

Sanderson, JM, 'UNTAC: Successes and Failures', in H Smith (ed.), *International Peacekeeping: Building on the Cambodian Experience*, Australian Defence Studies Centre, 1994.

—— *The Dilemma of Force: Don't Dabble in War*, Work in Progress – The United Nations University, vol. 14, no. 3, June 1995.

SarDesai, DR, *Viêtnam: the Struggle for National Identity*, Westview, 1992.

Schlesinger, A Jr, *Has Democracy a Future?* Foreign Affairs, September–October 1997.

Schwarz, B, *The Diversity Myth: America's Leading Export*, Atlantic Monthly, May 1995.

Bibliography

Secretariat News, UNHQ, New York (Phnom Penh), May–June, 1993.
Shawcross, W, *Cambodia's New Deal*, Contemporary Issues Paper no. 1, Carnegie Endowment for International Peace, 1994.
Simone and Feraru (eds.), *The Asian Pacific: Political and Economic Development in a Global Context*, Longman 1995.
Sisk and Reynolds (eds.), *Elections and Conflict Management in Africa*, United States Institute of Peace, 1998.
Smith, BC, *Understanding Third World Politics: Theories of Political Change and Development*, Macmillan, 1996.
Smith, H, (ed.), *International Peacekeeping: Building on the Cambodian Experience*, Australian Defence Studies Centre, 1994.
South China Morning Post.
Summary of World Broadcasts (BBC).
Taylor RH, (ed.), *The Politics of Elections in Southeast Asia*, Cambridge University Press, 1996.
Tessifore and Woolfson (eds.), *A Global Agenda: Issues before the 47th General Assembly*, University Press of America, 1992, p.84.
Thayer, C, *Prospects for Peace in Kampuchea: Soviet Initiatives and Indochinese Responses*, Indonesia Quarterly, vol. 17, Part two, 1989.
The *Cambodia Times*.
The *Nation*..
The *Spectator*.
The *Times*.
The United Nations in Cambodia, 1991–1995, UN Blue Book Series, vol. 2, 1995.
Thion, S, *Watching Cambodia*, White Lotus (Bangkok), 1993.
Thomas, T, *Into the Unknown: Can the United Nations Bring Peace to Cambodia?* Journal of International Affairs vol. 44, no. 2, 1991.
Turley, WS, *The Khmer War: Cambodia after Paris*, Survival, vol. 32, no. 5, 1990.
US Mission 'non-paper', 3 June, 1993.
Vatikiotis, MRJ, *Political Change in Southeast Asia: Trimming the Banyan Tree*, Routledge, 1996.
Vickery, M and Amer, R, *Democracy and Human Rights in Cambodia*, Final Draft Report, *SIDA*, 1995.
Vickery, M, *Cambodia 1975-1982*, Southend, 1984.
—— *Kampuchea: Politics, Economic and Society*, 1986.
—— *Cambodia (Kampuchea): History, Tragedy and Uncertain Future*, Bulletin of Concerned Asian Scholars, vol. 21, Nos. 2–4, April–December 1989.
—— 'Resignation of CPP candidates and Their Replacements: A counter analysis to "CPP Secessionism, Resignations from the Assembly and Intimidation of UNTAC: Background and Theories', by Stephen Heder"', Phnom Penh, 24 June 1993.
—— *Cambodia: A Political Survey, Regime Change and Regime Maintenance in Asia and the Pacific*, no. 14, Australian National University, 1994.
—— *The Cambodian People's Party: Where did it come from, where is it going?*, Southeast Asian Affairs, 1994.
Wade, R, *Governing the Market: Economic Theory and the Role of government in East Asia*, Princeton, 1990.

Bibliography

Washington Post.
Weiss, TG, (ed.), *The United Nations and Civil Wars*, Lynne Rienner, 1995.
Whitman and Pocock (eds.), *After Rwanda: The Co-ordination of UN Humanitarian Assistance*, Macmillan, 1996.
Will, G *The Elections in Cambodia: Taking Stock of a UN Mission, Aussenpolitik*, no. IV, 1993.
Williams, MC, *Keeping the Peace In Cambodia, Survival: IISS Quarterly*, vol. 38, no. 3, 1996.
Yearbook of the United Nations, 1981.
Young, T, 'A Project to be Realised': Global Liberalism and Contemporary Africa, *Millennium: Journal of International Studies*, vol. 24, no. 3, 1995.
Zakaria, F, *The Rise of Illiberal Democracy, Foreign Affairs*, November–December 1997.

Index

absolutism, 29, 36, 116, 117, 127, 138, 147, 150, 157, 159, 171, 174, 200, 202, 205, 206, 209, 210, 212
Amnesty International, 52
Angkar Loeu, 73
Anlong Veng, 98, 142, 146, 160
ARENA party, 125
ASEAN, 2, 12, 15, 16, 18, 22

Ben Kiernan, 15, 19, 43, 115
Buddhist Liberal Democratic Party, 40, 80, 92, 110, 120, 121, 124, 126, 128, 150, 157, 160, 162, 163, 176, 178, 181
Bou Thang, 9, 111

Cambodia Daily, 125, 151, 184, 188, 189
cantonment, 42, 88, 97
Chea Chamreoun, 181
Chea Sim, 89, 106, 127, 145, 151, 152, 153, 154, 195, 197, 209
Chhay Sung Yung, 154
Christophe Peschoux, 98
civil administration, 41, 74, 75, 76, 83, 85, 89, 90, 91, 93, 102
clientelism, 32, 33, 34, 91, 117, 129, 130, 154, 169, 200, 202, 203, 204, 205
Coalition Government of Democratic Kampuchea, 46
Communist Party of Kampuchea, 9, 10, 12

Constitutional Council, 179, 182, 183, 184
Cambodian People's Party, 35, 38, 39, 40, 41, 42, 65, 66, 67, 68, 72, 73, 74, 75, 76, 78, 80, 81, 86, 88, 89, 91, 92, 93, 94, 95, 97, 99, 102, 104, 105, 106, 107, 108, 109, 110, 112, 114, 115, 116, 117, 119, 121, 122, 123, 124, 126, 127, 128, 129, 130, 132, 133, 134, 135, 136, 137, 138, 139, 140, 141, 142, 143, 144, 145, 146, 147, 148, 150, 151, 152, 153, 154, 155, 156, 157, 159, 160, 161, 162, 163, 169, 170, 171, 172, 173, 174, 175, 176, 177, 178, 179, 180, 181, 182, 183, 185, 187, 188, 189, 190, 192, 193, 194, 195, 196, 197, 198, 201
CPP Assembly resignations, 109, 110, 113, 151

Dana Rohrbacher, 175
David Ashley, 30, 74, 117, 118, 120, 128, 129, 132, 137, 138, 139, 140, 141, 146, 156, 157
David Chandler, 48, 79, 200
Democratic Kampuchea, 6, 7, 11, 23, 46, 65, 66, 97, 143
disarmament, 23, 28, 37, 42, 43, 86, 88, 89, 93, 96, 103, 150

El Salvador, 125, 192

Index

elections, 2, 4, 28, 29, 32, 37, 39, 41, 44, 45, 46, 49, 66, 67, 68, 70, 72, 74, 76, 77, 80, 81, 93, 95, 96, 97, 101, 102, 104, 105, 106, 108, 110, 112, 115, 116, 118, 119, 132, 134, 135, 136, 137, 138, 140, 141, 150, 151, 155, 163, 164, 165, 166, 168, 173, 176, 177, 178, 179, 181, 182, 184, 185, 187, 192, 193, 194, 197, 199, 201, 204, 207, 208, 209, 211
electoral fraud, 77, 80, 105, 184, 187
Elizabeth Bork, 183, 184

'fall back to base area' strategy, 109, 110
Far Eastern Economic Review, 52, 64, 67, 68, 84, 131, 140, 145, 184
FUNCINPEC, 34, 40, 74, 79, 80, 81, 88, 89, 92, 105, 106, 107, 108, 110, 111, 113, 115, 119, 120, 121, 122, 123, 124, 126, 127, 128, 129, 130, 132, 133, 134, 135, 136, 137, 138, 139, 140, 141, 143, 144, 146, 147, 148, 150, 154, 155, 156, 157, 158, 159, 160, 161, 162, 163, 164, 170, 172, 173, 175, 176, 178, 179, 181, 182, 186, 187, 188, 189, 192, 193, 194, 196, 197, 198, 199, 200, 207, 208, 209
FUNCINPEC 1996 Congress, 136, 138, 157, 159, 160, 162, 163, 198

General Accounting Office (US), 115, 211, 212
genocide, 22, 24, 26, 28, 50, 51, 52, 53, 95, 190, 207, 211
Gerald Heeger, 173
Grant Curtis, 46, 121, 122, 128, 142, 143, 144, 146, 169

Heng Samrin, 9, 45
Henry Kissinger, 12, 36, 212
Ho Sok, 144, 170
Hok Lundi, 144
Hun Nheng, 41, 111, 112
Hun Sen, 9, 18, 19, 20, 21, 22, 23, 24, 25, 27, 28, 34, 35, 40, 41, 42, 45, 47, 103, 106, 111, 112, 113, 114, 115, 116, 118, 120, 122, 123, 132, 134, 136, 137, 138, 139, 140, 141, 142, 143, 145, 146, 148, 151, 152, 153, 154, 156, 157, 158, 159, 161, 162, 163, 166, 169, 170, 173, 174, 175, 176, 177, 178, 180, 182, 183, 185, 186, 187, 189, 190, 191, 192, 194, 195, 196, 198, 199, 201, 207, 210

Ieng Mouly, 162, 176, 178
Ieng Sary, 96, 97.
Information/Education (UNTAC), 109, 105
International Republican Institute, 125

Jarat Chopra 35, 56, 80, 84, 85, 86, 213
John Mackinlay, 84
John Pilger, 9, 12, 63
John Sanderson, 67, 68, 70, 71, 72, 84, 85, 87, 88, 118
July 1997, 2, 3, 4, 36, 83, 94, 119, 121, 124, 136, 146, 149, 150, 155, 156, 159, 160, 163, 168, 171, 172, 178, 179, 189, 200, 208, 212

Kampuchean National United Front for National Salvation, 6, 9, 12
Kate Frieson, 32, 33, 56, 61, 62, 79, 89, 128, 186
Khieu Kanharith, 108, 126, 170
Khieu Rada, 176
Khieu Samphan, 63, 94, 98, 102, 123, 141, 142, 143, 144, 172
Khmer Angkor Party, 176, 177
Khmer Citizen Party, 176
Khmer Nation Party, 160, 176, 179, 194
Khmer Rouge, 1, 3, 4, 7, 8, 10, 11, 12, 13, 14, 15, 16, 18, 19, 20, 21, 22, 23, 24, 26, 27, 28, 30, 34, 35, 37, 38, 39, 40, 41, 42, 43, 45, 50, 52, 54, 55, 63, 64, 65, 66, 67, 68, 69, 70, 71, 72, 73, 74, 75, 76, 78, 79, 83, 86, 87, 88, 89, 91, 92, 93, 94, 95, 96, 97, 98, 99, 100, 101, 102, 103, 114, 115, 116, 119, 121, 123, 124, 126, 140, 141, 142, 143, 144, 145, 146, 147, 148, 150, 154, 157, 160, 172, 182, 187, 189, 190, 207, 208, 210

Index

Khmer Unity Party, 176
khsae, 32, 128, 203, 204, 205, 207, 208
Kofi Annan, 212
Kong Mony, 176, 177
KR papers, 146

Lao Mong Hay, 126, 127, 149, 157, 166, 175, 180, 181
Lawyers' Committee, 52
Liberal Project, 81, 171, 213
Light of Liberty Party, 178
Lon Nol, 45, 158, 205
Loy Sim Chheang, 134, 136, 137, 160, 176

Mak Ben, 94
Mary Robinson, 169
McAuliff, 121, 151, 160, 194, 195
Michael Haas, 8
Michael Leifer, 18, 26, 29, 47, 57
Michael Vickery, 7, 10, 16, 20, 33, 53, 57, 58, 62, 73, 79, 111, 114, 127, 151, 155, 157, 164, 170, 192
Michel Loridon, 69, 70, 71, 72
Mikhail Gorbachev, 16

National Army of Democratic Kampuchea 22, 43, 65, 66, 67, 68, 75, 78, 96, 97, 98, 99, 101
National Assembly, 2, 40, 89, 104, 122, 123, 127, 131, 133, 152, 156, 160, 169, 176, 197, 198, 200, 203, 208
National Democratic Institute for International Affairs, 125
National Election Committee, 179
neak ta-sou, 116
neutral political environment, 37, 42, 74, 77, 88, 91, 178
Nguon Soeur, 176
Nguyen Co Thach, 28
Noam Chomsky, 172
Norodom Chakrapong, 109, 110, 111, 131, 153, 154, 155
Norodom Ranariddh, 95, 103, 106, 113, 116, 123, 125, 126, 127, 138
Norodom Sihanouk, 1, 7, 11, 13, 18, 19, 20, 21, 22, 23, 24, 26, 27, 40, 45, 46, 56, 61, 62, 65, 68, 70, 71, 79, 106, 107, 108, 109, 110, 111, 112, 113, 114, 116, 119, 122, 134, 142, 143, 154, 157, 158, 164, 171, 178, 192, 196, 205
Norodom Sirivudh, 122, 134, 155, 156, 158, 160, 161
Nuon Bunno, 97
Nuon Chea, 98, 141

Operation Dovetail, 70, 71
Opposition (concept), 35, 44, 148, 175, 189, 205, 206, 207, 209

Paris Peace Agreement, 6, 28, 31, 37, 88, 104, 118, 121, 171. 3, 5, 6, 11, 14, 19, 29, 30, 31, 32, 34, 35, 36, 37, 38, 39, 40, 41, 42, 43, 44, 46, 47, 48, 49, 50, 52, 63, 65, 67, 74, 76, 77, 81, 83, 84, 85, 86, 87, 88, 89, 91, 92, 94, 96, 98, 99, 100, 101, 102, 103, 113, 114, 115, 119, 121, 137, 138, 147, 148, 159, 207
Pen Sovan, 45, 169
People's Revolutionary Council, 11
People's Revolutionary Party of Kampuchea, 11
Perm-5, 31, 36, 38, 41, 43, 48, 81, 86, 98, 117, 212
Phnom Penh Post, 32, 124, 133, 155, 191, 193, 195, 197
Phok Samoeurn, 111
Pierre Lizée, 119, 148, 158, 163, 210
Pol Pot, 1, 2, 6, 7, 9, 10, 12, 13, 14, 19, 30, 39, 40, 45, 50, 51, 52, 53, 54, 55, 59, 60, 62, 63, 73, 94, 96, 97, 98, 99, 100, 101, 102, 127, 141, 142, 143, 157, 170, 190, 191, 194, 205, 212
powersharing, 4, 5, 21, 22, 23, 25, 26, 27, 29, 35, 46, 47, 105, 112, 115, 116, 119, 120, 121, 127, 128, 129, 136, 137, 139, 147, 149, 150, 153, 155, 157, 161, 164, 168, 172, 175, 196, 198, 200, 207, 208, 209
People's Republic of Kampuchea, 7, 8, 10, 11, 13, 18, 19, 21, 24, 50, 58
propaganda (western), 8, 9, 10, 16, 50, 60, 65, 79, 105, 190
Proportional Representation, 28, 110

Index

Raoul Garcia Prieto, 125
Raoul Jennar, 45, 48, 52, 56, 64, 65, 83, 108, 110, 113, 129, 134, 135, 183, 194
Reginald Austin, 110, 118
Richard Nixon, 12, 212
Roberto D'Aubuisson, 125

Sam Rainsy, 95, 106, 116, 122, 155, 156, 157, 159, 160, 161, 162, 164, 172, 176, 177, 179, 182, 183, 187, 188, 189, 190, 191, 192, 193, 194, 195, 196, 197, 198, 201, 205
Sar Kheng, 152, 154
secession, 4, 37, 41, 43, 80, 81, 109, 110, 111, 112, 113, 115, 116, 118, 119, 121, 131, 151, 153
Senate, 31, 130, 196, 197, 198, 199, 200, 203, 209
Sin Sen, 153
Sin Song, 109, 110, 111, 131, 153, 154, 155
Sixth Party Congress (of Viet Nam), 16, 17
SM Mohammed Idris, 212
Son Sann, 40, 92, 160, 162, 176, 178
Son Sen, 63, 98, 100
State of Cambodia, 26, 27, 34, 74, 89, 105, 207
Stephen Heder, 15, 46, 70, 71, 95, 96, 98, 99, 102, 109, 110, 111, 112, 156, 164, 191
Strategy of Provocation, 136
Supreme National Council, 26, 29, 46, 99, 119, 178
Sven Linder, 184

Ta Mok, 99, 100, 101, 141, 142
Tea Banh, 108

Tep Kunnal, 98
Thach Reng, 178
Thang Ol, 177
Thiem Bun Sron, 133, 135
Toan Chhay, 137, 160, 161
Tony Kevin, 169, 186, 195
Turley, 8

Ung Huot, 132, 172, 173, 174, 175, 176, 180, 183, 198
UNHCR, 76, 78
United Nations Advance Mission in Cambodia, 51, 63, 84
UNTAC, 2, 4, 21, 33, 37, 38, 39, 40, 41, 42, 43, 44, 46, 47, 49, 50, 51, 52, 54, 56, 60, 61, 62, 63, 64, 65, 66, 67, 68, 69, 70, 71, 72, 74, 75, 76, 77, 78, 79, 80, 81, 82, 83, 84, 85, 86, 88, 89, 90, 91, 92, 93, 94, 95, 96, 97, 98, 99, 100, 101, 102, 104, 105, 106, 107, 108, 109, 110, 111, 112, 113, 114, 118, 123, 124, 125, 127, 129, 130, 133, 144, 147, 148, 150, 162, 163, 165, 168, 169, 173, 179, 180, 181, 184, 190, 211, 212
US Mission 'non-paper', 107, 108, 113, 114
USAID, 125

Veng Sereyvudh, 127
Viêt Nam, 28, 36, 51, 65, 187, 190, 194
Vladivostock Initiative, 16

White Paper (CPP), 136, 139, 142, 145, 146

Yasushi Akashi, 47, 67, 68, 69, 71, 79, 80, 190